T0361373

Demystifying Big Data and Machine Learning for Healthcare

Advance Reviews

Data is quickly emerging as the greatest asset of the healthcare industry. The trend in our industry is to drive many decisions supported by data. The authors have done a great job putting together the issues, challenges and benefits of adopting a long view of Big Data. It is a walk of maturity with the real gold nuggets coming in Analytics 3.0 and beyond. This will not be solved with a product or purchased off the shelf. Big Data needs to be part of the DNA of an organization. Thanks to the authors for putting this together for us.

—Chris Belmont, MBA
Vice President and Chief Information Officer
MD Anderson Cancer Center

Intelligent decisions are best made with data that gives us rich context and a fuller view of all parameters and possibilities. However, how do we not drown in all this data we're generating? How do we stay afloat, swim, and surf—harnessing the tremendous power of this valuable resource? The authors attempt successfully to separate myth from reality with regard to the potential for big data and machine learning in healthcare. Great read!

—Rasu B. Shrestha, MD, MBA
Chief Innovation Officer, UPMC
Executive Vice President, UPMC Enterprises

This book is a must-read for any provider of healthcare services interested in practical recommendations and best practices about leveraging big data in its many ways and formats. The authors draw on their extensive practical experience to separate myths from realities and provide useful insights into the handling of the related challenges through the usage of real-world case studies.

—Prof. Dr. Diego Kuonen
CEO and CAO, Statoo Consulting, Switzerland
Professor of Data Science, University of Geneva, Switzerland

Big data has become so ubiquitous a term that its use conveys very little of value, particularly in healthcare. For those who want to actually understand this exciting area in meaningful way and how in turn it can add considerable value to their organisation's success, I would strongly recommend this book.

—Jonathan Sheldon, PhD
Global Vice President, Healthcare
Oracle Health Sciences

As the leader of analytics at a large national IDN of primarily community hospitals, our "small data" analytic needs alone can seem overwhelming at times. At the same time, we are seeing the greater value of advanced analytics and beginning to realize the promise of machine learning predictive algorithms. We are admittedly just beginning our journey into true "big-data" use cases, and I found this book to be an extremely useful overview of big-data and machine-learning analytic techniques and applications in healthcare. The book is written in an engaging format with simple definitions and descriptions leading to real-world applications. I recommend this book for healthcare leaders interested in a book that cuts through the hype of big data and effectively compiles the vast landscape of big-data analytic topics and terminologies into a single, practical volume.

—Nick T. Scartz
Corporate Chief Analytics Officer, Adventist Health System

Payers—not the least of which are Medicare and Medicaid—are demanding better value. Stuck with one foot in the past, policy makers think we might cut our way out of spiraling health costs. At the same time, Congress and the Administration are aggressively moving to at-risk, value-based models. Reimbursement economics has never been quite so precarious.

It is into this environment the authors insert important new insights, with key takeaways and action steps. Big data and machine learning are transforming how real-world evidence is collected and leveraged to enable data-driven transparency, collaboration, and improved patient outcomes. Written for a broad audience of healthcare stakeholders, this "first of its kind" book offers illuminating strategies, concepts, and best practices. The authors write in remarkably jargon-free language that makes this book an engaging and thought-provoking read for non-technical—and technical—readers alike. Highly recommended for those seeking not just to stay afloat, but to operationalize strategies and succeed in the new world of value-based care.

—Joel White
President, Council for Affordable Health Coverage
Co-author, *Facts and Figures on Government Finance*

This is the book that finally brings together in one volume the definitions and tools to understand big data, AI, and machine learning for the busy clinician, hospital administrator, or policy maker without requiring them to go back to school and take a graduate-level course curriculum to learn.

—Oscar Streeter, Jr., MD, FACRO
Chief Medical & Scientific Officer, CA Division of American Cancer Society
Radiation Oncologist, The Center for Thermal Oncology

The discipline of managing and analyzing big data continues to evolve at a rapid pace. The authors do a solid job of recognizing this growing complexity and offering an accessible introduction to the discipline in its increasing breadth. Presented is a discussion of both the art and science of big data; including the different sub-classes of big-data management and analysis, approaches to solve each challenge, and how these challenges map to healthcare problems of importance. Highly recommended for healthcare leaders interested in data-intensive advances for care delivery.

—Zeeshan Syed, MD, PhD
Director, Clinical Inference and Algorithms Program, Stanford Health Care
Clinical Associate Professor, Stanford University School of Medicine

It's my belief that the next dimension of clinical research and precision medicine will be built off the ability to not only access the vast amounts of data available but to be able to identify and quickly assess the valuable insights buried within. This book does a great job providing the perspective needed in practical terms to understand how far we've come and where we are in the access to and use of big data. It's a must read for those from health-care providers to data scientists looking to understand the tremendous potential and practical applications that machine learning and advanced analytics can and will bring. We have truly come to a point where health care has exceeded the capabilities of an individual person and must be augmented with machines that allow us to understand and apply health care appropriately. I strongly recommend this book to those who plan to be part of the analytically driven health-care environment.

—Matt Gross
Chief Solutions Officer, Duke Clinical Research Institute
Former Director of the Health and Life Sciences Global Practice, SAS

A comprehensive, timely, and truly invigorating book about machine learning, artificial intelligence, and big data in health care. These are topics that are shaping research and the practice of medicine—today. The authors show us the promise and potential pitfalls of this important topic and how this information will shape our future. Enjoyable and understandable—you will not need an MD or degree in computer science to gain a deep understanding of the future of big data and AI in healthcare. The handy "Common Uses in Healthcare" sections in Chapter 7 drive home the saliency of the topics.

A must read for health-care providers and patients alike.

—Phillip J. Beron, MD
Assistant Professor, Department of Radiation Oncology
David Geffen School of Medicine at UCLA

This is a deep dive into Big Data and Machine Learning for healthcare, yet these complex and challenging topics are made clear and comprehensible in this engaging exposition. It is a must-read for those who wish to understand these dominant forces that are rapidly reshaping medicine and to learn how best to apply them to their own healthcare enterprise.

—Pratik Mukherjee, MD, PhD
Professor, UCSF School of Medicine

Learning algorithms are as essential for extracting information from big data as a transmission is for a car to leverage the horsepower created by an engine. These algorithms have the potential for revolutionizing the healthcare industry by identifying new patterns and information in data, continuously adjusting themselves to changes, automating many aspects of big-data analysis, and operationalizing information extracted from big data.

This book demystifies machine learning algorithms by providing a solid overview of the state of the art and by presenting the relationship of big data and machine learning algorithms. The authors describe how machine learning can be used in the healthcare industry to support physicians' decisions, to improve the quality of care, and to detect new trends in healthcare data.

This book is a must-read for healthcare professionals who are entering the new world of big-data analysis.

—Michael Sassin, Dr. techn.
Director of Software Development, GBU Architecture
Oracle

The future of healthcare will be built on the back of data. Organizations that don't acknowledge and prepare for this are going to be left behind. This book serves as the perfect foundation for organizations that want to make sure they're prepared for that data-driven future. What makes this book particularly excellent is that it does a great job acknowledging past experiences and infrastructure, providing practical applications of what can be done today, and then looks to the future of where big data and machine learning are headed. The cherry on top are the case studies where they show how the concepts are working in actual healthcare situations.

—John Lynn (@techguy)
Founder of HealthcareScene.com

Global healthcare challenges and trends such as aging populations, increasing costs, patient engagement, ubiquitous devices and sensors, personalized medicine, changing reimbursement and economic models demand a new approach to informatics. This approaching tsunami of data, including clinical, financial, genomic, wearable, and device- and patient-generated data will overwhelm any clinician, patient, or researcher, as well as any traditional decision-making system. Machine learning and AI are going to be critical components of these new models, and this book will serve as a solid foundation for anyone attempting to rise to this challenge.

—Steve Jepsen
Vice President, Healthcare Integration Services
Global HealthSuite Lab Lead
Healthcare Transformation Services, Philips

Demystifying Big Data and Machine Learning for Healthcare

Prashant Natarajan

John Frenzel

Herb Smaltz

CRC Press
Taylor & Francis Group
Boca Raton London New York

CRC Press is an imprint of the
Taylor & Francis Group, an **informa** business

A PRODUCTIVITY PRESS BOOK

CRC Press
Taylor & Francis Group
6000 Broken Sound Parkway NW, Suite 300
Boca Raton, FL 33487-2742

First issued in paperback 2021

© 2017 by Taylor & Francis Group, LLC
CRC Press is an imprint of Taylor & Francis Group, an Informa business

No claim to original U.S. Government works

ISBN 13: 978-1-03-209716-9 (pbk)
ISBN 13: 978-1-138-03263-7 (hbk)

Library of Congress Cataloging-in-Publication Data

Names: Natarajan, Prashant, author. | Frenzel, John C., author. | Smaltz, Detlev H. (Detlev Herb), author.
Title: Demystifying big data and machine learning for healthcare / Prashant Natarajan, John C. Frenzel, Detlev H. Smaltz.
Description: Boca Raton : Taylor & Francis, 2017. | Includes bibliographical references and index.
Identifiers: LCCN 2017000343 (print) | LCCN 2017009297 (ebook) | ISBN 9781138032637 (hardback : alk. paper) | ISBN 9781315389325
Subjects: LCSH: Medical informatics. | Medicine--Information technology.
Classification: LCC R858 .N338 2017 (print) | LCC R858 (ebook) | DDC 610.285--dc23
LC record available at https://lccn.loc.gov/2017000343

Visit the Taylor & Francis Web site at
http://www.taylorandfrancis.com

and the CRC Press Web site at
http://www.crcpress.com

Dedications

To my wonderful parents, Saraswati and Dr. V.N. Iyer, my loving wife, Vishnu, and my darling daughter, Shivani. —Prashant Natarajan

To Elizabeth and Alexandra, my two beauties. —John Frenzel

To my wife Sandy, for her patience, love, and support throughout my career. —Herb Smaltz

To Tenne, my wonderful wife and dedicated, loving mother of our four amazing sons, who tragically died during the writing of this book. She will always be my inspiration. —Bob Rogers

The purpose of computing is insight, not numbers.
—Richard W. Hamming

Contents

Preface

The Plot

Big data, machine learning, predictive analytics, and AI are maturing in the hype cycle. In a short period, these emerging technologies have evolved from being novelty terms in e-commerce to ubiquitousness. By now, there are a few books on big-data technologies, methodologies, and management; however, the majority tend to be too generic (i.e., don't account for application to a specific domain, such as healthcare) or too technical. Business, clinical, and executive users in healthcare are looking for answers to fundamental questions, tailored recommendations, and domain-specific best practices. More important, they want to learn how to leverage current resources, data sources, and investments—without making each big-data or predictive-analytics effort a custom one-off or an *a priori* science project.

Intended Audience

Our audience for this book is intended to be diverse and includes

1. Clinicians, domain experts, and clinical/financial analysts
2. Managers, IT developers, consultants, and vendors
3. Policy makers
4. Patients and consumers
5. Executives and lines-of-business leaders
6. Researchers and academia

The Skeptical Questioner

The need for this book was driven by three catalysts, beginning in late 2013. The first of these catalysts occurred at a Q/A session following a conference panel discussion. I was moderating this panel on the coming applications of big data in healthcare and life sciences—and how we could replicate the successes in e-commerce and retail. The questioner (an experienced physician and über geek) expressed her keen interest—and her skepticism—in equal measure. She was already dealing with lots more new digital EHR data, regulatory reporting, and new BI dashboards and scorecards, and she was justifiably apprehensive about having to deal with more data (and more noise) coming out of new un- and semi-structured sources.

She asked a few important questions:

1. What is big data in healthcare beyond volume?
2. Had we accounted for the different types of semi- and unstructured data in healthcare, such as images, audio, video, and clinical narratives? What were the connections between these new data types and business value?
3. Were we ready with validated best practices that are domain specific and based on successful real-life case studies?
4. Given the increasing costs of care and reducing reimbursements, how could we ensure benefits for patients, clinicians, and organizations?

The Transformer

The second catalyst, in 2013, that led to this book was the successful analytics-driven transformation at MD Anderson: the FIRE program, which was built upon Oracle's healthcare analytics and translation research products. In the preceding years, I had many opportunities to collaborate closely with MDACC CMIO and dear friend, Dr. John Frenzel. As we were harnessing old and new structured and annotated healthcare data for the next generations of analytics, we were recognizing that the developments in big data in other verticals needed to be leveraged to bring new value and informed collaboration to healthcare.

The Visionary

Following discussions at HIMSS 2014, Herb Smaltz agreed to join us on this project. We were thrilled when Herb, an acknowledged leader and visionary in health informatics, agreed on the need for this book. His enthusiastic decision to join us was the third catalyst for me.

The Choreographer

We agreed that I'd choreograph this effort and also serve as case-study recruiter. To cut a long story short, we jointly submitted our proposal in mid-2015 and received an enthusiastic acceptance from HIMSS and CRC Press.

The Plot Thickens: Research and Interviews

Among the three of us, we performed several rounds of completed formal literature review of published papers, Internet resources (articles and videos), and conference submissions as a part of our proposal submission and throughout the writing process. In addition, I conducted interviews with 25 world-class executives, innovators, scientists, and practitioners in medicine, healthcare, and data science to both validate our ideas and to invite contrarian feedback. What you see here is an objective work that accounts for the still evolving nature of this field and current debates, but focuses on providing practical solutions instead of admiring the problems.

Keeping It Real

Any effort that involves new and still rapidly changing technologies requires practical, real-life experiences in order to connect text to practice. The book wouldn't have happened but for the enthusiasm and support of our contributing and case-study authors.

What's New?

In keeping with the theme of demystification, this book focuses on teaching you how to

1. Develop the skills needed to identify and demolish big-data myths
2. Become an expert in separating hype from reality
3. Understand the V's that matter in healthcare and why
4. Harmonize the 4 C's across little and big data
5. Choose data fidelity over data quality
6. Learn how to apply the NRF Framework (see page 26)
7. Master applied machine learning for healthcare
8. Conduct a guided tour of learning algorithms
9. Recognize and be prepared for the future of artificial intelligence in healthcare via best practices, feedback loops, and contextually intelligent agents (CIAs)

How Is This Book Organized?

This book has seven chapters and eight case studies. Given our broad intended audience, it is put together in a way that appeals to different reader types and interests. While we strongly recommend reading the book sequentially, you have the flexibility to start with the chapters that interest you more than others.

- Chapter 1 provides an introduction, makes the case for big data in healthcare, reviews evolutionary analytics, and creates a rich tapestry of high-value information sources that may be linked to an individual for healthcare.
- Chapter 2 describes the V's that matter in healthcare, makes a case for using data fidelity (as defined here) and the NRF Framework approach in addition to looking at data quality (as we do currently). The chapter also discusses how to use healthcare big data in current and next-generation analytics.
- Chapter 3 helps you get started in your organization while keeping the end in mind. The chapter makes important connections between Analytics 1.0/2.0/3.0. Key areas of

discussion include use-case selection, assessing your business and technical readiness, organizational optimization, and building a skills roadmap.

- Chapter 4 recognizes, identifies, and provides practical solutions to challenges specific to big data in healthcare. This chapter reviews how to apply what you know on data governance, MDM, and stewardship—and makes new connections to big data. The concept of data fidelity is discussed in the context of this chapter and why it is a more appropriate option than mere data quality.

- Chapter 5 lists and debunks common and uncommon myths related to big data and analytics, including the refutation of the existence of the "McNamara Effect" in healthcare quantitative analytics. Validated best practices collected via experience, research, and interviews are listed here for your immediate use.

- Chapter 6 covers the following advanced topics: NLP in healthcare and how to build a living, breathing knowledge-enabled healthcare organization.

- Chapter 7 introduces you to both essential foundational concepts and intermediate to advanced topics in machine learning, artificial neural networks, deep learning, and contextually intelligent agents in healthcare. It makes a compelling case (we think) for connecting big data to machine learning to AI. Other key topics covered here are the very useful "guided tour," best practices, and all-important discussions on healthcare jobs, policy, and ethics.

We recommend you read the case study overview to get a bird's eye view of each case study's problem space and solutions. The case studies don't follow any specific order, and you can read them in any sequence.

The Sequel

Thanks for purchasing this book. We hope you will enjoy reading it as much as we enjoyed writing it. Given the evolving nature of these topics and still developing technologies and solutions, we will support this print edition with blog updates and select curated resources on this book's website, www.bigdatacxo.com. We invite you to join us in ongoing conversations, share your thoughts, provide answers, and learn together.

—Prashant Natarajan

Acknowledgments

It takes the efforts of many to bring a book to life, and the current zeitgeist encourages chapter-length acknowledgments.[1] As a result, it was tempting to keep up with the times and expand the list here by name-dropping and assorted publishing tricks. In addition, while I will always appreciate the efforts of my haircutter, my makeup artist, and the other individuals who keep me looking good, frankly, they had little to contribute directly to the writing of this book. So, despite the risks of fewer pages and not looking cool, I will keep it relatively short and acknowledge the people who did contribute in a meaningful way.

I thank co-authors John Frenzel and Herb Smaltz. Their leadership, vision, and passion in healthcare are legendary. The opportunity to learn from and collaborate with them for this book will remain one of my career highlights.

My parents, Saraswati and Dr. V.N. Iyer, continue to teach me how to enjoy scholarship, reading, and writing. Their unconditional love and sacrifices influence this work. Vishnu, certainly my better half, is a fountain of patience and understanding. I couldn't have written this book but for her unflagging love, encouragement, and the family time she sacrificed over the last two years.

To my little one, Shivani: "I wrote this story for you, but when I began it I had not realized that girls grow quicker than books."[2] Someday, I hope you will excuse the moments we missed that I spent writing this book instead.

Our contributing authors have boundless passion and enthusiasm for patients, wellness, and healthcare. For sharing their knowledge so freely and for "keeping it real," my everlasting gratitude to Brian Wells; John Frenzel; Tony Byram; Elizabeth Baca; Pratik Mukherjee; Marc Perlman; Larry Manno; Shalin Saini; Apparsamy Balaji; and Carla Leibowitz.

A very special thank you to Bob Rogers, who was one of my initial interviewees/sounding boards and later joined us as contributor to this book (Chapter 7)—even as he was dealing

---

[1] Malone, N. (2013). "Thank You to the Author's Many, Many Important Friends: How the Acknowledgments Page Became the Place to Drop Names." New Republic [online]. Available at https://newrepublic.com/article/112578/what-sheryl-sandbergs-acknowledgments-reveals

[2] Lewis, C.S. (1949). "Dedication to Lucy Barfield, his goddaughter, for *The Lion, the Witch, and the Wardrobe: A Celebration of the First Edition*. New York: HarperCollins (2009).

with personal tragedy. Bob was always generous with his time and his insights, and we have a better book as a result.

The following individuals were generous with their time during interviews or reviews, made introductions, or supported this book in significant ways: Brad Perkins, MD; Dave Chase; Khan Siddiqui, MD; David Talby, PhD; Itamar Arel, PhD; Mitesh Rao, MD, MHS; Zeeshan Syed, MD, PhD; Summerpal Kahlon, MD; Andy Alasso; Anjali Arora; Vikas Agrawal; Uli Chettipally, MD; Reza Alemy, MD; Shawn Dastmalchi, PhD; Shankar Kondur; Oscar Streeter, MD; Christoph Trappe; Joel White; Nardo Manaloto; Wen Dombrowski, MD, MBA; Jim Blodeau; and others whom I may have inadvertently missed.

Thanks to Taylor & Francis, CRC Press, and HIMSS. Bringing a book to fruition—from proposal to publishing to launch—is a complex process that involves many unseen hands. The following individuals deserve special mention. Kris Mednansky, Senior Editor, Taylor & Francis, was a pillar of support and then some. Her guiding hand, sage advice, and command over every detail made the entire process easy. Gratitude is due to Alexandria Gryder (CRC Press) for her efforts and help. Theron Shreve (DerryField Publishing Services) was a great project manager—he deserves credit for making sure we met our milestones during the editing, typesetting, and printing phases. And Marje Pollack, Production Coordinator at DerryField, kept a tight watch on the details as we all hustled to meet our deadlines.

Susan Culligan, also at DerryField, is the kind of editor, who, until this book, I thought only existed in fiction. She not only dotted our i's and crossed our t's but was also our reader-advocate extraordinaire. Susan kept us on our toes with a collaborative spirit and passion that went beyond the call of duty.

There are others who made introductions, answered specific questions, or acted as readers to critique late drafts.

We'd like to acknowledge permissions granted by authors Ian Goodfellow, Yoshua Bengio, and Aaron Courville to quote from their yet-to-be-published book, *Deep Learning*.[3] We'd also like to acknowledge the permissions granted by William H. (Bill) Wilson to quote from his online resource, *The Machine Learning Dictionary*.[4]

—Prashant Natarajan

---

[3] Goodfellow, I., Bengio, Y., and Courville, A. (2016). *Deep Learning*. Book in preparation for MIT Press. Information available at http://www.deeplearningbook.org

[4] Wilson, H.B. (1998, updated June 24, 2012). *The Machine Learning Dictionary*. http://www.cse.unsw.edu.au/~billw/mldict.html

About the Authors

Prashant Natarajan is Senior Director & Product Maker at H2O.ai where he is responsible for AI solutions for industry verticals: health, life sciences, & government. He is passionate about helping healthcare organizations maximize their technology investments to improve personal wellness, care access & affordability, clinician satisfaction, and health policy. Prior to joining the H2O.ai team, Prashant contributed to award-winning roles as a product manager, domain specialist, and expert consultant at Oracle, McKesson, Siemens (now Cerner), Healthways, and eCredit.com.

His current areas of focus are health insurance, drug discovery & safety, precision medicine, population health, and opioid crisis. He is a recognized executive leader, industry/domain expert, and hands-on solutions designer. Prashant received his master's degree in technical communications & linguistics from Auburn University. He has an undergraduate degree in Chemical Engineering from Manipal University.

Prashant is a best-selling author and contributor to books on business intelligence, big data analytics, applied machine learning, and head & neck cancer. He is currently writing "Demystifying AI for the Enterprise" (2018), which separates reality from hype using validated use cases and best practices across multiple industry verticals.

Prashant is Industry Advisor for the California Initiative to Advance Precision Medicine (CIAPM) project at San Francisco VA. He is on the Board of Advisors at Council for Affordable Health Coverage, Washington DC. He enjoys teaching Applied Deep/Machine Learning & Artificial Intelligence as Co-Faculty Instructor at Stanford University, Palo Alto. Prashant also serves on Rutgers University's Big Data Advisory Board. He lives in Livermore, CA, with his wife, Vishnu; 6-year old, Shivani, baby Neel, and his Australian Cattle Dog, Simba.

John Frenzel, MD, is the Chief Medical Informatics Officer at MD Anderson Cancer Center and a Professor in the Department of Anesthesiology and Perioperative Medicine. He received his medical degree from Baylor College of Medicine and completed his fellowship training in Cardiovascular and Thoracic Anesthesia at the Mayo Clinic in Rochester, Minnesota.

In 2001, he received a Master's Degree in Informatics from the University of Texas Health Science Center Houston, School of Information Science. Dr. Frenzel has been active in applied Informatics throughout his career at MD Anderson.

In addition to several clinical leadership roles, in 2010 he was asked to lead the development and installation of MD Anderson's third-generation Clinical Data Warehouse, which sought to bring together all institutional clinical and genomic data. In 2012, he was asked to help lead the Institution's effort to install the Epic EHR and integrate clinical data back into the institutional warehouse.

John has published on various topics pertaining to clinical informatics. He is currently focused on the use of Time-Driven Activity-Based Costing (TDABC) to drive hospital revenue process optimization and labor costing efforts in preparation for bundled payments in oncology care. He is Board certified in both Anesthesiology and Informatics. John lives in Houston, Texas.

Herb Smaltz is the Founder, President, and CEO of CIO Consult, LLC, a strategic IT consulting firm. Prior to founding CIO Consult, Herb founded Health Care DataWorks, a healthcare business intelligence software company that earned the distinction of being a Gartner "Cool Vendor" prior to being acquired in 2015. Prior to his consulting and entrepreneurial career, Herb served as the CIO of the Ohio State University Wexner Medical Center, a $1.7B, six-hospital academic medical center comprising more than 1100 beds and over 13,000 FTEs. Herb has over 25 years of experience in healthcare management, with all but four of those years as CIO/CKO at various sized organizations including a 20-bed community hospital, a 300-bed tertiary referral medical center, an 1100-bed tertiary referral medical center, a five-state region, a seven-country international region; and at the corporate headquarters of a $6.2B globally distributed integrated delivery system.

Herb is a Fellow of the Healthcare Information & Management Systems Society (FHIMSS) and has served on the HIMSS Board of Directors from 2002–2005 and as the HIMSS 2004–2005 BOD Vice Chair. In addition, he is a Fellow in the American College of Healthcare Executives (FACHE).

His recent publications include *Information Systems for Healthcare Management,* 8th Edition, with Gerald Glandon and Donna Slovensky; *The Healthcare Information Technology Planning Fieldbook,* with George "Buddy" Hickman; *The Executive's Guide to Electronic Health Records,* with Eta S. Berner; and *The CEO-CIO Partnership: Harnessing the Value of Information Technology in Healthcare,* Smaltz, D., Glaser, J., Skinner, R., and Cunningham, T., III, eds.

About the Contributors

Elizabeth Baca, MD, is currently serving as the senior health advisor in the California Governor's Office of Planning and Research (OPR) and provides vision, leadership, and oversight for the California Initiative to Advance Precision Medicine (CIAPM). Previously, she served on the General Pediatric Faculty at Stanford Medical School and directed the Community Pediatric and Child Advocacy Rotation. Dr. Baca studied health policy at Universidad Simon Bolivar in Venezuela. She completed her Masters in Public Administration at Harvard Kennedy School of Government and her Doctorate of Medicine at Harvard Medical School.

Apparsamy Balaji has been involved in data management and analytics domain since 1996. He has an engineering degree in computer science from India and an MBA from Northern Illinois University. He is very passionate about helping organizations to make data- and analytics-driven decisions, including converting data into information of many kinds for the right people, at the right time, at the right place. His recent leadership of BayCare's patient engagement and operational analytics programs was recognized by Gartner for "Best in Class Domain Analytics."

Tony Byram is Vice President of Business Intelligence at Ascension, the largest not-for-profit health system in the United States. During 20+ years of service with Ascension, he has worked on bringing information to those in need—for instance, implementing clinical data repositories, ERP systems, integration technologies, business intelligence platforms, and now enterprise data warehouses and enterprise data lakes. As an electrical engineer, he enjoys puzzles, from myriad Rubik's types puzzles to solving population health data integration challenges.

Carla Leibowitz heads up Product and Strategy at Arterys. Before Arterys, she focused on strategic projects for Global 500 companies around precision medicine and SaaS as a consultant at Bain & Co. Prior to that, Carla led the innovation group at Medtronic Spine and Biologics and helped teach the BioDesign class at Stanford University. She holds 16 patents for medical device technologies. Carla earned a BS from MIT as well an MS and an MBA from Stanford University.

Larry Manno leads Deloitte Consulting's analytics and information management practice for the insurance sector. He specializes in technology-enabled business transformation for life insurers and health plans. Larry is passionate about data-driven finance and actuarial modernization for insurance. He helps insurers manage risk and create value through next-generation big-data platforms and advanced analytics.

Pratik Mukherjee, MD, PhD, is Professor of Radiology and Biomedical Imaging, Bioengineering, at University of California, San Francisco. He is a board-certified clinical neuroradiologist with an undergraduate degree in computer science, graduate-level courses in AI, and a PhD in computational neuroscience, and an MD from Cornell University. His work has spanned the spectrum from technique development to leading multicenter imaging projects to engaging with the FDA for imaging biomarker qualification for clinical trials.

Marc Perlman is the Managing Director and Global Business Development Leader for Deloitte LLP. With more than 33 years in healthcare, he has worked closely with governments, regions/provinces, health systems, payer organizations, system integrators, and vertical software companies in health information technology and next-generation analytics. Prior to Deloitte, Marc served as Global Vice President, Healthcare and Life Sciences Industry at Oracle. He currently serves as an advisory board member for the USA Health Alliance (USAHA) and the Council for Affordable Healthcare (CAHC).

Bob Rogers, PhD, is Chief Data Scientist for Analytics and Artificial Intelligence Solutions at Intel, where he applies his experience solving problems with big data and analytics to help Intel build world-class customer solutions. Prior to joining Intel, Bob was co-founder and Chief Scientist at Apixio, a big-data analytics company for healthcare. He has co-authored the book *Artificial Neural Networks: Forecasting Time Series,* which led to a twelve-year career managing a quantitative futures trading fund based on computer models he developed. He received his BS in Physics at UC Berkeley and his PhD in Physics at Harvard.

Shalin Saini is Manager, Life Sciences & Healthcare at Deloitte Consulting LLC. He has ten+ years' experience in technology consulting, leading, architecting, implementing, and supporting enterprise-wide information management programs. His experience has primarily been in the healthcare industry, where he enables health-plan organizations to leverage their enterprise data assets to create strategic value by resolving integration, regulatory, and operational challenges via end-to-end data analytics solutions.

Brian Wells joined Penn Medicine in 2007. He spent three years at The Children's Hospital of Philadelphia as the Project Director of two large Epic projects. For the 24 years prior to that, he worked in the healthcare software product industry. He earned his MBA from Villanova and his undergraduate Computer Systems degree from Rochester Institute of Technology. He became a Healthcare Information & Management Systems Society (HIMSS) Fellow in 2008.

Chapter One

Introduction

Herb Smaltz

Begin with the end in mind.

—Stephen Covey

"Big data"—healthcare practitioners hear the term discussed at nearly every professional conference they attend. Vendors are clamoring to educate, inform, and sell us on big data and what it can do for our respective organizations. We read about it in both the popular press and in our professional society literature and academic journals. In fact, the *Harvard Business Review* recently dedicated an issue to big data entitled "Getting Control of Big Data: How Vast New Streams of Information are Changing the Art of Management."[1] Yet at hospitals and health systems around the world, there continues to be a mystique surrounding this new management art. At the risk of oversimplifying it, we argue that at its core, big data is really just about leveraging information in its many and varied forms. What some find daunting within the healthcare industry is that more than a few hospitals and health systems have trouble effectively leveraging information that resides within its own proverbial four walls, or more specifically, that is generated from its own information systems and applications that it uses to support its clinical and business operations. Add to that the myriad information sources that exist outside a healthcare organization's four walls (e.g., police records, ancestry records, grocery store purchases, social media, health club memberships, etc.), and many healthcare organizations take pause in coming up with a viable strategy to harness the value of big data.

1.1 The Case for Leveraging Big Data Now

Despite these historical difficulties that healthcare organizations have experienced while trying to harness data to their benefit, powerful market forces will require ever increasing levels

---

[1] "Getting Control of Big Data." (2012). *Harvard Business Review,* Vol. 90, No. 10.

of efficiency and effectiveness in order for hospitals and health systems to survive, much less thrive. The healthcare industry is at a profound pivot point driven by rising healthcare costs. With healthcare now making up nearly 18% of the United States' gross domestic product[2] (and data suggests it is rising in a number of other countries around the world as well[3]), both governmental and private payors are putting increasing pressure on the providers of healthcare services to transform themselves to be more cost effective—and without negatively impacting patient access and health outcomes. With reimbursements from payors expected to continue to be ratcheted down, pressures to make operating margins will continue to be at the forefront of most hospital and health system leaders' minds. So how can data, and for that matter big data, help? In a recent McKinsey study,[4] researchers suggested that there were five ways in which big data can create value to organizations:

- **Creating transparency**. For example, making relevant data more accessible and consumable across disparate departments can significantly reduce search and processing time and hence time to management decision making.
- **Enabling experimentation to discover needs, expose variability, and improve performance**. For example, using data to analyze variability in performance (which either occurs naturally or can be generated by controlled experiments), organizations can more quickly identify root causes enabling leaders throughout the organization to manage performance to higher levels.
- **Segmenting populations to customize actions**. For example, leveraging data from both within and beyond the organization, big data allows healthcare organizations to create highly specific segments of their patient population and tailor services to precisely meet the needs of those patient segments.
- **Replacing/supporting human decision making with automated algorithms**. For example, leveraging data from both within and beyond the organization, healthcare organizations can increasingly develop and refine both predictive and potentially prescriptive algorithms that are gleaned from statistically significant correlations found in the data.
- **Innovating new business models, products, and services**. For example, the emergence of the Internet of Things (IoT), whereby most of the devices found in a healthcare setting such as infusion pumps are both network enabled and often real-time location enabled. This is daily creating ever larger data sets that when leveraged can inform whole new business models, products, and/or services. This presents significant opportunities for continuity of care/clinical integration across organizational boundaries and settings.

---

[2]   "National Health Expenditures 2014 Highlights." Centers for Medicare & Medicaid Services. Retrieved April 24, 2016, from https://www.cms.gov/Research-Statistics-Data-and-Systems/Statistics-Trends-and-Reports/NationalHealthExpendData/Downloads/highlights.pdf

[3]   Porter, E. (2013, June 27). "A World of Rising Health Care Costs." *The New York Times*. Retrieved April 24, 2016, from http://economix.blogs.nytimes.com/2013/06/27/a-world-of-rising-health-care-costs/

[4]   Manyika, J., et al. (2011). "Big Data: The Next Frontier for Innovation, Competition and Productivity." *McKinsey Global Institute*, June, pp. 1–146. Available at http://www.mckinsey.com/business-functions/business-technology/our-insights/big-data-the-next-frontier-for-innovation

The McKinsey study further suggests that in aggregate the use of big data in US healthcare alone can create value in excess of $300 billion annually, including a 0.7% annual growth in productivity.

What's more, regulatory compliance requirements continue to grow, particularly in the United States. For clinically integrated health systems that offer both outpatient and inpatient care delivery, the amount of reporting continues to increase. We argue that healthcare transformation will require us to look continually at new and better ways to manage insights—both from inside and outside the organization today.

One of the long-standing challenges in healthcare informatics has been the ability to deal with the sheer variety and volume of disparate healthcare data—and the increasing need to glean actionable insights that drive performance improvement. The variety of data in healthcare spans multiple business workflows, formats (structured, unstructured, and semi-structured), integration at point of care/need, and integration with existing knowledge. Furthermore, we argue that this ability to glean and operationalize new insights efficiently from these data sources must become so ubiquitous as to be seen as essentially a byproduct of an organization's day-to-day operations—a new core competency that will be a distinguishing factor in hospitals' and health systems' ability to survive and prosper.

Few would argue that the days of "old-school," "seat-of-the-pants," "gut-instinct" decision making are gone. Increasingly, managers in healthcare organizations require the kind of real-time pattern recognition and sense-making that only a deliberate data strategy and approach can yield. Yet most healthcare organizations do not have the information, processes, and tools to make informed, responsive enterprise decisions because of underinvestment in an information infrastructure at the *enterprise* level.[5]

In order to deal with these realities, this book proposes a new approach to creating a knowledge-driven, learning healthcare organization—based on new and existing strategies, methods, and technologies.

1.2 Business and Clinical Intelligence, Analytics, and Big Data— An Evolutionary Perspective

The problem with semantics is semantics. Terms used to describe the use of data to aid decision making within healthcare are many and sometimes confusing. Terms such as reporting, business intelligence, clinical intelligence, business and clinical intelligence, analytics, and big data, just to name a few, have all been used to describe the use of data to inform and aid decision making. Tom Davenport, co-founder of the International Institute for Analytics, and his colleagues provide a useful analytics framework for understanding the necessary evolution of leveraging data in our organizations that we'll use throughout this book (see Figure 1.1).

---

[5] "Gartner Reveals Five Business Intelligence Predictions for 2009 and Beyond." (2009). Gartner BI Summit 2009, The Hague, Netherlands, January 20–22, 2009. Available at http://www.gartner.com/newsroom/id/856714

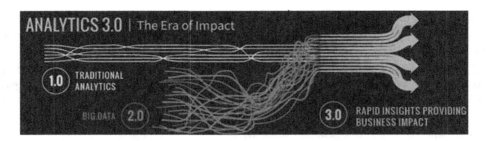

Figure 1.1   The evolution of analytics.

1.2.1 "Little-Data" Traditional Analytics

Analytics 1.0 or, as we like to refer to it, "little data," represents a traditional form of analytics characterized by data typically used for descriptive analytics ("what happened") via reports, performance dashboards, and scorecards normally found within your own organization's information systems. Data used in Analytics 1.0 is usually structured data that is created and leveraged either within the applications that generate the data (e.g., via the reporting capabilities built into many healthcare applications) or via a separate relational database, data mart, or data warehouse, in which data from an organization's main applications are copied and leveraged for descriptive analytics purposes via myriad potential data analysis and visualization tools. The latter are either created and maintained by the health systems themselves or purchased as a product or a web/cloud-based subscription service.

Figure 1.2 is a typical representation of such a traditional, little-data analytics capability. As depicted on the left-hand side of the Figure 1.2, hospitals, health systems, and/or group practices tend to have myriad applications that they have purchased or developed over the years to help them automate various business and/or clinical workflows/processes. Some examples are electronic health records (EHR) systems, time and attendance applications, and surgery information systems. As a byproduct of their use, they create quite a bit of data. In addition, many of these individual applications also come with a reporting module that typically provides a means to generate reports that leverage this data in a very siloed way. As a rule, data from other applications cannot be easily leveraged across application platforms' reporting modules. To overcome this, many healthcare organizations have made copies of the data generated within their main applications and either sent the data off to a third-party analytics service provider or placed the data into data marts or an enterprise data warehouse (EDW) that merges data generated across these various applications into a single, usually relational database (the EDW) from which end users can accomplish myriad analytics functions on the data and use it to guide business and clinical decision making. Examples include standard as well as ad-hoc report generation, web-based performance scorecards and dashboards as well as online analytics processing (OLAP), and data and text mining. EDW approaches to traditional little data must take care in constantly documenting how the data is copied/extracted from its original application, where it is created, how it is aggregated with similar data from other applications, if and how it is transformed, and the means by which it is cleansed and validated. This documentation is called *metadata,* or data about the data, and often is published for end-user

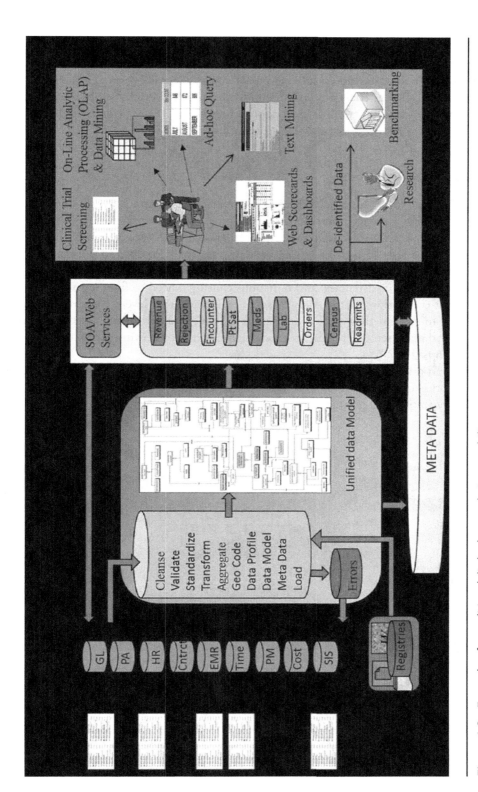

Figure 1.2 Example of a traditional, little data analytics capability.

consumption in the form of a data dictionary that describes each data element in each of the various data marts within the EDW. Some academic medical centers also have taken the extra step of creating a de-identification protocol to make it easy for researchers to leverage the same EDW to aid their clinical trials and grant submission opportunities. While there are many nuance variations of traditional, little-data approaches, Figure 1.2 is a generalized example of how most healthcare organizations are traditionally leveraging little data.

1.2.2 Big-Data Analytics

Analytics 2.0, or big data, is characterized as any collection of data set(s) so large (volumes) and complex (variety, velocity, veracity) that it becomes difficult to process using traditional data-processing applications and therefore typically (though not always) requires instead massively parallel processing software running on tens, hundreds, or even thousands of servers. These data are often unstructured and can be rather "dirty"—that is to say, these data may be fraught with errors, inconsistencies, and omissions causing a need to filter it and find statistically significant correlations in the data. As such, enterprises that leverage big data often find that they need to expand their staff to include statistically trained data scientists in order to help validate and make sense of big data sets (see Figure 1.3). (For a listing of big-data sets, please see Table 2.1 on page 23.)

Whereas traditional little-data analytics employs just a handful of means toward analyzing data (e.g., report generation, dashboards, and scorecards are typical), big data employs a number of generally statistically grounded means including, but not limited to:

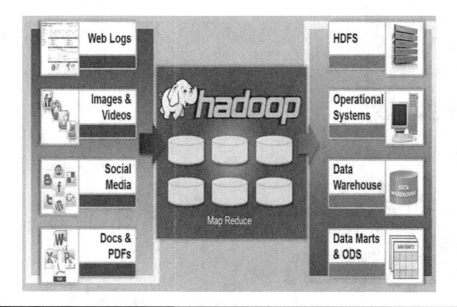

Figure 1.3   Representation of a typical Analytics 2.0 (big data) environment. (Copyright © SAS Institute Inc., Cary, NC, USA. All Rights Reserved. Reproduced with permission of SAS Institute Inc., Cary, NC.)

- **A/B testing** (statistical analysis of two groups of patients that are given different treatments to determine if one treatment produces better outcomes/results than the other)
- **Association rule learning** (takes large data sets and seeks to find statistically significant and meaningful associations among variables to inform process/service/performance improvement efforts)
- **Genetic/evolutionary algorithms** (a human-mediated methodology that allows, for instance, a predictive algorithm to continue to mutate and evolve, ideally, ever more accurate predictive power)
- **Machine learning** (a methodology that automatically learns to recognize complex patterns and make intelligent decisions based on data without human mediation)
- **Predictive modeling** (a methodology that uses historical data to predict future behavior, such as statistically analyzing patient data in order to predict the likelihood of readmission within 30 days for various conditions)
- **Prescriptive algorithms** (a methodology closely related to predictive algorithms that prescribes actions that should be taken when a given set of variables is present, typically to improve results/outcomes)

The technologies that are employed to facilitate these big-data methodologies are generally different from those leveraged in traditional, little-data analytics. For instance, traditional relational database query software is often unable to adequately handle the often non-relational and very large data sets in big-data analytics. Some of the more common technologies that are employed to analyze big data include, but are not limited to:

- **Hadoop** (an open-source software toolset that is built to analyze huge data sets, both relational and non-relational)
- **MapReduce** (another software toolset developed by Google to analyze huge data sets, both relational and non-relational in nature)
- **R** (an open-source tool that provides a means to develop statistical software and to statistically analyze large data sets)

1.2.3 Next-Generation Analytics (Analytics 3.0)

Finally, Analytics 3.0 is an emerging next-generation analytics evolution that produces superior descriptive, predictive, and prescriptive analytics insights by tightly integrating big-data and little-data traditional analytics to achieve insights and outcomes not previously possible.[6] (For a more detailed description, please see Section 2.5.1.)

Most contemporary business intelligence and/or analytics books have primarily focused on little data—the data that is primarily generated within their own proverbial four walls of the hospital or health system. These texts leave largely untouched the topic of big data—that is, an

---

6   Davenport, T. (2013). *The Rise of Analytics 3.0: How to Compete in the Data Economy.* Portland, OR: International Institute for Analytics.

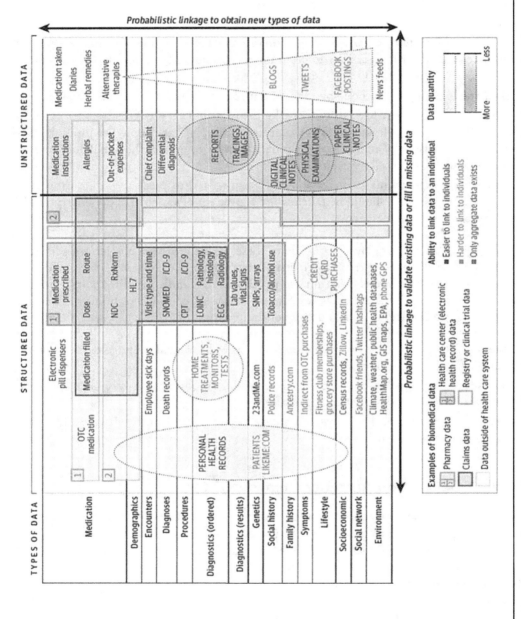

Figure 1.4 The tapestry of potentially high-value information sources that may be linked to an individual for use in healthcare. (Reprinted with permission of the *Journal of the American Medical Association.*[7])

exponentially increasing variety and volume of data and the ever-increasing velocity with which the data is being generated. At the recent 2016 CHIME Spring CIO Forum, Thomas Goetz, the opening speaker, highlighted an informative graphic recently published in the *Journal of the American Medical Association*[7] highlighting the rich tapestry of potentially high-value data sources that hospitals and health systems are largely ignoring (see Figure 1.4).

When one considers that the data healthcare professionals have about their patients is limited to what the patients tell them (with bias) plus what they have captured imperfectly within an EHR and other patient management systems, it is not surprising that patient adherence to treatment plans varies wildly (as do their respective outcomes and health status).[8,9,10] Imagine if a healthcare professional could easily have access to summarized data about their patient's over the counter medication purchases, fitness club attendance records, grocery store purchases, ancestry death records, and genetic data, to list just a few. Imagine an algorithm that parses your own panel of patients for those that are asthmatic, leverages publicly available weather data relating to heat and humidity, and sends out automatic alerts to remind patients of specific actions they should take to prevent an asthmatic episode. These are just some of the examples of next-generation Analytics 3.0 capabilities that are possible today, but that few healthcare organizations are yet leveraging in an effective way.

1.3 Conclusion

This book will suggest how hospitals and healthcare systems can leverage this tapestry of big data to discover new business value, use cases, and knowledge, as well as how big data can be woven into pre-existing little-data business intelligence and analytics efforts at hospitals and health systems to create a true Analytics 3.0 capability. Finally, this book will address challenges that healthcare organizations may face as they attempt to create Analytics 3.0 capabilities as well as provide pragmatic recommendations on how to deal with them.

[7] Weber, G., Mandl, K., and Kohane, I. (2014). "Finding the Missing Link for Big Biomedical Data." *Journal of the American Medical Association,* Vol. 311, No. 24, June 25.

[8] Garcia-Perez, L., Alvarez, M., Dilla, T., Gil-Guillen, V., and Orozco-Beltran, D. (2013). "Adherence to Therapies in Patient with Type 2 Diabetes." *Diabetes Therapies,* Vol. 4, No. 2, pp. 175–194.

[9] Martin, L., Williams, S., Haskard, K., and DiMatteo, M. (2005). "The Challenge of Patient Adherence." *Therapeutics and Clinical Risk Management,* Vol. 1, No. 3, pp. 189–199.

[10] Jimmy, B. and Jose, J. (2011). "Patient Medication Adherence: Measures of Daily Practice." *Oman Medical Journal,* Vol. 26, No. 3, pp. 155–159.

Chapter Two

Healthcare and the Big Data V's

Prashant Natarajan

If you don't know where you're going,
you'll end up somewhere else.

—Yogi Berra

2.1 Introduction

Worldwide revenues for big data and business analytics are forecasted to grow from nearly $122 billion in 2015 to $187 billion in 2019. Global organizations are preparing to use, are creating, or are already using a new generation of business solutions that leverage new data and technologies to adapt, transform, and create competitive differentiation in their markets. The fastest revenue growth is expected to occur in the following market segments: utilities, resource industries, healthcare, and banking.[1]

Healthcare is in the throes of a data revolution, and the numbers of innovative data-driven analytics applications are increasing by the day. "About 40 percent of [new applications] were aimed at direct health interventions or predictive capabilities. That's a powerful new frontier for health-data applications, which historically focused more on data management and retrospective data analysis."[2] The demand for such solutions is being motivated by a multitude of factors:

- Business and regulatory requirements for analytics at the macro (nation/state) and micro (individual/organization/department) levels

---

[1] Olavsrud, T. (2016). "Big Data and Analytics Spending to Hit $187 Billion." cio.com. Accessed July 6, 2016, from http://www.cio.com/article/3074238/analytics/big-data-and-analytics-spending-to-hit-187-billion.html

[2] Kayyali, B., Knott, D., and Van Kuiken, S. (2013). "The Big-Data Revolution in US Health Care: Accelerating Value and Innovation." McKinsey&Company. Available at: http://www.mckinsey.com/industries/healthcare-systems-and-services/our-insights/the-big-data-revolution-in-us-health-care

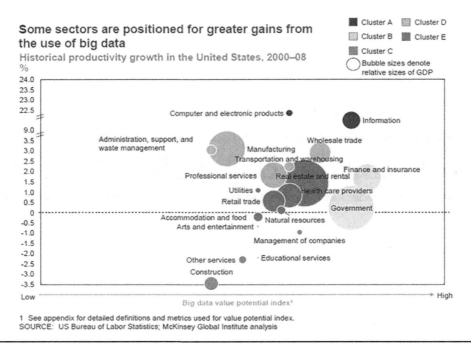

Figure 2.1   Data positioned for greater gains from use of big data. (*Source:* Exhibit from Manyika, J., et al. (2011). "Big Data: The Next Frontier for Innovation, Competition, and Productivity," May 2011, McKinsey Global Institute, www.mckinsey.com. Copyright © 2016 McKinsey&Company. All rights reserved. Reprinted with permission.)

- Digitization of the electronic health record
- Consumer healthcare, new models of data ownership/sharing, mobile health applications, and home monitors/devices
- Availability of technologies that allow users to unlock insights from existing/old data in more ways than before
- Fiscal concerns in organizations/governments and their desire to control spiraling costs or identify new revenue sources (collaboration, monetizing data, optimizing existing business processes)

Figure 2.1 shows how some sectors are positioned for greater gains from the use of big data, and Figure 2.2 exhibits how the type of data generated and stored varies by sector.

Developments in precision medicine, population health management, and preventive healthcare are requiring healthcare organizations to acquire all sources of data, integrate them into known and emerging lore/knowledge, and convert data into prescriptive insights. "By digitizing, combining and effectively using big data, healthcare organizations ranging from single-physician offices and multi-provider groups to large hospital networks and accountable care organizations stand to realize significant benefits."[3] Tomorrow's healthcare organization will be

---

[3] Raghupathi, W. and Raghupathi, V. (2014). "Big Data Analytics in Healthcare: Promise and Potential." *Health Inf Sci Syst,* Vol. 2, No. 3. Published online Feb 7, 2014. DOI: 10.1186/2047-2501-2-3; http://www.ncbi.nlm.nih.gov/pmc/articles/PMC4341817/

defined by how it accounts for and leverages big data—whether that data is created within an organization's four walls or outside. As we can see right now, ADL, SDoH, and observational data are generated by actors external to current organizational boundaries—humans, devices/smart phones, collaborative networks, and social networks (real and virtual).

The increasing diversity of big data from external sources also encompasses patient-generated data, environmental data, external references, third-party annotations, and real-time transactions, in addition to existing un-/semi-structured data such as medical imaging, clinical narratives, claims, log files, and gene/exome sequence results. Harnessing this big data successfully enables support for the following medical and healthcare improvements:

1. Wellness, patient engagement, and education
2. Predicting and avoiding care gaps, especially outside your healthcare facility
3. Disease surveillance and management
4. Individualizing therapy/treatment, drug regimes, and home/palliative care by integrating insights from genomic, phenotypic, and computational biomarkers
5. Clinical trial management
6. Medication adherence
7. Financial forecasting and planning

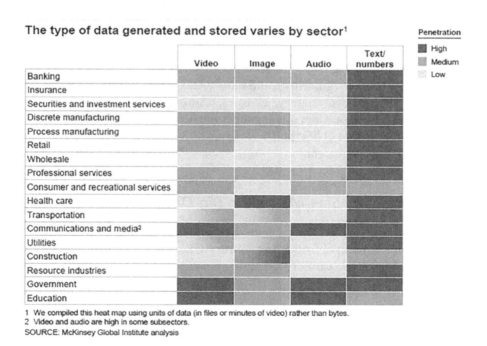

The type of data generated and stored varies by sector[1]

Penetration: High, Medium, Low

	Video	Image	Audio	Text/numbers
Banking				
Insurance				
Securities and investment services				
Discrete manufacturing				
Process manufacturing				
Retail				
Wholesale				
Professional services				
Consumer and recreational services				
Health care				
Transportation				
Communications and media[2]				
Utilities				
Construction				
Resource industries				
Government				
Education				

1 We compiled this heat map using units of data (in files or minutes of video) rather than bytes.
2 Video and audio are high in some subsectors.
SOURCE: McKinsey Global Institute analysis

Figure 2.2 Type of data generated by sector. (*Source:* Exhibit from Manyika, J., et al. (2011). "Big Data: The Next Frontier for Innovation, Competition, and Productivity," May 2011, McKinsey Global Institute, www.mckinsey.com. Copyright © 2016 McKinsey&Company. All rights reserved. Reprinted with permission.)

Transitioning from Analytics 1.0 to Analytics 2.0 and 3.0 requires the successful harnessing of big data. To do so, it is helpful to understand the definitions and roles of big data and the oft-quoted "3 V's." In this chapter, we will trace the history and evolution of big data, examine the 3 V's in detail in the context of healthcare, and posit that, in healthcare, we need to account for two additional dimensions: *Veracity* (or, more accurately, the degree of veracity, as we will discuss later) and *Value*. We will also discuss why these dimensions are not always equal and when it might be necessary to treat some V's as "first among equals."

2.2 Big Data and the V's: A Primer

The earliest definitions of big data focused on the size of data in storage. In his 2001 paper, Laney defined the 3 V's that make up big data as *Volume, Velocity,* and *Variety*. A popular definition of big data reflects this evolution—"high-volume, high-velocity and/or high-variety information assets that demand cost-effective, innovative forms of information processing that enable enhanced insight, decision making, and process automation."[4] Others define big data as "a combination of old and new technologies that help companies gain actionable insight" and "the capability to manage a huge volume of disparate data, at the right speed, and within the right time frame to allow real-time analysis and reaction."[5]

While there are active (and sometimes superfluous) attempts to add new V's to the original ones, this chapter focuses on the definition of big data that is driven by essential characteristics (Volume, Variety, and Velocity) and qualification for use (Value and Veracity). While doing so, we will review why it is important to avoid the "Death by a Thousand V's" syndrome. This syndrome is dangerous to your organization's digital health, as it is a navel-gazing semantic exercise on "the meaning of big data." To prevent this syndrome, the rest of this chapter provides domain-specific definitions, guidelines, and frameworks for each of the V's in healthcare big data so that you can focus on data strategy, use cases, teaming, and achieving progressive success. In addition, Chapter 5 book provides useful pointers on how to separate big-data myths from reality and a detailed examination of best practices. Figure 2.3 shows how the big-data definitions have evolved from 2001 to the present.[6]

2.2.1 Volume: Why Size Matters in Big Data

Information overload and the limits of human cognition in dealing with information are almost as old as written knowledge. In the first century CE, Seneca pointed out a possible solution to the problem: "Since you cannot read all the books you may possess, it is enough to possess

4 Laney, D. (2001). "Big Data." *Gartner IT Glossary*. Accessed March 22, 2016, from http://www.gartner.com/it-glossary/big-data/

5 Hurwitz, J., Nugent, A., Halper, F., and Kaufman, M. (2013). *Big Data for Dummies*. Wiley. Available at http://www.wiley.com/WileyCDA/WileyTitle/productCd-1118504224.html. p. 16.

6 Ylijoki, O. and Porras, J. (2016). "Perspectives to Definition of Big Data: A Mapping Study and Discussion." *Journal of Innovation Management*, Vol. 4, No. 1, pp. 69–91.

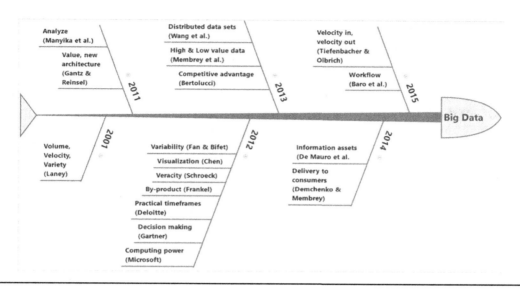

Figure 2.3   Evolution of big-data definitions 2001–2015. (*Source:* Reprinted with permission of Ossie Ylijoki.)

only as many books as you may read."[7] In the 13th century, Vincent of Beauvias described the causes of overload being "the multitude of books, the shortness of time and the slipperiness of memory." With the advent of the printing press, "Scholars in the 16th century were worried about not finding what they were looking for among so many books."[8] In the 20th century, discussions on the increasing size, storage, and management of large volumes of information predate modern computing. In 1944, librarian Fremont Rider wrote that Yale Library in 2040 will have "approximately 200,000,000 volumes, which will occupy over 6,000 miles of shelves . . . [requiring] a cataloging staff of over six thousand persons."[9] In 1966, while coining the "Law of Exponential Increase," Price postulated that "each [scientific] advance generates a new series of advances at a reasonably constant birth rate, so that the number of births is strictly proportional to the size of the population of discoveries at any given time."[9]

With the advent of modern computing, conversations in the 1970s through the 1990s focused on addressing the impact of Moore's Law, managing large digitized data volumes, creating optimized software to manage the creation (OLTP—online transaction processing systems) and management/storage/retrieval of digital data (RDBMS—relational database management systems). In 1980, I. A. Tjomsland said, "Data expands to fill the space available" because "the penalties for storing obsolete data are less apparent than are the penalties for discarding potentially useful data."[9] By 1990, the rapidly increasing need for digital data management is aptly recognized as an opportunity with its challenges (something that must

[7]   Seneca, L.A. (Republished 2016). *Letters from a Stoic.* Xist Publishing [e-book]. p. 8.
[8]   Blair, A. (2011). "Information Overload's 2,300-Year-Old History." *Harvard Business Review* [online]. Accessed July 6, 2016, from https://hbr.org/2011/03/information-overloads-2300-yea.html
[9]   Press, G. (2013). "A Very Short History of Big Data." Forbes.com. Accessed May 7, 2016, from http://www.forbes.com/sites/gilpress/2013/05/09/a-very-short-history-of-big-data/#7cdd8d7d55da

sound very familiar to today's CIO), leading Peter J. Denning to state, "The imperative [for scientists] to save all the bits forces us into an impossible situation: The rate and volume of information flow overwhelm our networks, storage devices and retrieval systems, as well as the human capacity for comprehension."[10]

The mid- to late 1990s resulted in two developments that dramatically accelerated data volumes. The first was that by 1996, digital storage became more cost effective for storing data than paper, and sharing/analysis of digital data became easier. The second was that by the late 1990s, the tremendous growth of the public internet coupled with the advent of e-commerce resulted in the creation of new data types (including semi- and unstructured data) and new storage and analytics solutions to manage this data. It is estimated that because of these and other developments in the 2000s, coupled with decreased cost of storage, the world's information storage capacity "grew at a compound annual growth rate of 25% per year between 1986 and 2007."[10] By 2008, the world produced 14.7 exabytes of new information—nearly triple the volume of information in 2003. In 2010, Eric Schmidt mentions that as much data is now being created every two days as was created from the beginning of human civilization to the year 2003.[10]

While the data revolution is in progress, the propensity to capture and store large amounts of data with no way of adequately analyzing it are lamented in an ACM paper in the late 1990s by Bryson et al., and we see the first mention of the words "big data" and its relationship to data size/storage. In 2001, Laney identifies and defines volume as one of the key characteristics of big data.[10]

Healthcare and Big Data Volumes

The healthcare industry—providers, public health services/government, pharma, payers—is no stranger to big data, as seen through its volumetric dimension, especially when one includes the entirety of digital and non-digital patient, medical, and epidemiological information. We generate, manage, and use large amounts of digital data for patient care, research, record keeping/billing/reimbursement, and compliance and regulatory requirements—and that has only become more so in a post-ACA environment in the US. While the trends within our organizations or the current regulatory regime may be well understood, there is a new world that exists beyond a healthcare organization's four walls and that will increasingly contribute data that may be complementary—or even contradictory—to the existing body of knowledge that exists within current transactional source systems such as EHRs, revenue cycle management systems, ERP, and so on.

The widespread adoption of smart phones, fitness monitors/trackers, network-enabled home monitors, and social networks by individuals and organizations are creating a world of truly big data in healthcare, where:

- Creation and consumption of data also happens outside the facility and today's systems of record.
- Patient longitudinal, self-reported data, and observational machine data need to be accounted for, integrated, explored, or curated in conjunction with existing data.
- The entirety of data not only relates to patient care or financial performance but also extends into wellness, prevention, education, engagement, and behavioral/environmental health.

---

[10] *Ibid.*

In addition to these new data sources, any healthcare organization also is creating and has access to huge volumes of historical unstructured data that has mostly been mined insufficiently for insights. Such unstructured data includes medical images, physician's notes, discharge summaries, annotations, OMICS sequencing, and even medical journals/publications. For example, "Every minute of the now most commonly used high-resolution video in surgeries generates 25 times the data volume (per minute) of even the highest resolution still images such as CT scans, and each of those still images already requires thousands of times more bytes than a single page of text or numerical data."[11]

In 2012, worldwide digital healthcare data was estimated to be equal to 500 petabytes; the data is expected to reach 25,000 petabytes in 2020.[12] The majority of this data is expected to be big data of the semi- or unstructured kind. While unstructured data has always been used in healthcare for qualitative and some quantitative insights (using NLP, DICOM post processing, etc.), the surface has barely been scratched when it comes to raw data analytics (via exploration and discovery), data mining, predictive and prescriptive analytics, or value-added transformations such as machine learning, cognitive computing, and analytics-driven workflows.

This increasing trend to capture data in all its forms and feeds to accomplish new functions is called *datafication* and is being driven by new opportunities, methods, and tools to deal with volumes in peta- and exabytes rather than giga- and terabytes. Datafication is already happening in e-commerce, retail, banking, and manufacturing. With the coming proliferation of IoT and mobile health, even smaller healthcare organizations and individuals will become participants in the datafication of healthcare.

Data volumes in healthcare will increase in greater than linear proportions compared to time. Barely five years ago, many enterprise operational data stores and warehouses required no more than a terabyte of storage. As we embrace new sources and unlock value from existing data, healthcare organizations are entering an era in which we will need to be able to store, manage, and use data volumes in the petabyte range and more. For example:

- Kaiser Permanente, the California-based HMO, which has more than 9 million members, is believed to have between 26.5 and 44 petabytes of potentially rich data from EHRs, including images and annotations.[13]

- The European Bioinformatics Institute (EBI) had approximately 40 petabytes of data about genes, proteins, and small molecules in 2014 in comparison to 18 petabytes in 2013.

Usually expressed in <<bytes>> of storage space, volume can also be defined in terms of number of historical records, current transaction volumes/CRUD frequency, number of connected devices, number of documents, or even as a function of duration/time. While volume is typically a function of size, business and technology decisions will be influenced by additional

---

[11] Manyika, J., et al. (2011). "Big Data: The Next Frontier for Innovation, Competition, and Productivity." Kinsey.com. Accessed May 5, 2016, from http://www.mckinsey.com/business-functions/digital-mckinsey/our-insights/big-data-the-next-frontier-for-innovation

[12] Smithwick, J. (2015). "Unlocking the Value of Unstructured Patient Data." *Becker's Health IT and CIO Review.* Accessed from http://www.beckershospitalreview.com/healthcare-information-technology/unlocking-the-value-of-unstructured-patient-data.html

[13] *Ibid.*

factors. Choosing the most appropriate storage and computing technologies must include an examination of the following factors on data volumes:

- **"Be specific" approach.** Data storage and management requirements are scoped for analytics/other secondary use cases. This approach is preferred for pilot projects/proof of concepts, when secondary use cases are known.
- **"Bring it all in" approach.** Expansive approach in which scoping is driven by the need to manage most/all data using big data technologies. This approach is used when there is a desire to do large data-set analysis, when taking sources offline, or when it is cheaper to use distributed storage for archiving purposes.
- **Types of data and metadata to be managed.** Un-/semi-/structured sources including large text, images, dark data, streams, etc.
- **Versioning.** Historical data, updates and corrections, change rate, slowly changing data.
- **Deployment model.** On-premise, cloud, hybrid.
- **Operations.** Data loading, migration, archiving, backup/restore requirements.
- **Future needs.** Planning for more sources and more use cases must be an early consideration, especially when your big data pilot is successful.

As we have seen so far, volume remains a key defining characteristic of big data. Decisions around enabling big data use cases must consider volumetric definitions and requirements based on the factors described earlier. However, it is important to acknowledge that volume is not the sole determiner of big data. In contrast to even a couple of years ago, the other 2 V's—Variety and Velocity—are clearly becoming as or more important than volume as identifiers of big data. This trend is being influenced by big data becoming more mainstream and accessible by organizations and individuals.

In any case, the interplay of the 3V's—even if volume is the initial defining characteristic of the data in question—has to be understood as a precursor for effective team organization, governance models, and optimal architecture/design. Each of these V's must be examined in relation to each other to determine if the data in question is big or little and to determine appropriate solutions.

2.2.2 Variety

Variety in big data refers to the diversity of data sources, data types, and use cases. Given its antecedents as a solution for large volume, semi-structured web analytics questions, and volume has been the most discussed of the 3V's. However, this emphasis on volume has been biased by the industry in which it was applied—e-commerce (specifically web advertising)—and the use cases it was used to enable. As a result, many people think of large volumes of data as a synonym for big data. "A common notion is that bigger is often better when it comes to data and analytics, but this is not always the case."[14]

---

[14] Bean, R. (2016). "Variety, Not Volume, Is Driving Big Data Initiatives." *MIT Sloan Management Review.* Accessed April 13, 2016, from http://sloanreview.mit.edu/article/variety-not-volume-is-driving-big-data-initiatives/

Increasing digitization in healthcare means more variety than the transactional sources used within the four walls of today's facility. The emergence of new data sources that did not exist 15 years ago (such as smart phones, social networks, and "intelligent" devices)—coupled with the need to integrate that data with what exists within essential business transaction systems (EHR, ERP, registries, etc.) creates an urgent need to recognize and address variety as the most critical in healthcare. In fact, variety may be a better predictor of what may be considered as big data than either volume or velocity.

It is not the ability to process and manage large data volumes that is driving successful big data outcomes. Rather, it is the ability to integrate *more* sources of data than ever before.[13] Variety in big data includes "traditional" data sources such as transactional source systems, spreadsheets, EDWs/data marts/cubes, as well as newer sources that include semi- and unstructured data direct from source. In addition to sources, understanding variety requires analysis and profiling of:

1. **Form/data types.** Numbers, text, graphs, video, audio, composite
2. **Function.** User requirements, economic, and emotional drivers that drove data creation and use
3. **Data fidelity.** Data quality *in the context of its use.* Focuses on whether data as a whole is "fit for purpose," as opposed to merely profiling/fixing data quality (which is usually measured at the entity/attribute/relationship levels). See section 2.4.2 for a fuller definition of data fidelity and why it may be a more appropriate dimension than data quality.

While many definitions of variety focus on heterogeneity in data sources, such definitions are incomplete. A significant enabler of the big data revolution is the diversity of applications for which this data is being used. Application variety includes:

- **Use cases.** Extraction, Analytics, Workflow, Collaboration via
- **Access points.** Laptops, tablets, smart phones, IoT, data services, application APIs for
- **Users.** Humans and machines

Profiling and analyzing application variety allows you to accomplish the following objectives:

1. Gather user and system requirements, including ownership/access/sharing/collaboration
2. Garner cost efficiencies by allowing you to manage storage and compute based on application and business need
3. Reuse existing data for new and related business applications, reduce data management needs, integrate/transform on demand
4. Expand use cases beyond regulatory reporting, BI dashboards, and descriptive analytics by incorporating
   - Discovery analytics
   - Predictive analytics
   - Prescriptive workflows (subject to human approval)
   - Machine learning and data science

As a result, any big data project in your healthcare organization must account for variety in both data sources and applications:

- Capture existing data and integrate/analyze/mine it.
- Go after new data sources.
- Integrate a small bit of unstructured data to existing structured sources.
- Investigate new use cases—bedside monitor, wearable, device, social media.

Many opportunities to harness big data will rely on the management of legacy data sources that have gone untapped in the past for technology reasons or cost of data storage. Therefore, these data sets have been ignored in existing analytics, reporting schemas, data marts, or warehouses. Big data technologies and machine learning allows us to gain insights from underutilized data as well. In the coming new world of healthcare data, data variety is increasing greatly. The data available will be semi-/unstructured, non-curated, and unwieldy, and applications will vary greatly. However, there are existing insights within such diverse data if we can separate signals from noise in an automated, timely, and cost-effective way.

2.2.3 Velocity

Velocity in big data usually refers to the rate at which data is collected and processed for analytics and other secondary uses. Today's healthcare organizations create and manage data from multiple transaction sources, such as research, EHR, ERP, billing, and surveys, in addition to HL-7/FHIR/EDI transaction messages and unstructured data. While these sources may be voluminous and varied, what's common among them is:

- Data and metadata are created or modified for clearly defined transactions that reflect current business process and workflows.
- Most analytics are driven by internally generated data, including patient-reported information.
- Latency is high; while transactional interoperability may happen in real-time, real-time alerting/analytics are limited in practice.

As discussed earlier in this chapter, new and faster sources of data will become the norm as healthcare organizations have to adopt streaming behavioral, wellness, and observational data from the Internet of Healthcare Things (IoHT)—smart phones, home/bedside monitors, implants, ingestibles (smart pills), and medical imaging devices, among others. Adding rich and relevant external, real-time sources such as weather reports, pollen counts, news reports, and even retail POS data will allow for more use cases in wellness and healthcare.

Figure 2.4 (on page 22) illustrates how consumer wearables can be used to create, track, manage, and optimize high-velocity wellness and healthcare data.

While it is useful to understand fast data and ways to deal with it with appropriate technologies and architectures, it is more important to examine the immediacy of user and business needs. Clinicians and administrators are already spending considerable time on capturing EHR data, and the last thing they need is new streams of unprocessed data and streaming analytics to add to the existing noise of IT-driven workflow alerts, problem list tasks, and billing/reimbursement follow ups. As a result, velocity must be carefully addressed for the following broad requirements:

- Receipt and processing: is high-velocity data being used "as-is" in real time or queued?
- Use case: what will the data be used for and by whom? What are patient care and performance use cases for streaming analytics and event processing?
- Data fidelity (discussed in Section 2.4.2) and quality.
- Business needs latency: duration for and rate at which insights are needed by humans or machines.
- Change rate of data (in-place updates or versions).

Any solution must account for velocity in big data by addressing *Data in Motion,* where data is processed and analyzed instantaneously and with subsequent physical storage; and *Data at Rest,* where data is physically stored for different types of analytics or for regulatory purposes. Techniques for dealing with Data at Rest are well described elsewhere and are beyond the scope of this book. However, real-time analytics or real-time analytics feedback into workflows are relatively new, and hence, a short description here of the process may be useful for readers.

In healthcare, high-velocity data can have large implications on computing or storage requirements. From legal and regulatory perspectives, traceable data lineage must be available when raw data is used for real-time decision support. Clinical use cases and interoperability require signals to be separated from noise, and they must be validated by an appropriate human user (clinician, care manager, etc.) prior to being used in workflows.

When don't you need high-velocity data management?

1. When the application doesn't need it
2. When there are easier ways of getting to data, for example, queued data (near real time), hourly batch, change data capture, etc.
3. When cost of processing/analytics outweighs user benefits

For time-sensitive secondary uses, value is directly proportional to velocity and indirectly proportional to latency. Creating quicker time-to-value for patients and providers will require us to expand the use of streaming analytics, real-time decision support, and using secondary (annotated, derived, or extracted) data to enable analytics-driven workflows. For time-sensitive uses, stale data is poor-quality data.

2.3 Sources of Big Data in Healthcare

Table 2.1 (page 23) lists types of big data, possible sources, and key characteristics.

2.4 Two More V's that Matter in Healthcare

Separate from Laney's original definition of the 3V's discussed earlier, there have been several attempts to expand the definition of big data. These new definitions have attempted to address some complaints that the original definition did not address usage. On a humorous note, I acknowledge the existence and eminence of a cottage industry that is devoted to discovering and adding new big data "V lists." Avoiding paralysis arising out of excessive semantic analysis is prerequisite to solution scoping and achieving RoI.

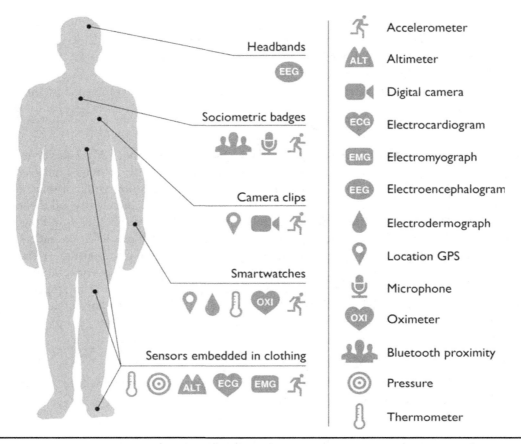

Figure 2.4   The coming age of consumer wearables, high-velocity data, and personal wellness/health analytics. (Explained on page 20.)

"Heart rate can be measured with an oximeter built into a ring, muscle activity with an electro-myographic sensor embedded into clothing, stress with an electodermal sensor incorporated into a wristband, and physical activity or sleep patterns via an accelerometer in a watch. In addition, a female's most fertile period can be identified with detailed body temperature tracking, while levels of mental attention can be monitored with a small number of non-gelled electroencephalo-gram (EEG) electrodes.

"Levels of social interaction (also known to affect general well-being) can be monitored using proximity detections to others with Bluetooth- or Wi-Fi-enabled devices. Consumer wearables can deliver personalised, immediate, and goal-oriented feedback based on specific tracking data obtained via sensors and provide long lasting functionality without requiring continual recharg-ing. Their small form factor makes them easier to wear continuously. While smart phones are still required to process the incoming data for most consumer wearables, it is conceivable that in the near future all processing functionality will be self contained."

(*Source:* Piwek, L., Ellis, D.A., Andrews, S., and Joinson, A. (2016). "The Rise of Consumer Health Wearables: Promises and Barriers." *PLoS Med,* Vol. 13, No. 2, e1001953. Retrieved from http://journals.plos.org/plosmedicine/article/authors?id=10.1371/journal.pmed.1001953. Used with per-mission of the authors; licensed under Creative Commons.)

Table 2.1 Sources for Big Data in Healthcare

Healthcare Data	Examples	Key Characteristics
Images	Radiographic images MRIs Ultrasounds Nuclear imaging	Increasing use of digital imaging resulting in rapid evolution from terabytes to petabytes of data. Storage size requirements are high and directly proportional to number of images. Still expensive to store/manage/use, including with distributed computing. Use cases that emphasize pattern recognition, automated attribute extraction, and "just in time" data mining/analytics/integration can alleviate active storage requirements. Consider cloud-based RIS storage and analytics deployment.
Un-/semi-structured text	Clinical narratives Physician notes Level 2,3 OMICS data Discharge summaries Pathology reports CDA/CCD	Contributes to large volumes in any healthcare enterprise, even with the increasing adoption of EHRs. Storage requirements lower than images, higher than structured-only data. Value not volume: raw text may require curation and/or clinician interpretation based on the use case. Use cases that emphasize data exploration and discovery, pattern recognition, relationship analysis, and NLP can justify actively storing and managing large volumes of such data.
Streaming	Bedside, remote monitors Implants Fitness bands and smart watches Smart phones	Volumes may be low in terms of storage size; however, frequency of receipt/use could be very high. Data/metadata are usually highly structured, unlike size-driven imaging and unstructured text. Managing large volumes of streaming data must address filtering noise, redundant versions, and elimination of false positives. Becoming more pervasive in healthcare, including in the developing world, as data capture, transmission, and storage costs are rapidly reducing. Use cases that emphasize observational data capture and analytics, self-reported clinical measurements, and device/implant integration with a person's wellness/health record justify the costs of managing this big data.

(continues on next page)

Table 2.1 Sources for Big Data in Healthcare (*continued*)

Healthcare Data	Examples	Key Characteristics
Social Media	Facebook Twitter Web forums	Volumes of data can be large and in real time. Storage requirements will be large for enterprise deployments if use cases are not well defined. Data/metadata are usually unstructured text or images. Becoming more pervasive in healthcare as a source for patient-provider engagement, wellness, and chronic/acute disease self-reported data. New frontier—regulatory requirements (HIPAA), data ownership/sharing, security may need to be addressed on an institutional level as prerequisite. Use cases that emphasize patient engagement, wellness/disease management, and patient satisfaction justify the costs of managing this big data.
Structured Data	All claims NLP annotations EHR/ERP/other structured data sources	Volumes of data can be large based on historical needs or number of sources. Storage requirements will be large for enterprise deployments. Represents little data that provides all-important context to big data. Data/metadata are usually structured—squatting, quality, and master data management (MDM) remain challenges. Should remain a significant source for big data efforts—where possible, combine with discovery/annotations/analytics from big data sources
Dark Data[a]	Server logs Application error logs Account information Emails Documents	Constitutes data sources of rich metadata that are already being stored in your environments. Volumes of data to be processed could vary from small to large depending on the type of data. Data is usually in a structured form but may not always be human friendly and may require a computer to pre-process first.

[a] Dark data is operational data that is collected by hardware and software systems during the course of normal business activity but finds limited use for business purposes. Dark data can also be categorized, based on latency, into hot data (immediate operations data) and cold data (non-essential historical data).

It's useful to examine Value and Veracity, as they specifically influence the use of healthcare data in decisions that go beyond financial implications—i.e., health, life, or death. Focusing on "what data needs to be" or "what data needs to do" in addition to its essential defining characteristics is foundational to understanding the role of big data in healthcare, timely identification of solutions and architectures, determining appropriate governance models, achieving RoI, and ensuring informed patients and clinicians.

2.4.1 Value

Most often, data are inconsequential and minimally useful. The value of data lies not in its existence or storage, but in how that data is put to use to improve business processes, workflows, and human/system behaviors. Therefore, value is defined as the usefulness of data for business or personal purposes. In healthcare, the value of big data must be measured via appropriate quantitative and qualitative analytics. Other secondary uses of big data analytics, such as data sharing, collaboration, monetization, and data-driven workflows, must also be measured as we determine the immediate and incremental value of big data efforts.

While healthcare organizations keep value in mind for their primary and secondary data uses today, the coming availability of big data from beyond the organization's four walls will require us to measure achievable value on an ongoing basis. Older methods of measuring analytics return on investment as a function of BI capital expenditure vis a vis number of reports and dashboards will need to evolve into measurement of value across the data lifecycle—from creation to analytics and machine learning to inculcating data-driven learning/behaviors.

Healthcare organizations will need to develop and standardize the equivalent of a metric from the web and CRM worlds: customer lifetime value (CLV). CLV is prediction of net profit attributable to a future relationship between an organization and its customers. A standard metric that measures big data analytics' impact, CLV provides formulae that quantify costs and benefits of customer acquisition, onboarding, retention, up-sell, and cross-sell, among other bottom-line indicators. CLV also measures corresponding improvements in operational efficiencies across the lifetime of the relationship using different types of analytics.

Given that healthcare is a microcosm of several industries, incorporates workflows from different verticals, and serves a multitude of information consumers (patients, clinicians, administrators), a framework for calculating the lifetime value of healthcare data must be broad enough to address the benefits to clinical care, financial performance, and patient engagement. Such a metric (or more likely, a KPI composed of constituent metrics) could also address value as determined by:

1. Clinical impact via measurable patient-specific outcomes
2. Behavioral modification (medication adherence, lifestyle modifications, increased interaction with coaches and providers)
3. Impact on business processes and workflows (time saved, steps reduced, etc.)
4. Number of users served "on demand" with relevant information and user satisfaction
5. Individual and organization progress in treating analytics as an asset, including improved data governance, quality, and fidelity
6. Monetization (financial value of de-identified data, value-based care, and value of integrating institutional and consumer healthcare data)

2.4.2 Veracity

The debate over data quality in big data is an enduring one in healthcare and will likely remain so. Hence, it is important to examine the role of veracity. Veracity in big data is more than data quality, and we must examine the role of data fidelity. Data fidelity is defined as data quality in the context and appropriateness of its use. Reasons for poor data quality can include:

- **Data entry.** Did the user enter the information correctly at the originating source? Are there any system errors?

- **Squatting.** Are two objects identified correctly to be the same or different based on semantics and structure? Does this same field in the source or target contain different types of data?

- **Data management.** Was the integrity of the information maintained during write/ retrieval/movement through the system?

- **Integration quality.** Is all the known information about a data element referenced to appropriate master and dependent data, de-duplicated, and integrated with other data sources?

- **Staleness.** Has the data aged enough that its validity is no longer relevant or trusted? Is data past its best-by and use-by dates for business or personal use?

- **Usage.** Is the information aggregated, transformed, and interpreted correctly at presentation? Is the data used as expected to achieve known business goals?

Data quality in warehousing and BI is typically defined in terms of the 4 C's—is the data clean, correct, consistent, and complete? When it comes to big data, there are two schools of thought that have different views and expectations of data quality. The first school believes that the gold standard of the 4 C's must apply to all data (big and little) used for clinical care and performance metrics. The second school believes that in big data environments, a stringent data quality standard is impossible, too costly, or not required. While diametrically opposite opinions may play well in panel discussions, they do little to reconcile the realities of healthcare data quality. Both schools of thought are right within their points of view; however, I also believe there is an urgent need for practitioners to recognize and use the "NRF Framework,"[15] which uses data fidelity in addition to data quality. This framework is based on the following assumptions and guiding principles:

1. To err is human. Perfect data quality in human-created/managed data is very difficult or very costly to achieve in reality.

2. Human data creation is context sensitive. What's appropriate for data entry and specific business processes may not be consistent or accurate enough for analytics/other secondary use cases.

---

[15] This Framework is developed by Prashant Natarajan, Bob Rogers, and John Frenzel and is designed to account for varying contexts of healthcare data in Analytics 2.0 and 3.0.

3. Fidelity over quality. *Where appropriate,* veracity of big data must be informed by data fidelity (validity and appropriateness of data for intended use) in addition to data quality (measuring/ensuring adherence of source data to the 4 C's—cleanliness, correctness, consistency, completeness—and independent of intended use). For example, certain secondary use cases (data discovery and some types of machine learning) don't require perfect data quality initially.

4. Unlike traditional data analytics and integration (ETL, profiling, etc.), cognitive analytics via machine learning does a better job of accepting data "as-is" and allows for data quality profiling and management to be less of an upfront exercise. Learning algorithms improve as the amount of data increases, with little or no additional spend in human resources. As more data is fed into a machine learning system, the more it can learn from the data and human feedback loops in order to identify appropriate patterns, self-correct, and refine insights.

5. For data and analytics that inform clinical care, we will invest in ensuring that data is of the highest fidelity and quality using the best of human resources (use-case definition, data stewardship, governance/oversight, and approval) combined with the best of machine learning (e.g., more accurate training models, labeled datasets, unsupervised machine learning, and human feedback loops).

6. When forced to work with less than ideal data quality, we will strive for a state in which data fidelity and quality improve continually as a result of analytics-driven workflows, learned user behaviors, and learning algorithms.

2.5 How to Use Big Data

The value of big data as discussed earlier is driven by the ability to convert that data into actionable insights that drive workflows and change behaviors. There are a few ways of classifying analytics, some of which are:

1. **Types of results produced.** Descriptive, discovery, predictive, and prescriptive
2. **Reasoning used.** Deduction, induction, diagnosis, and analogy
3. **Data type processed.** Structured (source systems of record and BI); semi-structured (documents, narratives, dark data); unstructured (images, video, audio)

Traditionally, most reporting and BI in healthcare have been deductive in nature, although big data analytics will also include inductive inferencing (and possibly diagnosis and analogy) via machine learning. Similarly, most reporting and analytics in healthcare today focuses on operational analytics or BI using highly structured source data. Examples of the former are operational data stores (ODS), silo EHR analytics (Epic Cogito, Soarian Operational Reporting, etc.) and ERP HR analytics. Examples of the latter include healthcare EDWs, purpose-built data marts, and/or OLAP cubes. Secondary uses of big data will need to expand to process more varieties of data types in their native formats and incorporate data mining/analysis/extraction through machine learning. A detailed examination of big data analytics as influenced by data types and inference used is beyond the scope of this chapter and will be addressed in Chapter 7.

2.5.1 Data Reduction, Big Data Analytics, and Result Types

Given the evolving definitions of big data and its secondary uses, it should not be surprising that there are slightly different nomenclatures for categorizing analytics based on the types of results that are produced. However, the most commonly used are *descriptive, predictive,* and *prescriptive* analytics. While there may be some overlap with the other analytics classifications listed above, these definitions provide an independent framework for understanding how number-crunching analytics can be used to achieve data reduction and different types of analytics results.

It is important to note that the evolution in analytics capabilities, while acknowledging the needs of human consumers, also reflects the reality that big data isn't necessarily created or managed for human consumption. As you will read below, deploying predictive and prescriptive analytics will require, as a prerequisite, the use of learning algorithms and appropriate machine learning techniques. (For a more detailed discussion, please see Chapter 7, *Applied Machine Learning for Healthcare.*)

1. **Descriptive analytics.** The purpose here is to provide hindsight. Descriptive analytics answers questions ("what happened?") about past events using historical data. The statistical basis for such analytics is mostly basic arithmetic operations and simple statistics (counts, sums, averages, percentages, min/max, and arithmetic operators), and the operators and consumers are mostly human. Usually, we also apply data filtering, hierarchy creation, and dimensional data modeling techniques to present the data via reports, BI dashboards, scorecards, and ad hoc reporting. An extension of descriptive analytics includes *diagnostic analytics,* the purpose of which is to determine the cause of an event or a trend that occurred in the past using questions that focus on the reason behind the event. Diagnostic analytics usually works on integrated data from multiple sources using data warehousing and OLAP/dimensional modeling. The analytics queries are typically more complex, are applied on integrated data, and use a combination of packaged BI and self-service tools. Given the large scale of big data, the nature of advanced analytics, and user diversity (machine learning or human cognition/feedback), the remaining two types of analytics will require us to apply machine learning, via appropriate heuristics, training models, and model validation (predictive analytics), or reinforcement learning, via continuous feedback loops (prescriptive analytics).

2. **Predictive analytics.** This is a second method of data reduction by analytics in which the focus is on generating insights using data that doesn't exist and by mostly extrapolating into the future. "The essence of predictive analytics, in general, is that we use existing data to build a model. Then we use [a properly validated] model to predict data that doesn't exist."[16] Predictive analytics leverages "data you have to predict data you don't have" in

---

[16] Wu, M. (2013). "Big Data Reduction 2: Understanding Predictive Analytics." Science of Social blog. Accessed June 30, 2016, from https://community.lithium.com/t5/Science-of-Social-blog/Big-Data-Reduction-2-Understanding-Predictive-Analytics/ba-p/79616

order to generate insights that can't be created by using simple arithmetic operations. It is important to clarify a couple of myths regarding predictive analytics. The first myth is that prediction is always based on time-series extrapolation into the future (also known as forecasting). This is not the case: predictive analytics can be applied to generate any type of unknown data, including past and present. In addition, prediction can be applied to non-temporal (time-based) use cases such as disease progression modeling, human relationship modeling, and sentiment analysis for medication adherence, etc. The second myth is that predictive analytics is a guarantor of what will happen in the future. This also is not the case: predictive analytics, due to the nature of the insights they create, are probabilistic and not deterministic. As a result, predictive analytics will not be able to ensure certainty of outcomes.

3. **Prescriptive analytics.** This is the third method of data reduction, in which "analytics goes beyond descriptive and predictive models by recommending one or more courses of action—and showing the likely outcome of each decision [based on the decision maker's actions.]"[17] Prescriptive analytics is similar to predictive analytics in that it also uses existing data to build and validate a model to create data that doesn't exist. The difference is that a prescriptive model is essentially a collection of multiple (and distinct) predictive models running in parallel, with each model supporting a different course of input/action and/or a desired outcome. Prescriptive analytics promises to be more relevant for healthcare big data for the following reasons:

- Focus is on action, not just visualization of information. Prescriptive analytics is by definition integrated into workflows and business processes to facilitate and complete user actions.

- Uses heterogeneous big data sources. For machine learning and prescriptive analytics to be useful, the focus is on large datasets that are usually beyond the limits of human cognitive processing. Machine learning can also be used to process native data types such as videos, images, speech, and large unstructured text more efficiently than humans can.

- Includes and integrates big data with important context from little data.

- Provides learning algorithms and feedback loops to enable reinforcement learning. Enables progressive validation of the predictive models via continuous feedback loops; modifies predicted data and generated insights with new feedback on data values, errors, anomalies, and adjusted or desired outcomes.

2.6 Summary

Going from Analytics 1.0 to Analytics 2.0 and 3.0 requires an understanding of what constitutes big data in healthcare, how to recognize it, and what to do with it. The preceding discussions of the 5 V's that matter in healthcare (Value, Veracity, Variety, Velocity, and Volume) provide definitions, examples, and healthcare domain-specific characteristics that serve as a

---

[17] Wu, M. (2013). "Big Data Reduction 3: From Descriptive to Prescriptive." Science of Social blog. Accessed June 30, 2016, from https://community.lithium.com/t5/Science-of-Social-blog/Big-Data-Reduction-3-From-Descriptive-to-Prescriptive/ba-p/81556

foundation for the rest of this book, including the case studies. For a more in-depth review of best practices and how to separate myths from realities in big data management, please read Chapter 5, *Best Practices: Separating Myth from Reality.* To better understand applications of the concepts discussed here in an Analytics 3.0 environment, please read Chapter 6, *Big Data Advanced Topics,* and 7, *Applied Machine Learning for Healthcare.*

Chapter Three

Big Data—How to Get Started

John Frenzel

Simply pushing harder within the old boundaries will not do.

—Karl Weick

3.1 Getting Started Within Your Organization

For many technology projects, success is measured with installation of an application or creation of a physical asset, such as a data center. Data warehousing has always been difficult, because leaders within an organization want to approach warehousing and analytics as just another technology or application buy. Viewed in this light, they fail to understand the complexity and interdependent nature of building an enterprise reporting environment. As the technology has matured, infrastructure such as computers and storage have become commodity items. Database management systems are robust, and there is a wide variety of off-the-shelf analytics tools to satisfy end users. Yet, for many organizations who are able to write the check and buy the best the industry has to offer, success often escapes them. In a recent survey, it was reported that while 25% of IT projects fail to go operational, 55% of big-data-focused projects never deliver any analytics.[1] Many organizations continue to approach warehousing as just another application, and therein lies the root of failure. Beyond the challenges of technology, warehouses and their associated analytics must reflect the current needs and future aspirations of the associated enterprise. Understanding these needs and helping to shape the expectations of the business customer are critical for programmatic success. Analytics 1.0, 2.0, and 3.0 require a walk of maturity in which business needs and technology leadership mature together. To be successful, organizations must take this walk and approach this journey as a team—a team with plans, strategies, budget, commitment, and an objective measure of success.

---

[1] "CIOs & Big Data: What IT Teams Want Their CIOs to Know." (2013, January 24). Retrieved from http://blog.infochimps.com/catagory/resources

Institutions embark on big-data journeys for many reasons. For some, it is a continuation of a successful "little data" Analytics 1.0 effort. Having built a foundation of traditional analytics, data governance, data quality, and vocabulary management, these organizations are looking to take the next step by moving into a world of alternatively structured data sets. For others, the Analytics 1.0 journey may be just in its infancy, but there is a senior thought leader or an obvious use case within the organization that could exploit the potential for Analytics 2.0. Understanding these reasons clearly from the outset is critical, as the approach within these two environments is different.

3.1.1 Sponsorship and Selection of Initial Use Case

Analytics 2.0 initiatives are by their very nature enterprise in scope, as they commonly reference non-traditional data sources and cut across traditional reporting silos. Matching scope of leadership to the scope of the project is critical, so engaging senior leadership for an enterprise investment in steering these efforts must be a priority. Sponsorship must be broad based. Organizations may get frustrated and fatigued as they walk the path of maturity. Results take time, because this is not just an application buy but the creation of and investment in an enterprise capability. That is why selecting the appropriate business sponsor, use case, and scope are critical. This task alone can ultimately mean the difference between success and failure. For many, big data is an abstract concept and, as such, can mean many things to many different people. For an organization new to the big-data space, the first use case is as much about education as it is about results. Finding a use case that provides a tangible return on investment with strategic benefits is ideal; however, selection of the use case must be done carefully. Many use cases, while meeting the requirement of ROI and strategic impact, have such large scope and complexity that success may be put at risk through over-reach. One must approach this carefully. Splitting one large effort into smaller, self-contained segments may be necessary, but this can impact time to delivery. The first project is an effort to set sponsor and institutional expectations. Clear measures of success coupled with project transparency must be defined at the inception of the effort, as they help advocates continually judge the trajectory of the effort and understand its status. Big data initiatives can be daunting but are absolutely amenable to the tenets of good project management.

Healthcare environments by their very nature are multidimensional, and because of this, some areas of the business will have greater data maturity than others. This may stem from previous investments, the underlying nature of the data, or a preexisting business need. Healthcare organizations tend to have greater data and analytics maturity on the finance side than on the clinical one. This is commonly due to the highly structured nature of finance data, which simplifies data governance and vocabulary management issues. Similarly, analytics maturity is often greater as a result of the clear recurring business needs within this vertical. Clinical and clinical/translational research data are oftentimes much less mature. Leveraging existing domain maturity as a component in the selection of the big-data use case can help reduce risk and improve time to delivery. In choosing a use case, the ability to create a successful analytics is paramount. Moving through the steps of data selection, ingestion, cleaning, and analysis must result in an analytics that is useful and gains adoption within the target environment.

This does not mean to suggest shying away from a strong use case with clinical data, an engaged sponsor, and an overwhelmingly positive ROI, rather it means that the risks must be carefully assessed and expectations managed.

3.2 Assessing Environmental and Organizational Readiness

The concept of analytics maturity embodied in the International Institute for Analytics (IIA) schema must be considered foundational in any organization's self-assessment prior to commencing a big-data project. Success at Analytics 1.0 creates a number of assets and capabilities that the organization has de facto mastered. These are critical building blocks for success in the transition into the 2.0 space. In the walk from a 1.0 little data world into the 2.0 big data one, complexity increases. In a 1.0 world, for example, a data quality team uses software tools to inspect source data, understand the deficiencies, and work either with the transactional source owner to remediate the business process or with the data integration developers to remediate it during the ETL process. These processes are robust and mature. The skillsets necessary to master these challenges are widely available, and there exists depth of knowledge around the optimal approach.

In the 2.0 environment, data quality is generally poorer and less amenable to remediation. Tools that work in a 1.0 world are not usually applicable. It is for this reason we recommend you use *data fidelity* (in addition to data quality) in Analytics 2.0 and 3.0 environments. Data fidelity is defined as *data quality in the context of its use* (see Section 2.4.2, *Veracity*). Alternative techniques using statistical analysis, variance measures, and other such methods become necessary. This is a different skillset and will most likely require individuals specifically trained in these methods. Finding individuals with these skills oftentimes requires searching outside the normal IS disciplines for people trained in applied math and statistics. Integrating them into a warehousing team takes time, as their skills and knowledge are widely divergent from those of the other members. As the data quality team grows to understand and incorporate data fidelity, the groundwork is being constructed for a move into an Analytics 3.0 environment, converging the little-data and big-data domains.

Does that mean that organizations without a strong Analytics 1.0 "little data" background should back away from a big data project? Absolutely not. The difference between these two organizations is that the speed and execution of a mature 1.0 organization moving into a 2.0 world would be expected to be greater than that of one less mature. For an organization with little experience in data warehousing, the scale of the effort will be greater and the time to delivery will be slower. In addition, because of the lack of existing infrastructure, the proportional cost will be higher. With this in mind, leaders of the effort must set and manage expectations as well as work diligently to constrain scope. The ultimate success of an effort often has already been determined at the time of project commencement. Extra care must be taken throughout the project so that the sponsors transparently understand the current state and challenges.

While big-data efforts have particular challenges, as noted above, core IS capabilities such as project management and requirements gathering remain critical. These become even more important when taking on a big-data effort. Over the past decade, waterfall project planning has slowly accepted scrum/Agile as a valid methodology. Many organizations have found Agile to be superior in more fluid environments. The ability to recognize deviation and rapidly correct course is important. Given the iterative nature of requirements gathering, analytics build, and data validation, the tighter this circle becomes, the more effective the effort. This is not to say that a strong team using the traditional waterfall approach could not be successful, but the agile approach more closely matches the analytics development workflow.

3.2.1 Technical Maturity

While the bulk of this chapter has focused on the organizational and people aspect of the big-data challenge, there are obviously technical obstacles to overcome as well. In the traditional world of relational databases, many vendors can create solutions from stock hardware that deterministically deliver a certain level of performance. In the Analytics 2.0 arena, the platforms are commonly based on open-source software stacks. Managing these platforms causes new wrinkles for an IS organization in which there may be no vendor to turn to and new releases may not exhibit enterprise stability. While these software packages are free to download, they certainly are not free to maintain and operate.

More widely adopted open-source platforms have gathered an ecosystem of support from third parties that take on the role a traditional vendor would play. They manage and certify releases, track and fix defects, and provide customer support. Some build proprietary tools that ease the burden of maintenance and application management. While outside the comfort zone of many IS organizations, open-source tools are the current cutting edge and lifeblood of Analytics 2.0.

For organizations planning to create an Analytics 3.0 capability in which data in traditional 1.0 RDMS models intersects with big-data 2.0 models, understanding how this is constructed from an architectural standpoint is important. While it is beyond the scope of this work to cover the various architectures in use with their associated strengths, an institution must constantly have visibility into the direction and changes happening in the software platform. The application technology underlying big data is extremely dynamic. In contrast to the world of relational databases, new software tools and approaches to specific problems are constantly coming into the marketplace of ideas. For an organization used to slow development and release cycles, this arena is much more chaotic. Having a strategy and a plan is helpful over the short to medium term, but there must be frequent re-evaluations of the strategy and direction. In walking down the big-data path, each organization will need to understand their priorities and goals. The role of little data and big data strategically and the institution's resource commitment will ultimately determine the scale and capabilities of the analytics environment.

3.2.2 Analytics Maturity of the Customer

The entire effort of undertaking a big-data project is to deliver tangible value to the target customer. That customer must be involved in the project build process and in helping to drive the final product. Moving from a 1.0 mindset in which data quality can be measured and controlled—a quantitative and retrospective appraisal—into the 2.0 world, in which data fidelity can be assessed in contextual and qualitative ways, directly impacts how the data can be used, as well as its weaknesses and caveats. As with all analytics, these must be well understood so that valid inferences from the data can be made. Most data-savvy consumers have a good grasp of how this works with 1.0 data, but they must mature in their understanding in a 2.0 world. The natural place for this to happen is during the project execution, during which these relationships and limitations are being dealt with by the project team.

3.3 Data and Use Cases

As mentioned previously, definition of the use case is one of the most critical steps of the entire project and will directly bear on its success or failure. The use case is commonly described as an analytics or insight to be delivered to the enterprise from the technology. It must be extraordinarily well defined. This is not to say that, after the outset of the project, there can be no flexibility as more information is uncovered, as it is reasonable to expect changes to occur, but rather that these should refine and sharpen the scope of the final product rather than redefine it. A well-defined use case begins to show value immediately, as the project team can rapidly seek and locate target data sets. This process also will help the project team to discover who the other relevant stakeholders are. In keeping with the enterprise nature of many big data projects, stakeholders tend to be spread throughout the organization. With a clear use case, these distributed data owners can understand how their buy-in will advance the interests of the institution. Their support is necessary: as the team prepares to ingest datasets, the data owner can provide insight and context that will be critical when the data comes together within an analytics. The discovery phase is important for the team to get a sense of the underlying complexity, data fidelity, and granularity. For the project, the use case must become a touchstone or guiding star. With a clear use case defined, teams can quickly and independently control scope, evaluate completion, and understand risks.

3.3.1 Metadata and Tools

Just as in the relational world, understanding a data source begins with the analysis of surrounding metadata. Broadly, metadata is data that describes the dataset. Systematically compiling and characterizing the metadata of source data sets is the foundation of a data catalog. This is an activity that requires maintenance over the life of the effort. Common attributes include relationships between and among the data elements, measures of quality, statistical measures of components, rules, and any structure that can be delineated. Creation of a data catalog helps analysts within an organization discover and use existing data resources. As these datasets are brought into production, limitations and caveats are characterized. These insights are added back into the catalog to help inform future users.

Many vendors have commercial tools to structure and streamline this process. Some suites of products include seamless user interfaces, which enable analysts to perform data discovery, fidelity/quality assessments, and metadata characterization, all from one platform and single repository. For organizations with a well-developed 1.0 understanding, many of these disciplines and toolsets already exist within the enterprise and can be adapted to the 2.0 use case. It is important to take an inventory of existing tools for manipulation and characterization of data. This creates a baseline to understand the current state of infrastructure and work toward a gap analysis.

Extending 1.0 platforms to big-data–enabled versions leverages the legacy investment and the knowledge base as well as the training of the workforce. So, what is the role of open source? As organizations gain knowledge and experience with the vendor-supplied tools, they begin to have a better understanding of the limitations of their platform. The rapid evolution within the open-source community sees customer teams characterizing open-source tools and capabilities that are not supported by their vendor. In showing value from these pieces of software, they begin to lead and drive vendor roadmaps.

Is this to say that a large capital investment in tools is a prerequisite for a successful big-data effort? While capital dollars are always useful, projects can take advantage of any number of common tools, such as Excel and open-source offerings. The tradeoff for lower cost is seen in slower time to market, steeper learning curves, and wasted efforts as a team attempts to create its own ecosystem toolset while simultaneously executing the big-data project. These hurdles can add additional external dependencies and uncertainties that can affect project execution. Their inclusion presents clear business tradeoffs impacting project budget, scope, and time to value.

3.3.2 Reference and External Data Sets

One of the advantages that an Analytics 2.0 effort brings to an organization is the ability to incorporate external data into internal analysis. The variety of external data is seemingly unlimited and should not be ignored. Geospatial, weather, population, and demographic data sets are readily available, some at no charge from government agencies. The value of inclusion of this type of data into an early use case is that these sources tend to be well characterized and understood. These elements are often considered novel within the enterprise and can help demonstrate the power of a 2.0 effort.

3.4 Effects of Organizational Structure

For organizations with an established 1.0 infrastructure, 2.0 efforts represent a logical extension of capability. In the early stages, existing personnel are employed to cross-train and use the initial forays into big data as a stretch assignment. Some individuals may already have substantial knowledge of the subject area and are logical choices. As this capability begins to grow and become more distinct, the ability to stretch reaches limits. The organization is at a crossroads at which further progress requires additional talent. Knowledge of statistics, math and data analysis, and visualization techniques becomes a critical skill gap. This is the role of the data scientist. Team dynamics also change, as the data scientist brings an ability to drive insights into the data, much like a subject-matter expert. These resources naturally become more closely aligned with the customer. Within clinical academic medicine, it is difficult to position these groups optimally within the organization. The natural tendency is to place them within the IS organization because their function is closely tied to the technology. Moving them into the business or clinical unit places the development effort much closer to the final customer, but separates them from the resources and support within the IS. Close coordination between the team and the target customer can be extremely helpful. Many organizations over the longer-term attempt to capture the best parts of both relationships with a matrixed approach. A team having the ability to draw on the IS bench of talent while at the same time becoming part of the customer organization can work very well.

3.4.1 Building a Skills Roadmap

In an initial big-data effort, a small team usually works closely together to accomplish their goal. As an organization begins more and larger projects, the number of individuals devoted to the effort will begin to increase. As this occurs, specialization of work increases and the team begins to subdivide along skill sets. While this is common in the workplace, creation of a set of functionally isolated silos is detrimental. An alternative approach is to build analytics delivery teams. These can be led by a project manager working with a data scientist. Dedicated to a project, this structure enables organizations to assemble teams focused on specific deliverables. Over the life of an analytics project, required skills change, and with a flexible delivery structure, team members can move from one effort to the next as their skills are utilized across several concurrent work streams.

3.5 Conclusion

Creating a successful Analytics 2.0 effort begins in the early stages of the project. Assembling the appropriate sponsorship and creating a clear and compelling use case is key. Without sponsorship, setbacks and difficulties can capsize an effort before a product is completed. The use case serves as the guide star for the project team and the sponsors to judge progress and trajectory. It can be used to limit scope creep and set the parameters for success by which the team is ultimately judged at delivery. Spending time in this step shows benefits throughout the entire project lifecycle.

Taking time to understand the technical infrastructure is important. While traditional RDBMS platforms are well characterized and extremely common within healthcare organizations, the Analytics 2.0 environment is typically constructed from open-source applications. While these applications are freely available, there exists a number of vendors that help to create an ecosystem of support so that institutions are not completely on their own when building and maintaining a production environment.

An initial inventory of the tools used to manipulate and manage data sets is necessary. Understanding what is already owned is helpful before looking to expand. Many vendors have already created a migration pathway from Analytics 1.0 into the 2.0 world. In staying with a current vendor, the organization can leverage existing training and relationships. Careful consideration must be taken in seeking to create one's own ecosystem of tools based primarily on open source. While reducing cost, this can increase time to delivery and overall project risk.

Understand the maturity of the organizational environment. For institutions with a mature Analytics 1.0 capability, many of the disciplines necessary for success in the 2.0 effort exist and need to be expanded and refined. For organizations with immature environments, capabilities such as data discovery, data characterization, and data catalog creation are critical. Tools necessary to support these efforts are widely available from vendors or are open-source alternatives. Focusing on building organizational capability in these areas is critical for success.

Understand the data sources available to the project. Including data from third-party vendors and government sources can help demonstrate the power of bringing in data to an analytics not previously seen. These sources tend to be well characterized and fairly inexpensive.

Understand the role of data fidelity in the Analytics 2.0 environment as compared to data quality in the Analytics 1.0 environment. Variety and Velocity of big data require a contextual understanding of Veracity as defined by data fidelity. Following the NRF Framework (described on page 26) provides practical recommendations on this topic.

Understand the maturity of the target consumer. If the use case is well crafted, the customer will adopt and use the insights to chart the trajectory of the business. Creating an organizational structure that moves the project team closer to the target user is helpful in keeping the vision of the end user in the loop.

As organizations mature in the 2.0 environment, machine learning, natural language processing, and the capabilities of the Analytics 3.0 world become the next big challenge. (For a more in-depth discussion of machine learning, see Chapter 7, *Applied Machine Learning for Healthcare,* and for more on NLP, see Chapter 6, *Big Data Advanced Topics.*) Building a solid platform to support these advanced initiatives is the ultimate goal. Lessons learned from deep experience in traditional analytics, as well as those from alternatively structured data sets, enable those organizations that invest in these capabilities to step into the 3.0 world naturally, as an evolutionary step rather than a risky leap.

Moving into the 2.0 world is a challenge, but it is within the grasp of most healthcare organizations today. While not yet widely adopted across the industry, Analytics 2.0 offers those who execute it effectively the benefits of first-mover advantage. As organizations more widely embrace this technology, it will become a necessary investment to remain competitive with those who had previously taken the plunge.

Chapter Four

Big Data—Challenges

John Frenzel

If you want to build a ship, don't drum up the men to gather wood, divide the work and give orders. Instead, teach them to yearn for the vast and endless sea.

—Antoine de Saint-Exupery, from *Citadelle,* 1948

4.1 Building Your Strategy

The hallmark of a successful analytics strategy ultimately is one that results in sustainable data delivery, as this demonstrates value to the enterprise and alignment of critical resources (infrastructure, personnel, and business use cases). All three of these elements are necessary, and while many institutions can stretch to produce a one-off product, this is rarely a path that ultimately leads to sustainability. The end result will be judged successful only if it is capable of delivering insights seen as valuable by the end user and can keep pace with the customer as they embark on the walk of analytics maturity within a subject area. In the early stages of an analytics journey, there is useful work for test cases or pilot efforts in order to better understand the skills, abilities, and needs in a particular area; however, a distinction must be drawn between limited experimentation and institutional competency.

[*Note:* Before proceeding further, it would be useful to review the definitions of Analytics 1.0, 2.0, and 3.0, as described in Sections 1.2.1, 1.2.2, and 1.2.3.]

As stated previously, the business use case must lead the effort; however, a strategy will not emerge if it is born only from a series of business use cases. Building a strategy implies synthesis, and with synthesis of purpose follows efficacy and agility. This cannot be achieved without institutional commitment and organizational change. Creating a sustainable data delivery pipeline requires change that is in itself difficult. This is one of the key reasons that organizations fail to make the leap from an Analytics 1.0 environment into the 2.0 world. Analytics 2.0 is complex and, for most organizations, represents uncharted territory. Sustainable institutional analytics competency delivers data in an agile manner from a platform that minimizes rework, rediscovery, and churn.

For the promise of an Analytics 2.0 effort to be fully realized, foundational investment with a strategic perspective must be embraced. There are two distinct challenges that emerge—technical and organizational; however, these challenges are intertwined. From the technical standpoint, data fidelity (validity and appropriateness of data *for intended use.* See Chapter 2, Section 2.4.2, *Veracity,* for a fuller description of data fidelity), and master data management (MDM) require a certain complement of tools, skills, and project management. These are all well within the grasp of most institutions looking to mount an Analytics 2.0 effort. From the organizational standpoint, however, there is much less certainty. Creating a data governance model requires buy-in from stakeholders across an organization, and building the case for this is time consuming. Potential stakeholders must understand how this will impact them and the role they will play.

Pursuing an Analytics 2.0 project is complex due to its multidimensional nature. As discussed in the preceding chapters, elements of technology, strategy, leadership, coalition building, and vision are all critical to the effort. For organizations coming to this with the maturity of proven people, processes, and information delivery, their ability to adapt to the 2.0 world represents an incremental change requiring some additive capabilities. However, most other organizations have strengths and weaknesses causing some of these disciplines to lead or lag. Effective data governance is a foundational element for sustained success. As stated previously, most organizations can come together to produce a "one-off" or "pilot" effort, and while this is a useful demonstration of Analytics 2.0 capabilities and its promise, it does not constitute a long-term approach. If an effort is seen as one with strategic value, then the business will expect sustainable results in terms of veracity, predictability, and ongoing investment cost. None of these are knowable when each effort is unique. Success flows from a system or process that is built on predictable and repeatable steps. Creating an environment in which this infrastructure exists is required to fulfill the vision and promise of Analytics 2.0.

4.2 The Need for Data Governance

The concept of data governance is not new; its roots date back to the beginning of enterprise mainframe applications. Organizations understood early on that the value of their data was not limited to providing a transactional legacy but could have utility to the business in and of itself. This secondary use of this data was seen as a potential business advantage, although one limited by siloed systems, lack of metadata, and immature governance structures. As data warehousing technology began to evolve, early leaders in this space created hand-crafted data models and analytics to deliver information. These were seen as risky ventures and warehousing as an expensive gamble. For healthcare environments even into the mid-2000s, a best-of-breed application landscape was common, and institutions with resources to devote to data warehousing faced the need to manage vocabularies, curate metadata, and understand data fidelity (validity and appropriateness of data *for intended use.* See Chapter 2, Section 2.4.2, *Veracity,* for a fuller description of data fidelity). Organizations such as the Healthcare Data and Analytics Association (HDAA, previously Healthcare Data Warehousing Association, HDWA) worked to share ideas and lessons learned. Many organizations became successful using these tools and leveraging the knowledge developed within these communities to build robust Analytics 1.0 environments.

As business computing evolved, the natural collapse of isolated best-of-breed applications into enterprise suites began to occur. Business and finance being a more mature application space led this trend with the evolution of increasingly comprehensive suites of products, as typified by Lawson and Oracle's PeopleSoft. Healthcare has lagged behind this trend, and it is only in the last decade that full-service, monolithic application suites have become available to meet the needs of complex hospital and ambulatory environments. Organizations worked to retire best-of-breed applications and gained real efficiencies in moving to a suite of solutions from a single vendor. With this evolution, reporting environments within these suites were created by vendors to service broader queries and became warehouses unto themselves.

The urgency for data governance within these environments lessened as the suite vendor took on much of this responsibility. HIMSS Analytics has regularly gathered data on the industry state of EHR adoption via the EMR Adoption Model (EMRAM). This model grades adoption on a scale of 0 to 7. Between 2006 and 2015, the rankings demonstrate a substantial shift. In 2006, 0.6% of hospitals were working at stage 5 or higher. In 2016, nearly 60% were at stage 5 or higher, and 25% were at stage 6 or 7. This is an enormous change and represents the widespread adoption of suite-based EHRs. Hospitals are now awash in data from the automated and integrated applications they have installed, and for many it has been a journey to understand and incorporate this data into operations.

With such a data-rich background and vendor support, why the call for Analytics 2.0? While many best-of-breed clinical silos have disappeared, the desire to join data between the EHR and other data types has not abated. The old problems of best of breed have been replaced with the problems foundational to Analytics 2.0. In academic and research environments, for example, genomic information as combined with the clinical presentation and history is difficult to produce but highly sought after.[1] Analyzing customer-sentiment data, understanding and predicting patient flow, and gaining insights into practice patterns driven by weather[2] all have the potential to improve the delivery of healthcare and the patient experience; but at this stage, no EHR is capable of ingesting these types of information. The need for environments in which to analyze this type of data is manifest, and this is the heart of the challenge of data governance in the Analytics 2.0 world.

4.2.1 Data Governance in the Analytics 1.0 Environment

The Data Management Association International (DAMA) defines data governance as "the exercise of authority, control, and shared decision making (planning, monitoring, and enforcement) over the management of data assets." Or from an operational standpoint: "the

---

[1] Wei, W.Q. and Denny, J.C. (2015). "Extracting Research-Quality Phenotypes from Electronic Health Records to Support Precision Medicine." *Genome Medicine,* Vol. 7, No. 41. Published April 30, 2015. DOI: 10.1186/s13073-015-0166-y

[2] Huang, Y. and Hanauer, D.A. (2014). "Patient No-Show Predictive Model Development Using Multiple Data Sources for an Effective Overbooking Approach." *Appl Clin Inform.* Vol. 5, No. 3, pp. 836–860. Published September 24, 2014. DOI: 10.4338/ACI-2014-04-RA-0026

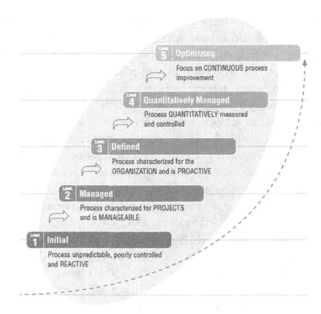

Figure 4.1   Data Governance Maturity Model. (Used Courtesy of International Business Machines Corporation, © 2007 International Business Machines Corporation.)

coordination of people, processes and technology in order to manage and optimize the use of data as a valued enterprise asset."[3] Over the decades, many models have been developed to help us understand an organization's maturity, including vendor-based models (as an example, from IBM [Figure 4.1]), consulting firms, and professional organizations. These exercises are usually comfortable for both the client and the consulting organization, as the outcome results in a series of well understood recommendations focused on attaining the next level of competency.

But that is not the point for organizations moving into an Analytics 2.0 environment. The utility and need of a maturity assessment is to systematically uncover and characterize where gaps exist within the enterprise so that they can be understood and potentially addressed prior to the commencement of a large capital project such as Analytics 2.0. If an organization has no capabilities in MDM, for example, this will become a critical impediment to success later on when the data exploration phase of the effort begins. Having the ability to proactively address this weakness helps improve the odds of success. Maturity assessments can be done fairly quickly using internal resources and publicly available information. The Capability Maturity Model (CMM) has a long track record and is well understood.

In 1989, the CMM was first described in the book *Managing the Software Process* by Watts S. Humphrey.[4] This project was the result of an effort by the US government and Carnegie

[3] *DAMA Dictionary of Data Management,* 2nd ed. (2011). Technics Publications, LLC. ISBN-10: 1935504118 ISBN-13: 978-1935504115

[4] Humphrey, W.S. (1989). *Managing the Software Process.* Addison Wesley Professional. ISBN-10: 0201180952 ISBN-13: 978-0201180954

Mellon University to better understand the ability of contractors to successfully implement software using objective measures to examine their business processes. The CMM created a set of structured levels that help to understand how well the behaviors, practices, and processes of organizations can sustainably produce the desired outcome. The level of maturity is commonly assessed on a five-point scale, from lowest to highest: *Initial or Chaotic, Repeatable, Defined, Managed,* and *Optimizing.* This was found to be a very useful framework upon which much effort was expended to address needs across the industry. As organizations began to embrace this methodology, applying multiple models that are not integrated across an organization created variations and points of conflict as to direction and goals necessary to reach the next higher state of function. In 2002, CMMI Version 1.1 was released. It incorporated the various models that had flourished over the past decade into a single coherent framework. Version 1.3 was released in 2010, and in 2014 CMMI released the Data Management Maturity (DMM) Model, which focuses on how organizations can better manage their data assets.

The DMM Model is comprehensive, with six categories, 15 component areas, 36 business process areas, 18 policies and procedures, and over 200 capability measures. IT organizations involved in analytics and data warehousing have an understanding of these disciplines with varying mastery. As an enterprise naturally matures in an Analytics 1.0 world, it must grapple with these concepts and gain experience in the problem space. Many of these elements are necessary for success in the Analytics 1.0 world, and organizations with a strong data delivery can effectively leverage them for success in the 2.0 world. For those organizations attempting to move directly into the Analytics 2.0 world without experience in the 1.0 space, caution is warranted and focus must be given to these topics, especially in the areas of standards, procedures, and building a framework for data fidelity (data quality *in the context of its use.* See Chapter 2, Section 2.4.2, *Veracity,* for a fuller description of data fidelity). Although these concepts are fairly well defined, they require organizational change, oftentimes in how processes are built and how people work, to actually derive the benefit of the discipline. In all areas that impact human interactions, this takes time and political capital. One must also keep in mind that the utility of a maturity assessment does not lie in the actual accomplishments of the organization, but rather in recognizing the strengths, gaps, and deficits. Organizations looking to undertake an Analytics 2.0 project would be well served by spending time reviewing the elements assessed in the DMM.

4.2.2 Elements of Data Governance in a 2.0 World

Success in an Analytics 2.0 environment is predicated on leveraging the capabilities and resources of an existing Analytics 1.0 infrastructure. Organizations lacking 1.0 infrastructure and experience will find that they will nonetheless need to build these capabilities as they mature, because while the data is different in structure, many of the needs are the same. A robust data governance program is one of these critical strengths, but it must be adapted to function with data sources and sets that are fundamentally different from the set rows and tables of an Analytics 1.0 world. Data governance is generally defined as the overall management of the availability, usability, integrity, and security of the data employed in an enterprise.[5]

---

[5] Thomas, G. (2013). "Defining Data Governance." Retrieved Sept 25, 2013, from www.datagovernance. com/defining-data-governance

The challenge here is clear. Healthcare organizations have large "pools" of alternatively structured data in the form of images, scanned documents, graphs, and text. Even this data within an electronic health record are poorly categorized and understood from an analytics perspective. Approaching this requires systematic effort to make this information available, usable, and representative.

4.2.3 Establishing Sources of Truth

In a mature Analytics 1.0 environment, analytics data should be clean, well understood, and trusted. Accomplishing this requires continuous effort using an iterative process. Many organizations begin with the identification of systems of record or sources of truth. Generally, these systems provide data that is foundational to the understanding of the institution. Examples would be PeopleSoft for employees or Cerner for patients. As the organization begins to pursue an analytics program, it identifies within these systems of record data quality issues and then work to modify the transactional environment to produce cleaner, higher-quality data. As slowly as the organization moves from a system-centric view toward an enterprise one, there emerges an advantage in building deep competency within certain domains. These domains oftentimes represent master data. What is characteristic of these data sets is that they are well known, deeply trusted, and of high quality. The early stages of a successful MDM effort require an organization to identify data sets that are critical to the enterprise. This is an important step and must be done in collaboration with the analytics team as well as the information owners.

Moving into the Analytics 2.0 environment, many of these certainties are challenged. Systems of record can be a Twitter feed driving a sentiment analytics or Natural Language Processing (NLP)-derived co-existing disease lists. The ability to influence the source systems to produce clean data is limited, and while these are sources of record, they will never be as clean or reliable as the Master Patient Index (MPI)-type information. Using data derived from these alternative sources represents a challenge. The contextual uses of data and the velocity of fast-data sources (as discussed in Chapters 2 and 3) drives the need to privilege data fidelity over data quality. In addition to building the analytics, the team must also supply insight into its limitations and help the customer understand what decisions the data can support and what inferences it cannot. This process of interpretation is iterative, requiring a much deeper engagement with the customer. The ability of the data analytics team to function at this level requires that they understand in detail the business use case. As they walk toward analytics maturity with that customer, they must help to educate them on the constraints found in the data, such as issues of data fidelity and quality.

4.3 Role of Master Data Management

Sustainable data delivery occurs when the underlying processes of data collection and quality are robust and reliable. Within every organization, core data elements exist that are used and reused. These data elements are candidates to belong within a Master Data Management

(MDM) effort. MDM creates structure and lineage around these elements so that they become trustworthy and regarded as sources of truth. Master data management efforts help organizations identify these critical data sets, standardize their characteristics, and assure their quality and fidelity in the future. This effort constitutes a fundamental step in creating a platform for sustainable data delivery. Efforts expended on mastering this data pay dividends not only through reuse but also with solid analytics that follow.

Within an Analytics 1.0 environment, mastered dimensions are important for sustainability, but many organizations have succeeded without highly mastered data. In an Analytics 2.0 organization, the creation of a robust MDM capability is critical for sustained success because mastered data is longitudinally stable. In the 2.0 world, lack of stability becomes increasingly problematic. Without an MDM program, analysts must use rules within the data integration tools, data exclusion, and other techniques to help clean these critical data sets in flight. In doing so, they can create uncertainty and bias within the data. As we saw in Section 2.4.2, in an Analytics 2.0 world, higher-quality data is being combined commonly with data sets of lower quality and higher variability. As analysts begin to stack uncertainties atop one another, the ability to understand underlying trends and insight declines. When the cleaning routines used to master the data on the fly change, data sets can fundamentally be altered and lead to skewed results.

MDM is designed to work with structured, relational data, and in the environment of Analytics 2.0, these data sets are typically unstructured or alternatively structured. While the alternatively structured data to be analyzed may not conform to the tools of the 1.0 world, there usually exist elements of MDM amenable to serve as guideposts of value within the data set. Web traffic from a patient wayfinding application, for example, could have wireless access point addresses embedded, indicating that location information and headers within the free text could have an MRN. While not directly mastering the alternatively structured data, those mastered Analytics 1.0 data sets become enabling. Master data management is the glue that couples datasets and their resulting insights together. Starting an analysis based on the dimensions that bear on the unstructured data to guide discovery seems intuitive. MDM causes institutions to focus on and systematize the understanding of data that is of critical importance to the organization. Beginning with these elements will help not just to tie the results to well-characterized dimensions but also to align results with issues that the business has deemed *a priori* important. Using the reverse approach to augment and absorb important understanding of the unstructured source into the mastered dimension enables the enterprise to grow and expand the sources it understands and uses independent of structure, thus expediting time to insight.

4.3.1 Getting Started with Data Fidelity

Data flows from transactional environments into data structures designed to serve the needs of the transactional system—its primary purpose. Most organizations pull data from these primary structures and repurpose it to serve a secondary function. As the context of the data moves further from the primary purpose, data quality issues become more pronounced and degrade utility. Moving from an Analytics 1.0 world in which data is confined to rows, columns, and tables into the alternatively structured universe of Analytics 2.0 magnifies the issue of data quality and management. There can be some objective certainty of data quality and context when data exists in columns and rows. Numerous applications exist that help organizations profile in these data sources and characterize the quality of the underlying data. Even so, data quality can be difficult to manage when just confined within these dimensions.

An Analytics 2.0 effort must have an unrelenting focus on characterizing and understanding data quality; however, most alternatively structured data sources return information that has a degree of ambiguity of context and inaccuracy of fact. For example, free text clinic notes that are processed into concepts via an NLP pipeline are stripped of surrounding textual history and, potentially, the narrative context. While annotators have parsed sentence structure, identified parts of speech, and attempted to account for logical negation, accuracy is not perfect. Nuances of language and complex semantic references irretrievably degrade the accuracy. Automated abstraction is not the root of this issue, but rather the variability of human expression. Trained human data extractors can study the same source material and arrive at different facts.

Data fidelity requires some measure of data quality to exist. For the 2.0 environment, this becomes complex and specific to the underlying data. In the NLP example, using manual extraction to create a baseline would be a logical first step. Building a known, correct dataset, while time consuming, would be extraordinarily helpful. This is commonly not part of a data quality effort in the 1.0 world, but solutions in the 2.0 world must account for data fidelity. Using the baseline data, statistical profiling harnessing frequency analysis and true positive/false positive rate for the various concepts begins to build an objective picture. Over time, a fundamental understanding of the data will emerge, illustrating its strengths or weaknesses and helping to inform the fitness of purpose.

Bringing an NLP-derived data source into production does not complete the process. In this case, it is critical to collect metadata around versioning of the pipeline and associated annotators. As improvements occur in the pipeline, the source data can be reprocessed and moved into production following additional characterization. On the change management side of this effort, consensus from stakeholders must occur as to how this reprocessed data is brought into production and how it will impact ongoing analytics series. Reprocessing source data with new concept extraction technology can improve accuracy but can potentially begin to skew derived analytics. Many organizations store multiple versions of derived data using metadata characterizing critical aspects to help the analytics user select the correct set. Similar issues arise in the genomics space when changes occur to sequencing pipelines and their associated variant call annotators. Data fidelity analysis in the 2.0 world must adapt to fit the data utilizing applicable tools and methodologies. These are new skills to a functioning 1.0 team and require study and education for both data provider and customer. (An example of one of these methodologies is the NRF Framework, described on page 26.)

The goal in an Analytics 2.0 effort is to create novel insights and enable improved decision making based on understanding of the data. Within mature 1.0 organizations, analytics producers and consumers have a reasonable expectation of the process and how the finished product appears. Organizations generally have a portfolio of Business Intelligence (BI) tools, and their analysts have a firm understanding of the context of the data. As one moves into the 2.0 arena, both these understandings become less certain. As referenced above, the alignment of the analytics team and the business case must be much closer. Visualization of data changes substantially, not necessarily in form, but in the details. For example, in addition to the analytics presentation, there will be an entire additional layer of data insights focused on the statistical accuracy and limits of the presented analysis. This second part requires customer education because it describes the accuracy and limitations of the analytics. In a 1.0 world, accuracy can be established through traditional data-quality metrics. Efforts to "perfect" the data can occur over years of fine-tuning transactional systems to produce clean information, yet misinterpretations still occur due to misunderstanding the context of the data. In a 2.0 use case in which critical information is derived from an NLP pipeline with a true positive rate of 72%, a true negative rate of 87% for hypertension, and a different set of values for diabetes, these explanations, understandings, and caveats are critical.

Analytics 2.0 commonly brings new stakeholders to the table who have not previously participated in data pooling or analytics efforts. These organizations oftentimes have widely varying understandings of the process and the product. It is within the walk of maturity with these new data consumers that the understanding of the nuances and limitations of data sources and techniques must take place. Clear alignment of the business use case and the analytics effort was emphasized earlier in this work. Delivering a stable, predictable product that informs the business requires a level of collaboration and education that is much more involved than in the 1.0 world. Without the foundational alignment and clarity of the use case at the start of an effort, success is difficult to achieve.

4.3.2 Organization

As institutions mature in their Analytics 1.0 efforts, their organizational structures have also had to grow and adapt. In the legacy world of isolated reporting environments built to serve individual applications, duplication of skills across the enterprise was common. Over time, areas of expertise emerged, and from that began a specialization of skill sets. In a successful 1.0 organization, these diverse groups consolidate and work more closely as a team. On the team, one sees skill-based verticals forming, such as data integration, data modeling, data fidelity/quality, MDM, and project management. A critical benefit to centralization of these individuals arises as they drive convergence on common software application platforms and common skillsets. Similar capabilities and training can bring a standard level of expertise across the team. Moving to a common data integration application, for example, also drives the development of methodologies and standards. As the team works together, they build an informal knowledge repository. Mature organizations make this repository explicit, and searchable cataloging approaches can be used to help train management and staff in adopting common approaches to data issues.

As the organization transitions into the 2.0 environment, this process tends to repeat. Instead of integration developers, now the organization is faced with the role of data scientists, for example, working in silos. Again, having the political will and organizational foresight to bring these individuals together is defining. By doing this, the organization gains not just economies of scale, as mentioned above, but agility of action. To sustainably deliver data to the enterprise, it is critical to build standard, repeatable processes at each step, driving out as much variation as possible. Foundational to this is the creation of methodologies. These can run the gamut from naming conventions through statistical approaches to understanding the quality and fidelity of NLP-derived data. Work by the team in building method-based approaches adds overhead at the outset but pays enormous dividends as the team grows. To achieve the goal of becoming sustainable, predictable, and agile, the time spent building and maintaining a library of methodologies is critical, as it tends to reduce costs and increase effectiveness through coordination of efforts. It builds a systematic process which then can leverage project management disciplines. These become the building blocks necessary for transparency, and as this approach matures, the ability to understand return on effort for resources expended naturally builds the case for future investment.

4.3.3 Stewardship

Across all modern organizations, there exists data that has been gathered, curated, and published from many sources, official and unofficial, in the quest to generate insight into business processes. Within academic medical centers, these commonly exist as Longitudinal Patient Disease Registries (LPDR), which serve the needs of individual researchers and scientists. For example, a surgeon collects and manages a 25-year case history of all appendiceal carcinomas (his specialty) presenting to the hospital practice. While clearly a niche against the broader backdrop of the institution, it represents a professional life's work and a wellspring of ongoing academic insight. Moving this data into the larger construct of the organization and potentially joining it with genomic sequencing data could add incredible value—but potentially at the cost of loss of franchise.

This concern of individual data privacy predates the dawn of electronic databases and continues to intensify today, as more personal data is produced and collected. Be it in the customer domain or the employee space, great care and forethought must be undertaken as data sources are collated.

Stewardship is a core component of data governance. Organizations have numerous sources of data, and as they are brought together, they gain increased value when seen in the context of other information. Creating this larger context is critical for the enterprise but potentially detrimental to the individual. Without some form of representative governance, individuals have little incentive to share, even when potential gains are large.

This task becomes one of data stewardship at the enterprise, but within the academic environment it can roll down to the level of individual efforts. Data stewards appropriate the role of ownership from the data management side of the task. They are responsible for understanding the fitness of the data elements and help to enforce policies, guidelines, and regulatory obligations. Within an academic environment they must also become the representative of that data stakeholder within the larger construct of the institution. For individuals to contribute, this process of stewardship and privacy controls must be explicit and well conceived. Independent of intentions, a ham-handed or clumsy engagement with this community can dramatically undercut partnership efforts. This is a process that will take patience and time. Building a broad-based steering team to help formulate policies is critical.

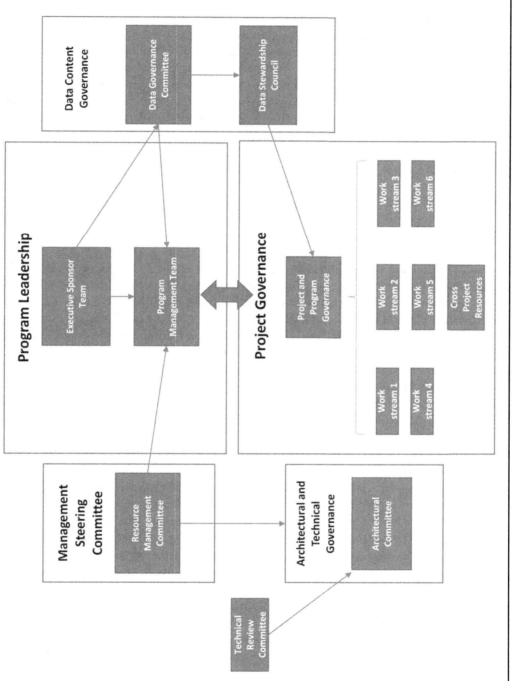

Figure 4.2 Sample framework currently in use at a major healthcare institution. (Explained on next page.)

4.3.4 Bringing It All Together—A Federated Approach

Bringing the components of data governance, stewardship, MDM, and technical oversight into an Analytics 2.0 effort is complex. Critical to the success is a framework which binds the analytics and warehousing teams to the customer and enterprise. Building this framework is time consuming but necessary for success. Represented in Figure 4.2 (on previous page) is a sample framework currently in use at a major healthcare institution. The framework is not an organizational chart or project plan, but spans the two in describing how issues and initiatives are directed and decided across the effort. The three verticals include architecture/technical governance, program governance, and data content/stewardship. While initially built to govern a classic relational warehouse model, the project takes a federated approach to subject-matter mastery and analytics deliverables.

Alternatively, structured data was brought into this effort as the institution moved into the 2.0 environment. Some modifications became necessary as, for example, streaming vital-sign–derived and NLP-derived information was incorporated. For a more mature organization, this was an evolutionary step in the governance model. Where an institution sits on the governance maturity curve dictates the level of disruption and reorganization necessary to accommodate the 2.0 effort. Underlying the governance model is an agile methodology for analytics development and content ingestion that is used to drive completion of business use cases. Classical waterfall or mixed methodologies can also be applied without great effect on the structure.

From a personnel standpoint, many healthcare organizations' data and analytics resources are distributed across the enterprise. This is usually a remnant from the best-of-breed silos or a department-based organizational focus. Within these teams exist deep resources with understanding of the specific transactional systems and local analytics needs. Effectively engaging these groups in an enterprise effort is difficult. The local resource owners are worried about loss of talent to a centralized project, and the IS team is concerned about lack of agreement with methodologies and data standards, resulting in project disruption. In order to succeed, each team must learn from the other.

Building federated teams is one successful approach. With this methodology, the central IS organization is responsible for creating the tools and artifacts for ingestion, curation, governance, and analytics constructs. This would include master data elements that are core to the business. These are foundational to the platform and embody strategic decisions made within the institution. In creating these constructs prior to the engagement, the project team is able to teach each federated group how the project works and the standards for participating. The distributed teams bring deep understanding of the subject matter, business needs, and processes. Each group contributes dedicated members to the effort with the understanding that this is a long-term commitment. The IS team would provide overall project management. Skill composition for a federated delivery team would include a data modeler, a data integration developer, a business analyst, and an analytics developer matched one for one by individuals from the distributed team. As the combined teams work together, diffusion of knowledge occurs, and an ongoing commitment to training is necessary to help fill skills gaps identified in the distributed team.

Rapid delivery of analytics insight is critical. Early in the project plan, analytics use cases must be clearly identified. These must serve the business need and bring early value to the customer. Working backward, data targets are identified for ingestion to support the analytics. Using an agile method for analytics delivery, multiple deliverable iterations are built over time.

With this approach, the business realizes value quickly from the effort, and the teams are naturally directed toward high-value data first. As the federated groups collaborate in this effort, they continue to grow in the understanding of the data, supporting structures, and methodologies. For the customer, they have the opportunity to size the teams dedicated to this effort as they see results. If the business finds value, augmenting the team with additional resources to proceed more quickly is the next step. If there is little value shown, or if other more compelling business opportunities arise, the contribution shrinks. Using this approach, the limited resources of the central IS team are concentrated in domains in which the data owners have high interest and need. Whatever the final outcome, the central IS organization continues to understand the customer data and to ingest, steward, and govern for the enterprise.

For IS organizations without distributed teams or limited resources, collaboration becomes even more critical. Building an inclusive structure to leverage individuals who have deep knowledge within these customer areas is the first step. Attempting to expropriate data or exclude local experts slows down any effort and results in political consequences. Focus on rapid analytics deliverables with many small additive iterations is important so that the customer can learn and understand what these products contain and begin to leverage them as soon as possible within the course of business. As the products become well understood, the customer is in a much more informed position to direct the next cycle of development and to bring business value. This walk of analytics maturity between the development team and the customer helps to build trust and understanding of the process between the partners.

4.4 The Skills Gap

An organization with an active Analytics 1.0 capability will encounter the need to augment the range of skills of a team beginning to explore alternatively structured data. While many technologies and skillsets are directly applicable in the 2.0 world, challenges exist where novel approaches must be embraced, and these require additional talent.

Most widely discussed is the role of the data scientist. This title has many different meanings and is filled by individuals with a wide variety of skills. The data scientist must have analytics ability, strong mathematics/statistics background, the ability to present/communicate their ideas, and most importantly, lead teams and delegate tasks. These individuals are in great demand and command substantial salaries. For many organizations, finding a suitable employee requires time, and once one is hired, the challenge becomes using the resource effectively. Being a highly skilled, independent agent with proficiency across multiple disciplines, these individuals can handle a variety of different data-focused tasks. They can assess data fidelity and quality, merge datasets, write SQL queries, perform statistical analysis, create PowerPoints, and so on. Leading organizations are realizing that in order to obtain the greatest value from this talent, it is important to surround these people with a team. Too often, because they are competent in all these various tasks, they become the ones who actually perform them. This is a waste of time and talent. Creation of a team led by the data scientist enables the scientist to focus on those issues and tasks requiring their particular expertise and offloading more mundane duties to less skilled resources. This also has the effect of multiplying their effectiveness, as they are able to work on several projects in parallel.

Constructing a team to support a data scientist is driven by the tasks and the skills required for that specific analytics use case. Commonly, team members include a data modeler, project manager, and business analyst. For smaller teams, these can be part-time roles, and in larger organizations, these are usually served through a pool of resources. Obviously, depending on the problem at hand, other skills exist that would be useful and would be pulled into the team as necessary.

Adding a data scientist role into an existing organization can be disruptive, as it changes the structure and reporting relationships. Many individuals do not grasp the role that this employee plays and what value they can bring to the team. Given the novelty of the position, oftentimes a data scientist is similarly confused and requires guidance and structure. This is a management challenge. Clarity of the role as understood within the organization is critical for their success. In some ways, these challenges exist more as a scaling problem. When an organization needs to add a second or third data scientist, the issues discussed above have resolved themselves. It is in the initial organizational shift when the role is introduced where the risk primarily exists.

4.4.1 Consultants

The use of experienced consultants to help initially structure and drive an Analytics 2.0 effort may be necessary, as the Analytics 2.0 space is more ambiguous than a 1.0 environment. However, there are no easy routes or simple solutions. Each institutional Analytics 2.0 effort is unique and must be constructed to fit the environment within which it was conceived. The structure necessary for success is driven from the maturity of the organization, business use case, and level of institutional commitment. Creating a sustainable delivery model comes from enterprise ownership and a recognition of enterprise value. This effort must be driven organically from within the organization. It is never turn-key and is not a cookie-cutter solution. That is what makes this difficult. While the organization is focused on the end product achieved through all the different processes and steps discussed above, it is necessary for leadership to yearn for the sea of data all around them and, in doing so, grow the capabilities the 2.0 environment from within.

4.5 Conclusion

A multitude of challenges exists when embarking on Analytics 2.0. Information Services must focus on those elements that are core competencies. The use of the CMMI-DMM is a good starting point to benchmark the organization, but a specific level of accomplishment is not the endpoint, but rather is a structured tool to help in gap analysis.

Creating core competencies around data governance, which includes data stewardship, data fidelity, and MDM, are critical to building a sustainable program, as financial limits exist for all projects, and these components, if executed well, enable institutions to scale analytics without a lockstep increase in cost.

The project team must build the environment, methodologies, project management, and artifacts to support and guide the effort. Core data elements must be identified and mastered first. Without stability within these areas, rework, confusion, and cost increase.

The tasks of data governors are to create an understanding of institutional data sources and build an efficient process for access and knowledge of the information contained within. This spans the domains of stewardship, quality, and MDM. Integrating these functions into a comprehensive view helps to bridge the gap between project plan and organizational structure. With this, members new to the effort can more easily join and contribute.

Whether utilizing a federated project plan or not, there are multiple work streams that must be coordinated for a project such as this to be successful. Due to the multidisciplinary needs, IS must step out of its comfort zone and lead diverse project teams. If it cannot, then it must find a capable partner within the organization to take on this function. If this path is chosen, the partner must be IT and organization savvy.

Analytics 2.0 requires new ways of understanding data from the perspectives of data fidelity and MDM. While many Analytics 1.0 constructs and skills are easily adapted, the need exists for new resources and capabilities. Data scientists are a critical addition to the team. Learning what skills are important and how to leverage these resources effectively is important to the overall success of the effort. A good deal of thought needs to be put into the structure of the role and selection of the individual. Creating an environment in which they can be maximally engaged and rapidly productive is critical.

Chapter Five

Best Practices: Separating Myth from Reality

Prashant Natarajan

Practice does not make perfect—only perfect practice makes perfect.

—Vince Lombardi

As we saw in Chapter 2, big-data analytics has been around for a few years now, especially in e-commerce. However, as the technologies have matured and other industries have adopted big-data analytics in the last two to three years, we are not only seeing the results but are also getting a better understanding of what leads to success. Recent studies show that big data in each industry is defined according to domain-specific needs and uses. For example, again as we saw in Chapter 2, what constitutes such data in e-commerce is not identical to what constitutes it in healthcare, manufacturing, or other industries—even when we are looking through the lenses of the V's, discussed earlier. When I began researching for this book in early 2015, most big-data analytics projects were happening outside of healthcare and the life sciences. Operational reporting, Meaningful Use, and regulatory reporting were the primary foci of most healthcare provider analytics efforts, and big-data analytics success stories were still being written.

Best practices are propagated through a vertical or industry after success has been demonstrated. This is apparent in the case of big-data best practices as well. In order to write this chapter, I began by interviewing users, practitioners, executives, and academicians from verticals as diverse as e-commerce and retail, entertainment (video gaming), finance, manufacturing, and life sciences, among others. As the first healthcare providers started going live with big-data solutions in early 2016, I added them to my list of expert interviewees (prominent successes are included as case studies in Chapter 8). As a result, and over the course of the last two years of research and interviews, it became clear that there was a corpus of best practices that:

- Reliably led to desired results, on-time project completion, and organizational success
- Were independent of the domain or vertical in which they were applied

This chapter collects these best practices and organizes them into the following six categories in order to provide a ready reference that has been validated by others' successes and, as importantly, failures.

1. Determining purpose—understanding your journey
2. Organization readiness and preparation
3. Deployment options—cloud, on-premise, hybrid
4. Communication and collaboration
5. Technical considerations
6. Learning algorithms and machine learning

5.1 Debunking Common Myths

The field of big-data analytics is still littered with a few myths and evidence-free lore. The reasons for these myths are simple: the emerging nature of technologies, the lack of common definitions, and the non-availability of validated best practices. Whatever the reasons, these myths must be debunked, as allowing them to persist usually has a negative impact on success factors and Return on Investment (RoI). On a positive note, debunking the myths allows us to set the right expectations, allocate appropriate resources, redefine business processes, and achieve individual/organizational buy-in. So, without further ado, let's get started on debunking the most prevalent big-data myths still in existence.

5.1.1 Myth 1: Everyone Is Doing It

Big data gets many headlines and interest in big data is at a record high—within enterprises and in the popular press. According to Gartner, 73% of organizations surveyed in 2014 were investing or planning to invest in big data by 2016. However, in 2012, Gartner found that only 13% of those surveyed had actually deployed big-data solutions.[1] Fast forward to 2015: among 3,000 surveyed organizations, 17% were actively using big-data (defined here as exclusively Hadoop-based) solutions.[2] In other words, if you are a provider and are not yet live on big-data solutions, don't despair. You are not terribly behind the adoption curve yet—and you're not alone.

However, keep in mind that per various analysts, healthcare organizations, and research conducted by this author, 2016–2018 are expected to be banner years for both cross-industry and healthcare use of big data.

---

[1] "Gartner Debunks Five of the Biggest Data Myths." Gartner Business Intelligence & Analytics Summit, 2014, October 21–22. Accessed at http://www.gartner.com/newsroom/id/2854917

[2] Maguire, J. (2016). "The Surprising Truth about Big Data." Accessed at http://www.datamation.com/applications/the-surprising-truth-about-big-data.html

5.1.2 Myth 2: Big Data Is Hype

Despite current adoption, the promise of big data is real, and large majorities of businesses and organizations (within and outside of healthcare) see big data as critically important. The relatively low rates of adoption are not reflective of the realities or capabilities of relevant vendors or technologies—but are reflective of the current challenges with learning curve, organizational inertia, resourcing challenges, and the challenge of having enough out-of-the-box tools/applications around Hadoop (as it is among some other big-data solutions). According to Gartner, "the biggest challenges that organizations face are to determine how to obtain value from big data, and how to decide where to start. Many organizations get stuck at the pilot stage because they don't tie the technology to business processes or concrete use cases."[3]

In 2016, 40% of the companies polled by Forrester were already implementing or expanding their big-data technology adoption, while 30% plan to step up their usage within the next year.[4] In a 2016 IDC Health Insights report, there's evidence that the era of massive post-ARRA/MU EHR implementations and spending are behind us. Provider spending beyond 2016 is expected to be driven by analytics, and big data is here to stay.[5]

5.1.3 Myth 3: The McNamara Fallacy Applies to Big-Data Analytics in Healthcare

The McNamara Fallacy, named as such by Daniel Yankelovitch after Robert McNamara, refers to decision making that is supposedly based solely on:

1. Measuring what can be easily measured
2. Disregarding what can't be easily measured
3. Presuming that what can't be measured is not important
4. Presuming that what can't be measured does not exist[6]

This fallacy has been examined at some length in relation to healthcare and clinical trials. It is somehow seen as an indictment of quantitative measurement and analytics in healthcare. Such a view may have been relevant in the days of purely paper health/medical records when the lack of digital data contributed to low-value and limited reporting. It may still hold true when it comes to obtaining meaningful and actionable clinical analytics out of EHR data (that is

---

[3] "Gartner Debunks Five of the Biggest Data Myths." *op. cit.*

[4] Wheatley, M. (2016). "Forrester: Big Data Market to Grow Three Times Faster than Tech Overall." Accessed at http://siliconangle.com/blog/2016/10/03/nosql-vendors-to-lead-the-charge-in-fast-growing-big-data-market-forrester-says/

[5] "40% of U.S. Healthcare Providers Report IT Budgets are Growing, According to IDC Health Insights" (2016). Accessed at http://www.businesswire.com/news/home/20160201005324/en/40-U.S.-Healthcare-Providers-Report-Budgets-Growing

[6] Basler, M.H. (2009). "Medical Education and the McNamara Fallacy." *BMJ*, Vol. 339, No. b2863. DOI: http://dx.doi.org/10.1136/bmj.b2863. Accessed at http://www.bmj.com/rapid-response/2011/11/02/medical-education-and-mcnamara-fallacy

primarily managed for billing and reimbursement). However, to apply the McNamara fallacy to healthcare big data misses a few key points:

1. McNamara said famously that "not every conceivable complex human situation can be fully reduced to the lines of a graph, % points on a chart, figures on a balance sheet"—which is certainly true in the case of wellness and healthcare.

2. Data sources are becoming more varied and existing outside traditional OLTP source systems. Such data has value as it represents human participants' actions and behaviors—outside the four walls of the healthcare organization (see Chapter 2). As a result of these rich and fast data sources, the extent of what can be measured increases greatly and is no longer limited to the EHR.

3. Moore's Law continues to govern the cost of big-data compute and storage—it will become easier (and cheaper) to keep data rather than disregard it.

4. With new developments in machine learning (see Chapter 7, *Applied Machine Learning for Healthcare*), the ability to process data with methods other than traditional deterministic reasoning expands to probabilistic reasoning, inferencing, and prediction. The data that doesn't exist can now be predicted—and learning algorithms can work on healthcare big data with more efficiency and performance than can the average human being.

5. The purpose of computing is insight, not numbers. Big-data analytics, for the first time in the era of digital health data, will allow us to capture qualitative metrics—sentiments, emotions, behaviors, moods, and relationships—in addition to existing/new quantitative metrics. The net result is a more complete picture of the individual—and their interactions with other animate and inanimate entities.

6. For these reasons, workflows and analytics that integrate little data, big data, and machine learning will form the basis of cognitive healthcare and repudiation of this myth. In other words, big-data analytics is the antidote to the current limited practice of organizational/departmental performance measurement and mandated regulatory reporting.

5.1.4 Myth 4: We Don't Have any Big Data (or) We Need Large Volumes of Data to Begin Our Efforts (or) It's All About OMICS

All healthcare organizations have big data (see Table 2.1 in Chapter 2, page 23). This table also describes data sources other than OMICS, and they are varied and numerous. To examine the role of the four other V's in relation to volume, see Chapter 2.

5.1.5 Myth 5: You Need to Clean All the Data First

As reviewed in Chapter 2, data quality is important but context- and user-driven. Getting all the data to a state of perfect quality is costly and time consuming and contributes to data staleness. As stale data is also poor-quality data for the appropriate use case, data quality enforcement in entirety for each source/use case must not be a showstopper. While use cases that involve patient care and health require the highest-quality data, we must also acknowledge that there will always be use cases that will allow for data to be used in its current state—e.g., discovery analytics, feature or representational learning in machine learnin, and operational analytics.

The advantages of deploying analytics also include getting a better idea of data quality from profiling, determining appropriate data governance, and establishing corrective actions as close as possible to the point of data origin. Hence, it is possible to obtain value out of existing unclean/unclear data while implementing progressive data correction improvements.

5.1.6 Myth 6.a: Data Lakes Are the Universal Solution to All Big-Data Questions.

Myth 6.b: The DW Is Dead in This Age of Big Data. There's Little Value in Little Data/BI Anymore.

The originators of these myths are vendors with service or product biases, "experts" who don't understand the variety of health data sources or purists who believe in a single cure-all (data lake) for everything that ails healthcare analytics today—real and imagined. While it's beyond the scope of this book to examine each of these myths in detail, it's useful to understand some definitions.

- **Schema on Write.** Data in a warehouse is loaded based on semantics and structure and is validated based on pre-defined logical and physical data models.
- **Schema on Read.** In a data lake, we load the raw data, as is—warts, blemishes, and all. When the data is ready to be used, we apply a data model or interface/API on it to provide semantics and structure.

In our world, there will always be a need for both schema types. Existing source systems and analytics will stay and thrive—just as new data sources will come into existence requiring advanced analytics beyond BI. The data warehouse and the data lake will need to co-exist.

In summary:

1. Data lakes are flexible and useful. However, they are only one component of a big-data management/analytics solution.
2. Data lakes are not *in situ* replacements of your existing data warehouse or data marts. Use the lake to supplement your DW—establish bi-directional relationships between these stores—and combine little and big data.
3. The DW provides important context via little data and serves as a lodestone that establishes semantics and governance beyond any single source/department silo.
4. The cure for the difficulties in managing a data warehouse is not a data outhouse. In reality, for data in a lake to be usable for analytics, it needs to be organized, queryable, and well understood and trusted by users and domain experts alike.

5.1.7 Myth 7: Big Data = Hadoop & HDFS. IT Department's <<preferred arch/tech>> Is Big Data.

Clearly, as you've read in previous chapters, the scope of what constitutes healthcare data is large and diverse—as are its intended secondary use cases. While Hadoop and HDFS have a key role to play in your unified big-data architecture, your solution must also account for the variety of newer, alternative, and traditional technologies. Business users have a greater stake in obtaining all data—and that's not limited by a single technology or architecture. Data strategy and analytical use cases should be kept independent of technology, as much as possible, in order to take advantage of fast and new development/methods/tools in big-data storage/management/analytics.

5.1.8 Myth 8: Big-Data Projects Are Expensive (or) We Need Legions of Data Scientists to Manage Big Data

As you will see in the best practices section that follows, the key is to start small, be focused, and establish frequent RoI analysis. Storage in distributed computing environments and big-data appliances are becoming cheaper for on-premise environments—while storage and compute costs are also reducing drastically on cloud options. The availability of open-source technologies, increasing adoption by commercial software vendors, and integration with existing services/products will continue to lower the upfront cost and maintenance thresholds.

You will need data scientists to lay the groundwork for data science—statistical modeling, learning algorithm design, training model creation, and advanced analytics. However, good data scientists who possess healthcare domain experience are not too easy to find, and trying to hire a legion is not easy—nor is such hiring needed. The important thing for organizations is to leverage the data scientists you have by enabling them to focus on their strengths and skills. Your big-data analytics team must also contain users, domain experts, business analysts, and systems engineers from your existing teams.

5.2 Best Practices

"A method or technique that has consistently shown results superior to those achieved with other means, and that is used as a benchmark."[7]

The best practices here are a compilation of extensive interviews with seasoned data management and analytics practitioners—in and out of healthcare. In order for the community to take advantage of others' successes (and avoid their failures), it was clear that these recommendations be neither high-level and generic nor around a single tool or technology. As a result, you'll find the best practices to be practical and based on actual experience/knowledge from real-life deployments.

The intent of this section is not to be prescriptive but to inform you about what has worked successfully for others and let you determine what's relevant for you. Admittedly, some of these

---

[7] *Merriam-Webster.* Accessed at http://www.merriam-webster.com/dictionary/best practice

practices may be reiterations of what you already know or are already using in your analytics environments. If so, these points will serve as additional validation.

5.2.1 Determining Purpose and Scope

Avoid Big Bang and overly ambitious scope until your teams have gotten a handle on the use cases, workflows, data, and technologies. Any multi-destination journey, including this foray into big data and machine learning, starts with small steps. The best practice is to progressively define the scope of the analytics and data sources. If your team is new or inexperienced in designing/developing such solutions, they should start with known structured data/analytics and add a new big-data aspect to it. Similarly, scope of should begin at the department level before scaling up to the facility or the enterprise.

5.2.2 Solve a Pain Point or Create a New Opportunity for the Business, Providers, and Patients

Bringing in new data should be accompanied by opportunities to generate new insights. Avoid the temptation to structure your big-data efforts only around existing ad hoc querying, regulatory reporting, or existing BI. Leverage your existing reporting/BI applications for the data they contain, but integrate with new data to discover new use cases. Be proactive about demonstrating progress, ROI, and value on a rolling basis via appropriate metrics.

5.2.3 Use More Data Variety—Not Just Volume

While there will always be IT-driven use cases that may require big-data solutions for storage, backup, etc., keep in mind that analytics that draws upon greater variety of data sources (even with the accompanying variable data quality) is more impactful to business and users than the most optimal storage option. Unstructured data is a great option for business use cases, as they usually represent under-analyzed data and insights.

5.2.4 In Some Instances, It's OK for IT to Determine Use Cases

In some cases, it's appropriate for IT to determine the use cases—especially in the technical realm—as long as the solution also supports business needs. Big-data technologies are currently used by IT for:

- Backup and archiving: also addresses "sunsetting" challenge where legacy applications may not be available in the distant future.
- Managing active data storage on the cloud or in big-data appliances.
- Creating data repositories/lakes that can hold data in a wide range of formats—totally unstructured to highly structured Hadoop and other big-data storage/tools have costs

and resource needs too. For example, data retention should be considered in advance even for HDFS folders—consider moving/archiving out of HDFS to lower-cost storage when the retention period expires or the need for the data has passed.

5.2.4 The Hammer-Nail Conundrum

Big data is not a "one-size-fits-all" solution. Don't be afraid to say no to the latest big-data vendor or technology. Frankly, not every use case requires big-data management. RDBMS, DW/marts, and BI may be the better/cheaper option for your next project than the latest big-data technologies. Determine the benefits of the new technology compared to the cost of deployment/ maintenance/migration as a pre-condition to investing at scale across your enterprise.

5.2.5 The Need for Integration

The reality is that the space is changing fast and newer technologies are still maturing. For the foreseeable future, structured data will continue to be created in OLTP sources for existing business process, regulatory, or reimbursement needs. Many predict that a consequence of big-data management will result in increased creation of structured data and integration between little and big data. Expect to integrate structured and unstructured data. Big data considerably broadens the integration challenge as it expands the universe of opportunities.

What this means is that your data management and analytics infrastructure will likely be a hybrid architecture that includes Hadoop/HDFS, RDBMS, document DBs, traditional grid computing, on-premise and cloud computing, machine learning, and even your mainframe. Platform as a Service (PaaS) providers offer an attractive option that can help you assemble a compatible set of tools and test it out.

Plan for the V's and design multiple ingestion and access points in your hybrid arch. Build unified big + little data ecosystems that integrate the different sources in Table 2.1 for data ingestion. Access to the data must also be varied and support the different types of analytics, discovery, and machine learning discussed in Chapters 2 and 7.

5.2.6 Resourcing

Executive sponsorship is essential—change starts from the top for any transformational exercise. One of the consequences of datafication is the increased recognition of the need for a Chief Data Officer (CDO) or Chief Analytics Officer (CAO) whose team is responsible for all data and uses across your enterprise.

Team composition depends on each org and context. Finding skilled human resources is hard (and expensive); consider collaborating and sharing with peers/other HC organizations.

5.2.7 Storytelling

The role of data visualization is well described, but that's not the case for data-driven storytelling. Demonstrating success with analytics is more than displaying pretty charts with clean

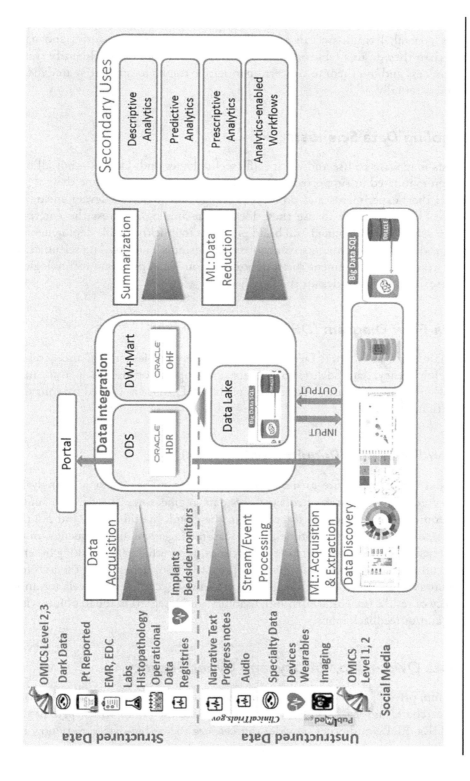

Figure 5.1 Example conceptual model for big data and machine learning. (*Source:* Prashant Natarajan and Greg Jones, © 2016 Oracle.)

data. Analytics-driven workflows and their impact must also be conveyed via data-driven storylines. In general, I think we can agree that humans respond to stories and narratives much better than they do to a table or chart with targets or benchmarks. Identify storytellers early in the process and use them to convert quantitative results to qualitative understanding, internally and externally.

5.2.8 Enabling Data Scientists

Data scientists may want to use and try specific technologies and datasets—not all of which may have been mandated or supported by IT. Allow data scientists to define their algorithms and construct their experiments and prototypes using their preferred development environments. While IT doesn't have to use these identical technologies across the enterprise, IT must embrace sandbox development and build processes to quickly enable deployment of such solutions in production environments. When needed, business analysts, data scientists, and IT must also be ready to re-implement the sandbox solution via appropriate technologies, standards, processes, and technologies for the long haul.

5.2.9 Data-Flow Diagram (DFD)

Build and maintain a conceptual DFD with multiple repositories, stages, and access points that account for latency, data fidelity, governance, and application use cases. You can choose to implement—on a phased basis—those parts of the DFD that are needed by your use cases and organization.

5.2.10 Non-Functional Requirements (NFRs)

Non-functional requirements are as important in big-data management and analytics programs as they are in other areas of software systems engineering. The need to understand and define requirements on security (especially in the cloud, hybrid cloud, and multi-tenant environments), data ownership, real-time access, load management and frequency, migration, regulations, retention/backup/recovery, response times, and performance, among other NFRs, are critical to all big-data efforts. In addition, be proactive in understanding the uses for data/metadata such as timestamps, data lineage aka provenance, confidence levels (of annotated data), accuracy of results (machine learning), usability, and integration touch points with other data sources and/or feedback loops.

5.2.11 Data Ownership, Privacy, and Cyber Security

Data ownership, privacy, and cyber security are getting more attention than before from practitioners, researchers, and legal/regulatory experts. Unlike the era in which patient data was limited to EHRs, ERPs, and other provider sources, healthcare big-data variety now includes social network/mobile/wellness data in which ownership, privacy, and sharing are more distributed than before. Hence, these topics need to be acknowledged and addressed implementations as early as possible—starting from business planning and use case development. These requirements must not only account for existing national/state regulations but also address less frequently discussed requirements such as:

- Who owns the data that is created outside your enterprise?
- Who sees the data and for what purpose? How transparent are data sharing and permission protocols?
- Is data replicated or stored outside primary source? For how long and why? Will data be purged after it's used?
- Are IRB/access/security policies adequate for distributed data management and usage?

5.2.12 Understanding the Role of Data Fidelity

Understand the role of data fidelity and not just data quality (see Chapter 2, Section 2.4.2). Plan for variable and context-sensitive data fidelity but demand that veracity increase as latency increases. It's also important to understand the role of other determinants on data fidelity and quality—there is no one-size-fits-all approach in our hybrid conceptual model. For example, low latency (i.e., real-time) data is subject to limits on how much validation and curation can be done in short time intervals before the data becomes stale.

Checking for referential integrity or late-arriving data is more challenging on real-time/streaming data, as is the ability to integrate across sources or apply complex transformations. In these scenarios, real-time data feeds will not have the complete information to be useful beyond specific event processing or time-sensitive alerting use cases. As we saw in Chapter 2, some recommend applying context-sensitive data quality transformations at the analytics query run time because curation might delete important but unknown relationships or prevent detection of hidden patterns and other anomalies. Finally, we recommend profiling early and frequently at multiple touch points in the data-flow diagram, irrespective of human or machine source.

5.2.13 Data Governance

Ford's famous adage about the Model T applies to governance of big data. There is only one governance strategy and it must address both little and big data. Data governance—especially in production environments—must be inclusive yet comprehensive across your entire data ecosystem. Building a patchwork of strategies/solutions for each data source or analytics use case will reduce integration opportunities, decrease future reuse, and increase the costs of conformance. Even in sandbox environments and discovery analytics, there's a role for data governance—albeit via less formal mechanisms such as checklists, agile methods, and common master data.

5.3 Conclusion

Extracting tangible and timely value from healthcare big data isn't an exact, quantitative science yet—and it will always be influenced by known/unknown human and technology factors into the foreseeable future. However, the opportunities and rewards of harnessing big data for patient care, provider happiness, and personal wellness are transformational. We can greatly increase our chances of success by knowing what myths to avoid and why—and by using the tried and tested best practices described above as a framework for your organization.

Chapter Six

Big Data Advanced Topics

John Frenzel and Herb Smaltz

One man's "magic" is another man's engineering.

—Robert Heinlein, *Time Enough for Love*

With increasing computational power and continuing deflation in the cost of storage, commonly available commodity class hardware is now able to attack some of the more difficult computing challenges. Dating back to the 1950s with Alan Turing's article, "Computing Machinery and Intelligence,"[1] the quest for computers to understand and take action with information derived from natural speech and text has been compelling. This has now become a mainstream application, as voice-to-text translation coupled with computerized concept extraction has become a dominant means by which most Americans interact with first-level customer support.

While EHR technology has brought computers into the exam room, the field continues to gather a majority of data about the patient through unstructured and semi-structured text. In some ways, this is grounded in the ultimate purpose of a patient record. While it is a source of objective data about the patient, it is seen as a narrative that can convey a story of the patient's course of disease and the evolving understanding of its history. This use as a communication tool between providers is difficult to cast in structured format and not lose the expressive content that adds meaning to the narrative.

But there exists value in this data outside of the narrative. Physical findings, pre-existing conditions, family history, and diagnoses as discrete elements have value independent of the narrative context. These are sought-after attributes that can fuel research and therapeutic discovery. Within the healthcare space, Natural Language Processing (NLP) technology is being used to extract structured data from unstructured medical records and has become one of the signature use cases in Analytics 2.0. There are many facets to NLP as it applies to healthcare and use cases leveraging this technology abound.

---

[1] Turing, A.M. (1950). "Computing Machinery and Intelligence," *Mind,* Vol. 59, No. 236, pp. 433–460.

6.1 The NLP Toolbox

NLP is not a monolithic application, rather it leverages a number of specialized software tools that help characterize different aspects of the textual information. These are commonly built as focused applications called *annotators,* which ingest text and begin to extract and build metadata around the content. Annotators are typically organized into a pipeline architecture in which text data moves from application to application for the next stage of analysis. For example, there are specialized annotators that work to identify complete sentences. While this seems like a simple task, it is not. Although sentences end with a punctuation mark, not all punctuation marks signify the end of a sentence. A sentence boundary disambiguater annotator ensures that all downstream applications are working off of complete sentences for analysis.

At a fundamental level, NLP ingests text from either speech or the written word. Language analysis tends to be viewed in a hierarchical abstraction, with words at the base moving to concepts at the top. Not all use cases require a full conceptual view of the information and can use facts and features generated at one of the intermediate levels. At the sentence level of analysis, annotators exist that can identify parts of speech, disambiguate pronouns, and handle logical negation. These are combined to build an annotation pipeline, the product of which becomes an input for a further set of analytics. These analytics use machine learning concepts driven by various statistical models to infer context and meaning from the data supplied.

In the early days of NLP, much of the work focused on hand-coding rules and decision trees. This was laborious and produced a rigid structure that proved difficult to expand into other subject areas, because increasing the accuracy of a rule-based model required crafting additional rules. While straightforward in concept, this was a scaling barrier as these rule sets began to overlap and conflict. In the late 1990s, a statistical approach was developed using mathematical models that include weighting criteria of the various features obtained from the annotator pipeline. The value to a statistical approach was that accuracy increased as more data was exposed to the model. The complexity of the model was hidden in the weighting of the features and elements. During the learning phase, feedback would tune these weights to improve accuracy. It was resilient to instances of mangled data or misspelled words because these algorithms relied on statistical inference. Instead of a single converged answer, these models return a set of possible answers that include a probability qualifying the accuracy of the result. The results and associated probabilities can be aggregated with additional annotated findings to help converge on the correct concept.

All of these approaches require training to help tune and improve the accuracy of the results. Training can occur in a supervised or unsupervised context. Supervision refers to the use of previously annotated data sets as the training source. Creating a supervised training set requires work to validate the results via a "gold standard" reference. This is costly and time consuming, potentially limiting the size of the training set. Unsupervised training is much less labor intensive but suffers in regard to accuracy. This can be addressed with larger volumes of training data but generates complex models that are more difficult to tune. A hybrid approach is the semi-supervised training. Supervised data sets are used to initially calibrate the algorithm and configure the model. Larger unsupervised sets then are used to incrementally tune it. This approach combines the strengths of the two while reducing cost and time to delivery.

6.2 Healthcare Use Cases

- Recently, a large academic healthcare provider moved from a legacy best-of-breed–based EHR onto a single-vendor platform. With this transition, the institution wanted to jumpstart an effort to use problem-based charting.[2] An NLP pipeline was constructed to extract diagnoses and create a problem list from the legacy transcribed notes and pre-populate this into the patient record on the new system. The annotators used standard medical terminology such as CPT and ICD to serve as the vocabularies and discovered synonyms via a statistical method. Over 10 million documents were ingested, including history and physical notes, operative reports, discharge summaries, medication lists, and radiology notes. These were injected into the new EHR using a Continuity of Care Document (CCD) to display the data into the user interface, and providers would then validate these items as part of the new workflow.

  It would have been cost- and time-prohibitive to perform this work using contract medical personnel manually prior to conversion. If the data extraction was forced on the providers to be done by hand following the go-live, it would have been a big dissatisfier. Providers received the NLP-derived problem list suggestions well, and the organization made a significant step toward embracing problem-based documentation.

- A specialty hospital installed a data warehouse to focus on the interaction between therapeutic choices and disease outcomes. While there was some discretely structured data available from the EHR, the institution was interested in specific information that was mainly contained in free text. An effort had been undertaken to manually extract this information from patients' charts, but this was not cost or time effective to scale. An NLP process was assembled to extract these concepts and move them into the warehouse. The manually extracted content was repurposed as a training dataset for a semi-supervised approach to build analytics accuracy. As the training progressed, statistical measures were used to qualify the results, and these became metadata within the warehouse so that data scientists utilizing this information had a statistical foundation within which to interpret their results. This process was repeated across several additional disease foci, providing useful insight.

NLP represents one of the more developed use cases for healthcare in the Analytics 2.0 space. Analytics capabilities as demonstrated above can help institutions leverage alternatively structured data such as free text and bring real value to the enterprise and its customers. There are numerous sources of alternatively structured data beyond the medical record, such as Twitter feeds, Facebook APIs, and LinkedIn. Using annotator pipelines and sediment analysis algorithms, for example, organizations can build insights into what their customers are saying online about an institutional initiative or public campaign, be it theirs or a competitor's. The effort in the Analytics 2.0 space can create a first mover advantage for those organizations interested and willing to think outside the box when faced with unconventional challenges or looking to exploit unique opportunities.

---

[2] Weed, L.L. (1968). "Medical Records That Guide and Teach." *N Engl J Med,* Vol. 278, pp. 593–600.

6.3 The Knowledge-Enabled Organization

The widely referenced landmark Institute of Medicine study[3] suggests that each year up to 98,000 patients die as a direct result of errors made in the course of their care. Other more recent studies[4] suggest that the actual number of deaths in the United States that are attributable to medical errors may be significantly higher—up to 440,000, a staggering number. A key contributing cause of these errors, these reports conclude, is a lack of relevant information.

While information technology has great potential, a solution to these quality and patient safety problems transcends simple information. The complexity of healthcare delivery has expanded as diagnostic and therapeutic technologies expand. Another factor contributing to the complexity of delivering patient care is the exponential expansion of medical knowledge, making it virtually impossible for a physician to stay abreast of the latest medical information. Making the growth of information more of a problem, many physicians perceive that the impact of managed care practices has essentially limited the amount of time they spend with a patient and the amount of cognitive time they spend thinking about diagnoses and treatment options on any given patient.[5]

These dynamics create increasing decision complexity, which affects what a caregiver notices and what a caregiver ignores. Karl Weick, a pioneer researcher in *sensemaking* (the ability to more accurately make sense of any given situation), notes that "information load is a complex mixture of the quantity, ambiguity, and variety of information that people are forced to process. As [information] load increases, people take increasingly strong steps to manage it. They begin with omission, and then move to greater tolerance of error, queuing, filtering, abstracting, using multiple channels, escape, and end with chunking."[6] Weick's seminal work suggests that to adequately overcome complexity and information load, organizations must put in place deliberate systems of sensemaking. Leading healthcare organizations are adopting sensemaking strategies to reduce medical errors and increase operational efficiency. Knowledge management principles and practices adopted in a sensemaking environment help to optimize decision making within the limited time and ambiguous information available to contemporary providers.[7]

6.4 Knowledge Management and the Learning Organization

While a relatively new concept to healthcare delivery organizations, knowledge management is being successfully used by many other industries, particularly industries that gain from reusing knowledge (e.g., consulting firms), or quickly leveraging new discoveries into new

---

[3] Institute of Medicine (IOM) (1999). *To Err Is Human: Building a Safer Health System.* Washington, DC: National Academies Press.

[4] James, J. (2013). "A New, Evidence-Based Estimate of Patient Harms Associated with Hospital Care." *The Journal of Patient Safety,* Vol. 9, No. 3, pp 122–128.

[5] Morrison, I. and Smith, R. (2000). "Hamster Health Care: Time to Stop Running Faster and Redesign Health Care." *British Medical Journal,* Vol. 321, pp. 1541–1542.

[6] Weick, K. (1995). *Sensemaking in Organizations.* Thousand Oaks, CA: Sage Publications.

[7] Middleton, B., Christopherson, G., Rocha, R., and Smaltz, D.H. (2004). "Knowledge Management in Clinical Systems: Principles and Pragmatics." Paper presented at the International Medical Informatics Association Medinfo 2004 Conference, San Francisco, September 11, 2004.

products and services (e.g., manufacturing research and development). From Peter Senge's *The Fifth Discipline*,[8] to Nonaka and Takeuchi's *The Knowledge Creating Company*,[9] to Davenport and Prusak's *Working Knowledge*,[10] to Zipperer's *Knowledge Management in Healthcare*,[11] there are ample resources available to inform the healthcare field about the basics of knowledge management/the learning organization and how to apply its principles within a complex organizational setting. The key underlying tenet of the seminal knowledge management literature is that when individuals within organizations have the knowledge they need to be able to make decisions and accomplish their individual jobs, organizational efficiency and effectiveness are significantly improved. Often, however, healthcare workers do not have key information, and errors and suboptimal outcomes may follow.

Knowledge management is the organizational practice of explicitly and deliberately building, renewing, and applying relevant intellectual assets to maximize an enterprise's effectiveness.[12] Knowledge management practices seek to leverage as much of the information and knowledge that exists within and beyond an organization as possible. Smaltz and Cunningham suggest that "this knowledge can either be in explicit form (such as in databases, spreadsheets, presentation slides, or documents or other media) or in tacit form (such as the 'know-how' in an individual's head). The task of knowledge managers is to explicitly and deliberately build the organizational processes and toolsets that bring this knowledge asset to bear on the thousands of daily tactical and strategic decisions that are made each day in a healthcare organization."[13] While the topic of tacit knowledge management is certainly part of the practice of knowledge management, for the purposes of this manuscript, we will focus our attention on explicit knowledge management, as that, to date, has been the primary focus of both traditional Analytics 1.0 and big data Analytics 2.0 use cases.

The phrase "the learning organization" was coined by Peter Senge,[14] who suggested that organizations that learn more efficiently and apply what they learn more quickly have a competitive advantage over those that do not. He suggested that the following are characteristics of learning organizations:

- **Systems thinking.** The organization is thought of as a whole, and analytics are in place that provide performance monitoring holistically such that interdependencies and

---

[8] Senge, P. (1990). *The Fifth Discipline: The Art & Practice of the Learning Organization.* New York: Doubleday.

[9] Nonaka, I. and Takeuchi, H. (1995). *The Knowledge-Creating Company.* Oxford, UK: Oxford University Press.

[10] Davenport, T. and Prusak, L. (1998). *Working Knowledge.* Boston MA: Harvard Business School Press.

[11] Zipperer, L. (2016). *Knowledge Management in Healthcare.* London, UK: Routledge Taylor Francis Group.

[12] Wiig, K. "Knowledge Management: An Emerging Discipline Rooted in a Long History." *Knowledge Horizons: The Present and the Promise of Knowledge Management.* Depres, C. and Chauvel, D., eds. Woburn, MA: Butterworth-Heinemann.

[13] Smaltz, D.H. and Cunningham, T., III (2015). "Data Rich, Information Poor: Building a Knowledge-Enabled Organization." *The CEO-CIO Partnership: Harnessing the Value of Information Technology in Healthcare.* Smaltz, D.H., Glaser, J., Skinner, R., and Cunningham, T., III, eds. Chicago: Healthcare Information and Management Systems Society. p. 126.

[14] Senge, *op. cit.*

consequences of action (or inaction) can easily be seen and acted upon. This is an aspi-rational characteristic—that is, such connectedness in information visibility is difficult to achieve in practice, but learning organizations explicitly attempt to achieve it in their continual performance improvement efforts.

- **Personal mastery.** While this characteristic relates to the mastery of individuals in orga-nizations to learn, in an organizational theory context it really is more about creating a cultural expectation of continual learning. In other words, organizations must invest in helping their individual members learn more quickly by investing in capabilities to that end (e.g., training, analytics, etc.).
- **Mental models.** This characteristic is also a cultural expectation to challenge long-held beliefs or assumptions that may be outdated. In essence it is a characteristic that encour-ages open dialog in a non-attributional way to ensure that the assumptions underlying management strategy and actions are constantly updated and validated. By doing this, it is thought that the learning organization is rarely out of step with its competitive environment.
- **Shared vision.** Learning organizations are most effective when their individual members have a shared goal or vision that they can readily rally behind and adopt as their own.
- **Team learning.** Learning organizations have cultures that embrace dialog and commu-nication that are not hierarchical but rather horizontal, crossing departmental or unit boundaries with ease. They also tend to have strong knowledge management capabilities for the collection, aggregation, validation, and dissemination of data, information, and knowledge.

We mention these learning organization characteristics to make an important point. Creating the robust Analytics 3.0/knowledge management capabilities is a necessary but insufficient condition for achieving superior organizational performance. It also may explain why invest-ments in analytics and other knowledge management capabilities may not always reap the benefits expected. Unless an organization has achieved these largely cultural characteristics of a learning organization, investments in analytics and other knowledge creation and dissemina-tion systems are at risk, and that is largely a responsibility of senior leadership in a healthcare organization. The moral is, unless the characteristics of a learning organization are adopted and constantly reaffirmed via leadership actions, investment in analytics may still serve a great purpose, but its full potential will not be achieved.

6.5 Building the Knowledge-Enabled Healthcare Organization

So for the moment, let's assume that the organization's leadership team has created a culture, or is working on creating a culture, with the characteristics of a learning organization. How does a healthcare organization then get started with knowledge management—with the practices of explicitly and deliberately building sensemaking capabilities that maximize an organization's effectiveness? One mistake that many healthcare organizations make is that they expect to achieve better decision making, more efficient operations, and better healthcare outcomes by simply providing more and more data to caregivers and administrators. As noted previously, such approaches merely increase the information load on caregivers, thereby making it more difficult to arrive at quality decisions. In response, leading healthcare organizations are taking systematic and deliberate steps to reduce the information load on caregivers by focusing attention on the data and information that truly matter in a given situation. They accomplish this primarily by using the following two practices:

1. **"Baking in,"** or embedding, knowledge into clinical and administrative workflows (e.g., via alerts, reminders, evidence-based order sets, and "click through" capability to relevant medical literature and evidence).

2. **Achieving excellence in analytics.** This excellence is achieved by applying the principles and practices described throughout this book—namely, traditional analytics, or Analytics 1.0, via robust logical enterprise data warehouses (EDWs) that provide automated performance dashboards and robust ad hoc (what if) reporting capabilities; big-data analytics, or Analytics 2.0, leveraging large, complex, and often unstructured data sources via new analytics techniques such as predictive modeling and machine learning; and ideally, leveraging both of these together into an Analytics 3.0 robust and comprehensive analytics capability.

Table 6.1 Baking-In Healthcare Knowledge with Workflow Examples

Types of "Baked-In" Knowledge	Workflow Example
Alerts	Within an electronic health record system, an alert is triggered when a provider orders a new drug for a patient that interacts negatively with another drug that the physician has either ordered previously or that the patient is already taking.
Reminders	On a nursing unit, a nurse is reminded that a patient is due for another dose of a particular medication at a prescribed time.
Evidence	Within an electronic health record system, providing "click-through" capability to access relevant medical literature (often via an electronic subscription service) pertinent to the current patient situation.
Order Sets	Within an electronic health record system, physicians often place orders for various drugs or treatments; creating order sets is the practice of pre-populating orders into groups that evidence has shown to be effective together; rather than having to place individual orders, a physician may select an entire order set.
Automatic Billing Codes	During an outpatient visit, Evaluation & Management (E&M) codes are automatically generated to facilitate billing via information that the caregiver team annotates in the electronic health record.

(Described on following page)

6.5.1 Baking In Knowledge—Knowledge-Enabled Workflows

There are literally thousands of workflows in the typical twenty-first-century healthcare organization. Some examples of such workflows include the process of admitting a patient to the hospital, a patient appointment in an outpatient clinic, or assessing a patient's condition in the emergency room. On the surface, these seem fairly innocuous examples, but consider the implications of missing information, too much information, or ambiguous information on any of these workflows. Being alerted that a patient is allergic to amoxicillin, is currently already taking a beta-blocker for an unrelated condition, or is epileptic can make a profound difference in the treatment plan initiated by the caregiver team, not to mention the patient outcome. Table 6.1 (on previous page) provides some examples of how healthcare organizations are baking in knowledge into their workflows to increase patient safety and ensure more quality outcomes for the services they provide.

While not infallible, the practice of placing relevant knowledge directly within the workflow creates an organizational system that will maximize quality decision making, reduce medical errors, and significantly increase the quality of care provided to patients.[15,16]

6.5.2 Achieving Excellence in Analytics

In the last chapter, we provided a number of examples of some of the bright lights within our industry and how they are successfully applying advanced analytics capabilities to improve their organization's performance. One of the great ironies that the authors of this book continue to find puzzling is that, with some notable exceptions, hospital and health system investments in advanced analytics appears largely fragmented and isolated rather than as a systematic, explicit enterprise strategy for investing in advanced analytics. Despite the fact that the healthcare provider industry is among the most information-intensive industries on the planet, and despite the fact that the management literature, such as *Harvard Business Review*'s recent full issue on big data,[17] highlights the increasing importance of advanced analytics on organizational performance, healthcare organizations' investments in analytics have not reaped the kinds of benefits that accrue when truly integrated, automatic sensemaking capabilities of an Analytics 3.0 capability are in place.

These capabilities have been outlined in this manuscript but are worth summarizing here. Excellence in analytics is achieved by:

- Managing information as a strategic asset and incorporating master data management techniques, including, but not limited to, explicit and vibrant data governance, metadata management, and data profiling.

[15] Bates, D., et al. (1998). "Effect of Computerized Physician Order Entry and a Team Intervention on Prevention of Serious Medication Errors." *Journal of the American Medical Association,* Vol. 280, No. 15, pp. 1311–1316.

[16] Berner, E. and La Lande, T. (2007). "Overview of Clinical Decision Support Systems." *Clinical Decision Support Systems,* 2nd ed. Berner, E., ed. New York: Springer.

[17] "Getting Control of Big Data." *Harvard Business Review,* October, 2012.

- Mastering traditional Analytics 1.0 capabilities such as enterprise dashboards/scorecards and accurate and reliable reporting capabilities to aid ongoing continuous performance improvement across the spectrum of hospital and health system departments and processes.
- Investing in big data Analytics 2.0 capabilities to tap into the myriad largely ignored, complex, often unstructured data sources using advanced techniques such as predictive modeling and machine learning to gain new insights into patient populations and their individual behaviors and how these affect patient care and outcomes.
- Ensuring that the enterprise analytics strategy "begins with the end in mind," with a goal to achieve an Analytics 3.0 capability whereby both an organization's traditional Analytics 1.0 capabilities work seamlessly with its big data Analytics 2.0 capability (i.e., ensure that the two capabilities are not fragmented and isolated but are built and maintained to be used together).

Knowledge management is not a new concept in the field of organizational theory and management science. And individual components of knowledge management are common in healthcare, such as knowledge bases built into electronic health record (EHR) systems for drug-drug interaction checking or the maintenance of evidence-based order sets to reduce variability of patient outcomes. However, the practice of holistically, explicitly, and deliberately managing *all* of the knowledge assets available to a healthcare organization remains largely fragmented and isolated. By reimagining how they think about analytics and by systematically and deliberately investing in an enterprise approach to achieving robust Analytics 3.0 capabilities, healthcare organizations can place themselves into a better position to not only survive, but thrive in an increasingly competitive industry. (For a deeper discussion of machine learning used in Analytics 3.0, please see Chapter 7, *Applied Machine Learning for Healthcare*.)

Note: Section 6.3 onward have been reproduced with permission from Health Administration Press and have previously appeared in Glandon, G., Smaltz, D.H., and Slovensky, D. (2014). *Information Systems for Healthcare Management.* 8th ed. Chicago, IL: Health Administration Press.

Chapter Seven

Applied Machine Learning for Healthcare

Prashant Natarajan and Bob Rogers

Computers are useless. They can only give you answers.

—Pablo Picasso

7.1 Introduction

Collecting, managing, and storing big data is a costly exercise if we can't convert such data into high-value, actionable insights or influence workflows in a timely fashion. Generating knowledge from big data increasingly requires the use of machine learning for various reasons—cognitive, organizational, technical, and operational. Any discussion on big data must include a corresponding discussion on machine learning; frankly, they can seldom be separated anymore. "To be useful, data must be analyzed, interpreted, and acted on . . . [and] attention has to shift to new statistical tools from the field of machine learning that will be critical for anyone practicing medicine in the 21st century."[1]

In order to obtain the most value of out of large, diverse, and fast data, we need to consider options beyond rules-based deductive reasoning, "traditional" systems engineering, and descriptive analytics. Artificial intelligence, specifically the sub-fields of machine and deep learning, provides optimal and cost-effective options to expand the universe of knowledge and solutions in healthcare.

---

[1] Obermeyer, Z. and Emanuel, E.J. (2016, September 29). "Predicting the Future—Big Data, Machine Learning, and Clinical Medicine." *New England Journal of Medicine*, Vol. 375, p. 1216.

Machine learning enables new use cases by:

- Ameliorating the effects of certain human limitations—cognitive (repetitive accuracy, human limitations and information overload), physical (fatigue), emotional (mood, human biases, etc.)
- Enabling new knowledge creation or data reduction via learning and prediction
- Learning to generate computational biomarkers—finding hidden patterns/insights that are not visible to the eye
- Processing repetitive data management tasks more efficiently, consistently, and with greater performance
- Serving as the foundation for clinical workflows and comprehensive secondary use that includes predictive and prescriptive analytics, intelligent search, speech-to-text conversion, real-time image processing, among other uses

7.2 Chapter Overview

While there is a plethora of books, videos, websites, and other resources on machine learning, most content is either too rudimentary or, on the other end of the spectrum, requires an advanced understanding of linear algebra, probability, statistics, and/or computer science. In addition, there appears to be a paucity of resources on applied machine learning—in which learning algorithms, data sets, and best practices are optimized for and applied in a specific domain/industry such as healthcare. As with any emerging technology, ensuring the successful design/deployment and "production" use of machine learning requires knowledge that enables you to connect theory to practice and convert general principles into domain-specific applications.

If you are interested in learning more about this exciting field, or just want a better understanding of the truth behind the hype of "how <<Brand X>> <<machine/deep learning>> can cure <<disease 1>>," then this chapter is for you.

7.3 A Brief History

AI and machine learning are not new topics. They have been researched, argued over, and used by computer scientists, applied linguists, engineers, etc. for more than 60 years. The mathematical foundations of machine learning are rooted in algebra, statistics, and probability developed over the last 2000 years. However, modern development of AI and machine learning in the 1950s and '60s began with the works of Alan Turing, John McCarthy, Arthur Samuels, Alan Newell, and Frank Rosenblatt, among others. Samuel's self-learning and optimizing Checkers program is recognized as the first working instance of a machine-learning system. Rosenblatt was instrumental in creating the Perceptron, a learning algorithm inspired by biological neurons that became the basis for the field of artificial neural networks, which we will touch upon later in this chapter. "Feigenbaum and others advocated the case for building expert systems—knowledge repositories tailored for specialized domains such as chemistry and medical diagnosis."[2]

---

[2] "One Hundred Year Study on Artificial Intelligence, Appendix I, A Short History of AI." Stanford (2016). Available at https://ai100.stanford.edu/2016-report/appendix-i-short-history-ai

In the 1990s, research on machine learning moved from knowledge-engineering–based expert systems to statistical and data-driven approaches. The subsequent time period saw the refinement of backpropagation ("the workhorse algorithm of learning in neural networks"[3]) as also the development of the precursors of what we call *deep learning* today by Hinton and others.[4,5] "Something that can be considered a breakthrough happened in 2006: Hinton et al. [. . .] introduced Deep Belief Networks (DBNs), with a learning algorithm that greedily trains one layer at a time, exploiting an unsupervised learning algorithm for each layer, a Restricted Boltzmann Machine (RBM)."[6]

A more in-depth history of machine learning is beyond the scope of this chapter.

7.4 What's Different About Machine Learning Today?

After many fits and starts over the past decades, machine learning has come out of the hibernation that happened during the "AI winter" that followed the last hype cycle in the 1980s and '90s.[7] Machine learning is also no longer a knowledge-engineering effort as it once was. It's been redefined and optimized to be data intensive instead, hence its appropriateness to handle big data. Today, machine learning (and for that matter, deep learning) is maturing to a point where targeted applications are practical and real. There is definitely increasing market demand, and machine learning is here to stay.

Machine learning is ready for prime time for the following reasons:

1. **Moore's Law.** Continuing advances in computing and storage are allowing us to store and process very large data sets in a cost effective and scalable manner.

2. **Availability of more data.** Machine learning is primarily a data-driven endeavor. As a result, the creation/availability of large data sets coupled with the ability to share/transport such data are allowing us to get further than ever before in predicting or determining new knowledge.

3. **New sources in native unstructured data formats.** Several big-data sources such as the ones discussed in Table 2.1 in Chapter 2 ("Table 2.1 Sources for Big Data in Healthcare" on page 23) are unstructured. Machine learning is ideally suited and is rapidly evolving to better support the generation of insights and analytics directly off native formats such as videos, images, voice, and large un- or semi-structured text.

---

[3] Nielson, M. (2016, January). "How the Backpropagation Algorithm Works." Retrieved from http://neuralnetworksanddeeplearning.com/chap2.html

[4] Hinton, G.E. and Salakhutdinov, R.R. (2006, July 28). "Reducing the Dimensionality of Data with Neural Networks." *Science,* Vol. 313. Available at https://www.cs.toronto.edu/~hinton/science.pdf

[5] Rumelhart, D.E., Hinton, G.E., and Williams, R.J. (1986, October 9). "Learning Representations by Back-Propagating Errors." *Nature,* Vol. 323, pp. 533–536. Retrieved from http://www.nature.com/nature/journal/v323/n6088/pdf/323533a0.pdf. DOI: 10.1038/323533a0

[6] Bengio, Y. (2009). *Foundations and Trends in Machine Learning,* Vol. 2, No. 1, p. 6. DOI: http://dx.doi.org/10.1561/2200000006

[7] Katz, Y. (2012) "Noam Chomsky on Where Artificial Intelligence Went Wrong." *The Atlantic* [online]. Available at http://www.theatlantic.com/technology/archive/2012/11/noam-chomsky-on-where-artificial-intelligence-went-wrong/261637/?single_page=true

We interact with machine learning (and learning algorithms) on a daily basis; examples include self-driving cars, email spam filters, Netflix movie suggestions, Amazon shopping recommendations, and postal-code–based mail sorting using handwriting recognition. Machine learning applications are rapidly being deployed and used in the commercial space across diverse verticals—retail and e-commerce, government, finance, healthcare (providers, payers, and pharma, and personal/public health), cyber security, transportation, agriculture, space exploration, and manufacturing, among many others.

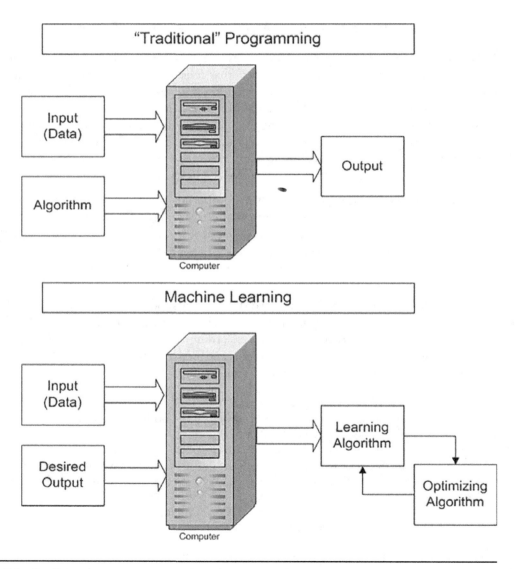

Figure 7.1 Traditional programming and machine learning: a comparison.

7.4.1 What Is Machine Learning?

Arthur Samuel is credited with defining machine learning as the the field of study that gives computers the ability to learn without being explicitly programmed. While its simplicity ensures that this definition is oft-quoted, others provide added perspectives and useful clarifications:

> Machine Learning is a paradigm that enables systems to automatically improve their performance at a task by observing relevant data. Indeed, machine learning has been the key contributor to the AI surge in the past few decades, ranging from search and product recommendation engines, to systems for speech recognition, fraud detection, image understanding, and countless other tasks that once relied on human skill and judgment.[8]

> One useful perspective on machine learning is that it involves searching a very large space of possible hypotheses to determine one that best fits the observed data and any prior knowledge held by the learner.[9]

As we will review in the next section, machine learning is different from traditional software programming due to its emphasis on:

- Learning algorithms versus "traditional" algorithms
- Reasoning that is primarily induction and abduction, with a selective emphasis on deduction
- Dealing with uncertainty ("the unknown unknowns") via the use of mathematical models that are driven by probability and statistics as compared to deterministic rules
- Prediction: using data you have to extrapolate data you don't have in order to infer probability of outcomes

7.5 How Do Machines Reason and Learn: A Crash Course in Learning Algorithms

"A learning algorithm is an algorithm that is able to learn from data."[10] Machine learning is different from traditional programming (see Figure 7.1). "In machine learning, we provide the input (data), the desired result and out comes the [learning] algorithm."[11] Learning algorithms—also known as *learners*—are algorithms that create new knowledge or demonstrate new skills by learning from old (training) data and new (generalized) data. A learning algorithm uses data and experience to self-learn and also to perform better over time. During the process, a learner also optimizes itself to progressively come up with better predictions (see Figure 7.1).

---

[8] "One Hundred Year Study on Artificial Intelligence, Appendix I, A Short History of AI." *op. cit.*

[9] Mitchell, T.M. (1997). *Machine Learning.* McGraw Hill. p. 27.

[10] Goodfellow, I., Bengio, Y., and Courville, A. (2016). *Deep Learning.* Book in preparation for MIT Press. Information available at http://www.deeplearningbook.org. p. 98.

[11] Domingos, P. (2015). *The Master Algorithm: How the Quest for the Ultimate Learning Machine Will Remake Our World.* Basic Books. p. 5.

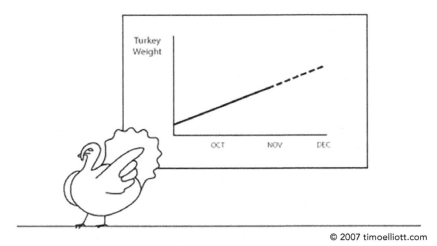

THANKSGIVING PREDICTIVE ANALYTICS

© 2007 timoelliott.com

"I see no reason why excellent growth shouldn't continue . . ."

Figure 7.2 Prediction is not certainty. (*Source:* Timo Elliot; used with permission.)

Learners are the foundation of any machine-learning system, and they help us achieve generalization via induction or abduction. *Generalization* is a core concept in machine learning; to be useful, machine-learning algorithms can't just *memorize* the past, they must *learn from* the past. Generalization is the ability to respond properly to new situations based on experience from past situations.

We will introduce two basic concepts here: *Training Dataset* (the data you have that is used as input to the learner to train the model), and *Test Dataset* (dataset is used by the learner for validation and optimization).

Training model refers to the ML artifact that is created coming out of the training process. Training is supplying the learning algorithm with training data to learn from.

A *cost function* is something (usually, a function) that you want to minimize in the ML system. For example, your cost function might be the sum of squared errors over your training data set.[12]

In summary, a machine-learning system consists of the following basic components:

- Learning and optimizing algorithms
- Training and test datasets
- Training model
- Cost function[13]

---

[12] "Can someone explain to me the difference between a cost function and the gradient descent equation in logistic regression?" (2012). StackOverflow, StackExchange. http://stackoverflow.com/questions/13623113/can-someone-explain-to-me-the-difference-between-a-cost-function-and-the-gradien

[13] Goodfellow, I., et al. *op. cit.* p. 99.

Table 7.1 Some Example Learning Problems[a]

Example Learning Problem	Task T	Performance Measure P	Training Experience E
Learning Checkers	Playing checkers	% of games won against opponents	Learner playing practice games against itself
Handwriting recognition	Recognizing and classifying handwritten words within images	% of words correctly classified	Training dataset of handwritten words with given classifications
Self driving car	Driving from Cupertino to Livermore on public roads	Average distance travelled before an error (as judged by a human overseer)	Sequence of videos, still images, and steering commands recorded while observing a human driver

[a] Table adapted from Mitchell, T.M. (1997). *Machine Learning*. McGraw Hill. pp. 3–4.

In summary, "a well-defined learning problem requires a well-specified task, T; performance metric, P; and source of training experience, E."[14] A formal (and personal favorite) definition of learning states, "A computer program is said to learn from experience E with respect to some class of tasks T and performance measure P if its performance at tasks in T, as measured by P, improves with experience E."[15]

7.6 Mastering the Basics of Machine Learning

Now that we've reviewed Mitchell's definition, let's take a look at Task T, Performance P, and Experience E using examples in Table 7.1.

7.6.1 Task, T

A *Task* is something that we want the machine learning system to do: "the process of learning itself is not the task. Learning is our means of attaining the ability to perform the task."[16] To illustrate further, a task for a self-driven car would be to make the journey autonomously from Peoria, Illinois, to Livermore, California. The learning algorithms and the rest of the machine learning system that the car uses to learn and recognize street signs, sidewalks, other vehicles, people, etc. constitute the means by which this task is completed successfully. Examples of tasks that can be done by a machine-learning system are classification, classification with missing inputs, regression, transcription, machine translation, structured output, anomaly

[14] Mitchell, T.M. *op. cit.*
[15] *Ibid.* p. 2.
[16] Goodfellow, *op. cit.* p. 99.

detection, synthesis, density estimation, denoising, imputation of missing values, named entity recognition, etc.[17]

In machine learning, "a *Dataset* is a collection of Examples."[18] "A *Task* is defined in terms of how the learning system should process an Example. An *Example* is defined as a collection of features that have been quantitatively measured from some object or event that we want the system to process. A *Feature* is the combination of an attribute and its value." For instance, "Color is blue" is a feature, where color is the attribute and blue is the value. Another example: "The features of an image are usually the values of the pixels in the image."[19]

Note that some authors prefer to use the terms *Feature* and *Example* as synonyms.

In machine learning, we are very interested in understanding and addressing *dimensionality,* which is defined as the number of features that contain most useful or actionable information, as well as *Parameters,* which are attribute values (of high-value features) that control the behavior of the learning system. Parameters are important, as they can be modified by the learning algorithm to determine better performance (accuracy) or contextualization of prediction. So for example, the predicted sale price of a house may be impacted more by parameters such as nearness to school or number of bedrooms, rather than the type of roof shingles or color of exterior paint.

As we saw in earlier chapters, with big data, it has become easier to collect/store/manage data than to obsess over or minimize what is collected. "We are in the era of massive automatic data collection, systematically obtaining many measurements, not knowing which ones will be relevant to the phenomenon of interest. Our task is to find a needle in a haystack, teasing the relevant information out of a vast pile of glut. This is a big break from the past, when it was assumed that one was dealing with a few well-chosen variables—for example, using scientific knowledge to measure just the right variables in advance."[20]

Understanding Dimensionality allows us to discuss *dimensional reduction,* which is reducing the number of features required in an example. Dimensional reduction refers to the algorithmic processes by which a dataset having high dimensions is converted into a dataset with fewer dimensions so that as much information as possible about the original data is preserved. This is done in machine learning to address what is known as Bellman's *Curse of Dimensionality,* in which "many learning algorithms that work fine when the dimensions are low become intractable when the input is high-dimensional. But in machine learning [the curse] refers to much more. Generalizing correctly becomes exponentially harder as the dimensionality (number of features) of the examples grows."[21]

Dimension reduction can be accomplished via *Feature Extraction* and *Feature Selection.* Feature extraction creates new features resulting from the combination of the original

---

[17] *Ibid.* pp. 100–103.

[18] *Ibid.* pp. 104.

[19] *Ibid.* pp. 99.

[20] Donoho, D.L. (2000). "High-Dimensional Data Analysis: The Curses and Blessings of Dimensionality." Stanford University. Retrieved from http://statweb.stanford.edu/~donoho/Lectures/CBMS/Curses.pdf. p. 17.

[21] Domingos, P. (2012, October). "A Few Useful Things to Know about Machine Learning." *Communications of the ACM,* Vol. 55, No. 10, p. 81.

features; and feature selection produces a subset of the original features. Both attempt to reduce the dimensionality of a dataset in order to facilitate efficient data processing tasks.[22]

Weights determine how each feature affects the prediction. If a feature receives a positive weight, then increasing the value of that feature increases the value of our prediction. If a feature receives a negative weight, increasing the value of that feature reduces the value of our prediction. If the weight is 0, there is no effect on prediction.[23]

One of the primary purposes of machine learning is for the system to perform on "unknown unknowns," or new, previously unseen data—not just the training dataset with which the model was trained. A good machine-learning system generalizes well from the training dataset to any data from the problem domain. This allows the system to extrapolate and predict on "never seen before" data. Wilson explains further:

> Learning in backprop seems to operate by first of all getting a rough set of weights which fit the training patterns in a general sort of way, and then working progressively towards a set of weights that fit the training patterns exactly. If learning goes too far down this path, one may reach a set of weights that fits the idiosyncrasies of the particular set of patterns very well, but does not interpolate (i.e., generalize) well.[24]

> Generalization is the ability to perform well on previously unobserved inputs. Generalization Error (also called Test Error) is defined as the expected value of the error on a new input.[25]

Overfitting has significant impacts on the performance of the machine learning system. Overfitting happens when a learner mimics random fluctuations, anomalies, and noise in the training dataset, thus adversely impacting the performance of the system on new data. "[W]ith large complex sets of training patterns, it is likely that some errors may occur, either in the inputs or in the outputs. In that case, it is likely that [the learner] will be contorting the weights so as to fit precisely around training patterns that are actually erroneous."[26]

7.6.2 Performance, P

In order to evaluate the abilities of a machine-learning algorithm, we must design a quantitative measure of its *Performance, P*. Performance is usually measured on the task being carried out by the machine-learning system and is typically measured in terms of *Accuracy,* which is the "proportion of examples for which the model produces the correct output," or *Error Rate,* which is the "proportion of examples for which the model produces the incorrect output."[27]

---

[22] Dash, M. and Liu, H. (n.d.). "Dimensional Reduction." Retrieved from: http://www.public.asu.edu/~huanliu/papers/dm07.pdf

[23] Goodfellow, I., et al. *op. cit.* pp. 107–108.

[24] Wilson, H.B. (1998, updated June 24, 2012). *The Machine Learning Dictionary.* http://www.cse.unsw.edu.au/~billw/mldict.html#generalizebp

[25] Goodfellow, I., et al. *op. cit.* p. 110.

[26] Wilson, B. *op. cit.*

[27] Goodfellow, I., et al. *op. cit.* pp. 103–104.

We conclude our brief discussion on performance by reviewing *Noise,* which in machine learning refers to "errors in the training data for machine learning algorithms. If a problem is difficult enough and complicated enough to be worth doing with machine learning techniques, then any reasonable training set is going to be large enough that there are likely to be errors in it. This will of course cause problems for the learning algorithm."[28]

7.6.3 Experience, E

Experience in machine learning is primarily determined by the amount of supervision (during the learning process) and the availability of labeled data in the dataset.

In *supervised learning,* "algorithms experience a dataset containing features but each example is associated with a *Label* (AKA *Target*)."[29] Wilson defines supervised learning as "a kind of machine learning where the learning algorithm is provided with a set of inputs for the algorithm along with the corresponding correct outputs, and learning involves the algorithm comparing its current actual output with the correct or target outputs, so that it knows what its error is, and modify [*sic*] things accordingly."[30] Input data is labeled based on existing knowledge (for example, is the email in the training dataset spam or not-spam?) The model continues to train until it achieves a desired level of performance on the training dataset, and the training model is then fed new and unknown data, as described earlier.

In *unsupervised learning,* input data is not labeled, and furthermore, "the system is not told the 'right answer'—for example, it is not trained on pairs consisting of an input and the desired output. Instead the system is given the input patterns and is left to find interesting patterns, regularities, or clusterings among them."[31]

In *semi-supervised learning,* as the experience suggests, input data may be only partially labeled, and the expected results may or may not be known. The machine learning system will include both supervised and unsupervised learners.

Active learning is a semi-supervised learning experience in which "the model chooses by itself what unlabelled data would be most informative for it, and asks an external 'oracle' (for example, a human annotator) for a label for the new data points."[32] The learner aims to "achieve high accuracy using as few labeled instances as possible, thereby minimizing the cost of obtaining labeled data (something that remains challenging in healthcare)."[33]

Deep learning is a type of machine-learning experience that uses learning algorithms called *artificial neural networks* that attempt to simulate or replicate the functioning of the human

---

[28] Wilson, B. *op. cit.* http://www.cse.unsw.edu.au/~billw/mldict.html#firstN

[29] Goodfellow, I., et al. *op. cit.* pp. 105.

[30] Wilson, B. *op. cit.* http://www.cse.unsw.edu.au/~billw/mldict.html#firstS

[31] *Ibid.*

[32] Gal, Y. (2016). *Uncertainty in Deep Learning,* PhD Thesis, University of Cambridge. Retrieved from http://mlg.eng.cam.ac.uk/yarin/blog_2248.html. p. 11.

[33] Settles, B. (updated 2010, January 6). "Active Learning Literature Survey." *Computer Sciences Technical Report 1648,* University of Wisconsin–Madison. Retrieved from http://burrsettles.com/pub/settles. activelearning.pdf

brain. Think of deep neural networks as "ANNs with lotsa depth."[34] Before we review deep learning, let's take a quick look at artificial neural networks and understand why they serve as a basis for understanding what deep learning does.

7.7 Artificial Neural Networks: An Overview

- **Biological neuron.** "From the artificial neural network point of view, a biological neuron operates as follows: electrical pulses from other neurons cause the transfer of substances called neurotransmitters (of which there are several varieties) from the synaptic terminals of a neuron's axon (think "output") across a structure called a synapse to the dendrites of other neurons (call them downstream neurons). The arrival of the neurotransmitter in the dendrite of the downstream neuron increases the tendency of the downstream neuron to send an electrical pulse itself ("fire"). If enough dendrites of a neuron receive neurotransmitters in a short enough period of time, the neuron will fire."[35]

- **Artificial neuron.** "A simple model of a biological neuron used in neural networks to perform a small part of some overall computational problem. It has inputs from other neurons, with each of which is associated a weight—that is, a number which indicates the degree of importance which this neuron attaches to that input."[36]

- **Artificial neural network.** "An artificial neural network is a collection of simple artificial neurons connected by directed weighted connections. When the system is set running, the activation levels of the input units is clamped to desired values. After this the activation is propagated, at each time step, along the directed weighted connections to other units. The activations of non-input neurons are computing using each neuron's activation function. The system might either settle into a stable state after a number of time steps, or in the case of a feed forward network, the activation might flow through to output units. Learning might or might not occur, depending on the type of neural network and the mode of operation of the network."[37]

7.8 Deep Learning

"*Deep learning* is a specific kind of machine learning. In order to understand deep learning well, one must have a solid understanding of the basic principles of machine learning."[38] It is a "kind of learning where the representations you form have several levels of abstraction, rather than a direct input to output."[39] Think of "deep" in deep learning as having many more layers

---

[34] @natarpr (author) on Twitter. (2016, December 8).

[35] Wilson, B. *op.cit*. http://www.cse.unsw.edu.au/~billw/mldict.html#bioneuron

[36] Wilson, B. *op.cit*. http://www.cse.unsw.edu.au/~billw/mldict.html#neuron

[37] *Ibid*.

[38] Goodfellow, I., et al. *op. cit*. p. 98.

[39] Norvig, P. (2016, March 18). "Deep Learning and Understandability versus Software Engineering and Verification." Available at http://youtu.be/X769cyzBNVw

(or *Depth*) than were possible with ANNs and as the ability to deal with very large datasets due to Moore's law and data availability. The principle driving deep learning is "guiding the training of intermediate levels of representation using unsupervised learning, which can be performed locally at each level."[40]

Deep learning particularly does well on sequential, unstructured, or analog data such as images, audio, and video and is becoming very popular today due to its high performance. "Deep Learning discovers intricate structure in large data sets by using the backpropagation algorithm to indicate how a machine should change its internal parameters that are used to compute the representation in each layer from the representation in the previous layer."[41]

Deep learning currently excels at supervised learning. However, we see as much or greater potential for using deep learning in unsupervised learning, "primarily because large data-sets contain greater amounts of unlabeled data that require labeling, which is time- and effort-intensive."[42]

Let's discuss some types of deep neural nets, including Feed Forward Neural Networks; Recurrent Neural Networks; Convolutional Neural Networks; and Reinforcement Neural Networks.

- **Feed Forward Neural Network.** A "kind of neural network in which the nodes can be numbered, in such a way that each node has weighted connections only to nodes with higher numbers. [. . .] In practice, the nodes of most feedforward nets are partitioned into layers—that is, sets of nodes, and the layers may be numbered in such a way that the nodes in each layer are connected only to nodes in the next layer. The first layer has no input connections and is termed the input layer. The last layer has no output connec-tions and is termed the output layer. The layers in between the input and output layers are termed hidden layers, and consist of hidden units."[43]

- **Recurrent Neural Network.** Sequence-based neural networks that play a key role in natural language processing, machine translation, video processing, and many other tasks.[44] "The idea behind RNNs is to make use of sequential information. In a tradi-tional neural network, we assume that all inputs (and outputs) are independent of each other. But for many tasks that's a very bad idea. If you want to predict the next word in a sentence you better know which words came before it. RNNs are called *recurrent* because they perform the same task for every element of a sequence, with the output being depende[nt] on the previous computations. RNNs [. . .] have a 'memory' which captures information about what has been calculated so far."[45]

[40] Bengio, Y. (2009). "Learning Deep Architectures for AI." *Foundations and Trends® in Machine Learning,* Vol. 2, No. 1, p. 7. Information available at http://dx.doi.org/10.1561/2200000006

[41] LeCun, Y., Bengio, Y., and Hinton, G. (2015 May 28). "Deep Learning." *Nature,* Vol. 521, pp. 436–444. Retrieved from http://www.nature.com/nature/journal/v521/n7553/abs/nature14539.html

[42] Ng, A. (2014, August 26). "Deep Learning: Machine Learning via Large-scale Brain Simulations." Invited Talk: Deep Learning, Stanford University. http://youtu.be/W15K9PegQt0

[43] Wilson. *op. cit.* http://www.cse.unsw.edu.au/~billw/mldict.html#firstF

[44] Yarin, G. *op. cit.* p. 5.

[45] "Recurrent Neural Networks Tutorial, Part 1: Introduction to RNNs." (2015, September 7). Retrieved from http://www.wildml.com/2015/09/recurrent-neural-networks-tutorial-part-1-introduction-to-rnns/

- **Convolutional Neural Network.** A "type of feed-forward artificial neural network in which the connectivity pattern between its neurons is inspired by the organization of the animal visual cortex."[46] CNNs excel at dealing with sequential, analog, or unstructured data and are showing great promise in healthcare—particularly in image/audio/video recognition, recommender systems, and natural language processing. The model is made of a "recursive application of convolution and pooling layers, followed by simple NNs. A convolution layer is a linear transformation that preserves spatial information in the input image. Pooling layers simply take the output of a convolution layer and reduce its dimensionality."[47] An excellent example of how deep learning and CNNs are being used in healthcare is the work being done by Pratik Mukherjee MD and his team at UCSF (see UCSF Case Study on page 149).

- **Reinforcement Neural Network**. Neural networks in which the learner learns and performs tasks via trial and error, much like a child learning to ride her bicycle. Reinforcement learning is inspired by behaviorist psychology and focuses on how software agents ought to take *actions* in an *environment* so as to maximize some notion of cumulative *reward*.
  "Reinforcement learning differs from supervised learning in that correct input/output pairs are never presented, nor sub-optimal actions explicitly corrected."[48]

7.9 A Guided Tour of Machine-Learning Algorithms in Healthcare

Every machine-learning algorithm is good at answering a specific kind of question. Let's take a look at some of the most important algorithms in healthcare and the questions they are being used to answer.

Don't be intimidated by the sheer number of machine-learning algorithms that are out there. While there are currently 54 Wikipedia pages dedicated to specific machine-learning algorithms, all of these are really variations on a few major themes.

The list of algorithms described below is not exhaustive. Our goal is to give examples of the most commonly used methods to answer different types of questions in healthcare analytics. In addition to the type of question being answered, there is another useful way to characterize machine-learning algorithms: whether or not they need input data that is labeled with known answers to create them. Methods that require input data with known labels are called *supervised training* algorithms, and those that do not require any prior knowledge of what answers are expected are called *unsupervised.* The majority of the algorithms below are supervised learning algorithms. We indicate the unsupervised learning algorithms with an asterisk (*).

7.9.1 Classifier

Does data belong to class A?
Example: Is this really a heart failure patient?

---

[46] "Convolutional Neural Network." https://en.m.wikipedia.org/wiki/Convolutional_neural_network
[47] Yarin, G. *op. cit.*
[48] "Reinforcement Learning." (n.d.) Wikipedia. https://en.m.wikipedia.org/wiki/Reinforcement_learning

- **Logistic regression.** Logistic regression is the workhorse of classifiers. It is a linear classifier, which means it uses a single, straight cut to divide the world of possible features into two groups. If a patient's characteristics fall on one side of this cut, they are in class A (i.e., they are judged to have heart failure), otherwise they are not in class A. In problems with many features (some problems can require millions of features), logistic regression is the preferred method because it works well and is straightforward to compute.

- **Support Vector Machine (SVM).** SVM is a linear classifier with a twist: the world of possible features is split by a single line as in logistic regression, but this line can be curved. This additional flexibility makes SVM highly adaptable, but because of the way the curvature is introduced (though something called a kernel), they are still simple to compute and to interpret.

- **Decision tree, random forest, boosted trees.** Trees and forests are an entire family of algorithms, all based on the idea of creating a tree of decisions about features that lead to a specific classification. For example, to identify heart failure, the algorithm may start with ejection fraction. Is ejection fraction above or below 50? For each of these paths, a new question would be considered, such as: does the echocardiogram show Left Ventricle Hypertrophy? At the end of each series of questions, the patient falls into either a "heart failure" or a "not heart failure" bucket. Random forests improve upon decision trees by dividing the input data into many different subsets and creating a different decision tree for each of these subsets. All of the different resulting decision trees then vote to determine the final classification of the input. This process reduces the risk of making the final buckets too small and subsequently being fooled by random variations in the original labeled training data. Boosting is a trick for creating decision trees and random forests that can significantly improve their ability to generalize from example data. We call them out specifically here because boosted tree classifiers tend to be among the best-performing algorithms in public classification competitions such as Kaggle (www.kaggle.com).

- **Deep Learning.** Deep learning, and indeed neural networks in general, can take raw data as input and produce a class (or a vector of probabilities for many classes) as output. All neural network models consist of multiple layers of "neurons": each neuron in a layer receives the outputs of neurons in previous layers, combines these inputs, and uses a threshold to determine whether to output a value closer to 0 or closer to 1 for processing by the next layer. Deep-learning algorithms are unique in their ability to automatically generate features of interest in input data, as long as they are provided with a sufficient number of training examples (usually in the millions). Deep learning is already extensively used in image, video, and audio understanding in healthcare, and it will eventually become more common in other classification problems in healthcare as larger sets of labeled training data become available for healthcare applications.

Common uses: Classifiers are the most commonly used machine learning algorithms in all analytics applications, including healthcare. In healthcare, classifiers are used to:

- Suggest possible patient diagnoses
- Identify patients with high readmission risk

- Automatically alert care providers early in the development of sepsis
- Define the thresholds for "abnormal" lab results
- Automatically differentiate between clinical and administrative documents
- Recommend the most effective wellness or disease management intervention for a patient
- Many, many more

7.9.2 Memory-Based Learning*

How does this new piece of data compare to past data?
Example: Who are the patients most like this patient?

- **Associative memory.** An associative memory system compares incoming data with past data to identify what the new data is most like. The comparison can be based on any subset of the attributes of the data, so no assumptions need to be made about what is "important" in the data, and very large numbers of features can be included. This makes these algorithms especially useful in healthcare applications, because the number of conditions and measurement results that could be applicable to a patient is very large.

Common uses: Memory-based learning is commonly used in healthcare to:

- Create cohorts of patients with which to compare a specific patient. This is the "patients like mine" question that plays a role in treatment planning, pharmaceutical research, and risk adjustment modeling.
- Identify insurance fraud.
- Calculate risk of readmission and other costly future events.

7.9.3 Topic Modeling

What is this document about?
Example: What conditions are being addressed for this patient in this SOAP note?

- **Latent Dirichlet Allocation (LDA).** LDA assumes that content is made up of a combination of underlying topics. A single doctor's note may be 80% about a patient's diabetes and 20% about pain management. LDA can identify the combinations of terms and phrases that make up the underlying topics. LDA can be applied to many different sources of information, from single documents to groups of documents, to even a patient's entire clinical history.
- **Probabilistic Latent Semantic Analysis (pLSA), Latent Semantic Analysis (LSA).** These algorithms are similar to LDA but make stricter simplifying assumptions about how topics are distributed in documents and how words are distributed in topics. With modern computing and large datasets available for analysis, these assumptions are no longer necessary, so LDA is the dominant methodology.

Common uses in healthcare:

- Reliably identify the conditions that a patient has based on clinical text combined with structured data for use in acute disease detection, such as:
  - Sepsis detection
  - Heart failure detection for prevention of hospital readmission
  - Drug-seeking and drug fraud

7.9.4 Forecasting

How much will this time series change in the next time period?
Example: How likely is this CKD patient to progress in the next six months?

- **Linear regression.*** Draws a straight line through the time series of past data, assuming that the current linear trend will continue. This approach requires that the predicted output is a continuous variable.
- **Neural networks.*** A neural network, which can be as simple as a Multi-Layer Perceptron (MLP) or as complex as a recurrent deep-learning model (e.g., Long Short-Term Memory, LSTM), takes past values as inputs and produces the predicted next value as output. All neural network models consist of multiple layers of "neurons": each neuron in a layer receives the outputs of neurons in previous layers, combines these inputs, and uses a threshold to determine whether to output a value closer to 0 or closer to 1 for processing by the next layer.
- **Exponential smoothing.*** This is a simple but surprisingly useful method for predicting the next value in a time series based on a weighted average of the most recent past values. It gives the most weight to the most recent measured value, then reduces the weight by multiplying by a number between 0 and 1 for each subsequent previous value, resulting in an exponential decrease in the impacts of older previous time-series values.
- **Auto-Regressive Integrated Moving Average (ARIMA) modeling.*** This is a general group of forecasting methods (of which exponential smoothing is actually a member) that uses weighted averages of past time-series values, past differences between time-series values, past differences between rates of change of past values, and so on, to calculate future values of the time series.

Common uses in healthcare: The expected next value of a time series is often used as part of a larger predictive modeling or clinical decision-support application. For example:

- Chase lists for disease management: the predicted future values of key diagnostic measurements such as Hemoglobin A1C or creatinine are used to determine who should be included on a chase list for chronic disease management.
- Risk prediction for individuals: a number of healthcare companies, payors, providers, and third-party analytics vendors use predictive models to compute the likelihood that a patient will convert to a new diagnosis within future time periods ranging between six months and two years.

- Very time-sensitive detection of disease: acute applications, such as sepsis detection in the hospital, commonly include time-series forecasts of key measurements such as temperature, white blood cell count, or respiratory rate.

7.9.5 Probability Estimation

What is the most likely interpretation of the data?
Example: What is the most likely diagnosis, given the patient's signs, symptoms, and measurements?

- **Probabilistic Graph Model (PGM).** PGM algorithms, such as Bayes networks, identify key observations, measurements, and outcomes and link them together to identify causal relationships. Each of these factors would be represented as a node in a graph, with connections between nodes indicating causal relationships. These graphs can be learned directly from data or constructed by human experts. The PGM algorithm then uses actual data to determine the amount of influence each combination of variables (nodes) has on the others.
- **Logistic regression.** Logistic regression models assume that the log of the odds of an event occurring (or an interpretation being applicable) can be calculated from a simple weighted average of a set of observations. In practice, this means that they can be used to predict the likelihoods of categorical values such as diagnoses or specific outcomes.

Common uses in healthcare: Sepsis detection, readmission prevention.

- CDS and diagnosis tools: For example, a model for diagnosing COPD might include historical and demographic information such as age, sex, smoking history, exposure to chemicals, and signs and symptoms such as coughing, dyspnea, and blood oxygen saturation, along with comorbidities such as bronchitis, diabetes, and lung cancer. Each of these factors would be represented as a node in the graph, with connections between nodes indicating a causal relationship. The presence or absence of a combination of these factors will influence the probability that a COPD diagnosis is applicable to the patient.
- Disease risk forecasting: PGM and logistic regression can both be used to compute the probabilities of different diagnoses or interpretations of data.

7.9.6 Image and Video Understanding

What is in this image? What is happening in this video?
Example: Is there a nodule in this chest x-ray?

- **Deep learning.** Deep-learning systems, especially convolutional neural networks (CNNs), are very powerful methods for recognizing objects or patterns in complex images. The power of deep-learning algorithms is that, given enough data, they can learn what is important for understanding an image without being explicitly told. In practice, to recognize a cat in a photo, or a nodule in a chest x-ray, a deep-learning system may need to be shown millions of images, each labeled with the desired answer for that image. This training process can be very computationally intensive and require long times to complete (hours, days, and even weeks), but once the algorithm is trained, it can easily be used to quickly recognize the objects it has been taught—a process called "inference" or "scoring."

Common uses in healthcare: This area is exploding right now. At the time of writing, there are compelling deep-learning results being developed for:

- Automated detection of "findings" in radiology images: for example, features such as nodules, pneumonia, or pneumothorax can be automatically detected in chest x-rays using deep-learning systems. These results can be used to route time-sensitive cases to radiologists or to enhance the productivity of radiologists without sacrificing accuracy. Development is underway to develop commercially viable radiology detection systems for all modalities, including MRI, CT, and ultrasound.

- Workflow monitoring and procedural compliance: prototype systems have been developed that can use video and other data streams (such as RFID-based location tracking) to track compliance with standard workflows and procedures. For example, nosocomial infection prevention, in which deep-learning systems have been developed to recognize activities in hospitals that increase the risk of nosocomial infection. These systems, for instance, can flag when a wound is handled but hands are not washed before an IV is placed.

- Patient safety monitoring: Patients can be monitored via video to predict their fall risk in general and to identify when they are getting out of the bed or performing a risky activity, so that personnel can be alerted to assist.

7.9.7 Speech to Text

What is the transcribed text for this audio stream?
Example: What did the clinician dictate?

- **Hidden Markov Models (HMMs).** HMMs assume that there are underlying processes that we can't see—but which are nonetheless consistent and predictable—that create outputs that we can see. For example, in a sentence, if the word "mellitus" is detected, the previous word is far more likely to be "diabetes" than it is to be "disabilities." This is very valuable in speech-to-text processing, because it is not possible to clearly hear or identify each word in an audio stream. The HMM can help choose the right interpretation of the sounds to result in the correct overall transcription. HMM has been used historically in a number of commercial dictation transcription systems.

- **Deep learning, especially Long Short-Term Memory (LSTM).** LSTM models, like the Convolutional Neural Networks described above, can automatically learn what attributes of an audio stream are important for predicting what words it represents. Given sufficient data, which is readily available to online service providers such as Google and Baidu, it is possible to train LSTM models to accurately convert spoken language into text in almost any language. This technology has become the state of the art for spoken language understanding applications and will likely play an increasing role in clinical transcription applications.

Common uses in healthcare:

- Dictation and clinical note transcription.
- Interpretation and automated documentation of clinical encounters, including speech from clinicians, patients, and support staff.
- Voice controls for computer systems in the clinic and in the surgical theater.
- Call-center resources and agent coaching to help call-center operators provide appropriate information and resources to patients or members.
- Patient coaching: applications are being developed in which patients are given context-dependent coaching for disease management, wellness, and particularly behavioral health applications.

7.9.8 Recommender Systems

What was the behavior of other people like you?
Example: What chronic disease management intervention is most likely to be effective for this patient?

- **Collaborative filtering.** Collaborative filtering includes several different methods for predicting a user's rating for a specific item given the user's history of ratings for other items, combined with the history of all users' ratings for all items. Intuitively, if a user rates an item highly, then that user is likely to give a high rating to a very similar item. For healthcare, users could be patients, items could be treatments or interventions, and ratings could be outcome or level of compliance.
- **Memory-based learning.** Memory-based learning systems, such as Saffron, compute the difference between a new data point and previously seen data, for a number of different contexts. When the new data is near previous data, it is possible to predict the outcome based on what happened in the past. These systems tend to learn continuously on an ongoing basis as they are exposed to more data, and they can be used to reason on very complex data.
- **Association rules.** Association rules are a data-mining method in which algorithms use historical data to identify items or events that commonly occur together. For example, a patient needing health education and weight management is also highly likely to need nutrition management.

Common uses in healthcare:

- Matching patients with interventions and coaching resources
- Detecting fraudulent claims
- Call-center optimization and customer experience

7.9.9 Clustering

Can the data be grouped into natural categories or buckets?
Example: Are there natural groupings that can help me understand my patients?

- **Unsupervised Clustering.*** Unsupervised clustering algorithms, such as K-Means, can automatically identify naturally occurring groups of similar items. Typically, the algorithm is given a set of attributes for each item (for example, diagnoses and lab measurements for each patient) and a number of clusters to create. The algorithm will then work out which combinations of attributes most accurately divide the items into that number of groups. The resulting "clusters" can usually be interpreted by humans by looking at which attributes are most important in the cluster.
- **Hierarchical clustering.*** This family of methods creates a tree or dendogram of clustering scenarios for data, creating a single cluster containing all the items, which then splits into two clusters, each of which further splits into two clusters, and so on until each "cluster" contains only a single item. Based on the problem under consideration, this process can be stopped at any point to create meaningful clusters.

Common uses in healthcare:

- **Risk adjustment.** Risk adjustment is a crucial analytical tool for many applications in healthcare, from clinical-outcomes studies to determination of reimbursement for patients in capitated care delivery programs (such as Medicare Advantage). The problem is that, when calculating the impacts of different activities on outcomes, the baseline level of illness for each patient needs to be computed to create a consistent baseline for comparison of methods across all patients. Clustering can be used to group patients into meaningful groups of similar comorbidities or risks.
- **Patients like mine.** In the care of complex or rare disease, it is valuable to understand how different treatments have worked on other patients in similar situations, but this information is only useful if the past patients are similar enough to the current patient to have predictive value. Clustering can be very useful to identify the most similar patients.
- **Population health management and chronic disease management.** Current population health management methods rely on identifying broad groups of patients for whom interventions can be implemented to improve outcomes in general. Clustering is very powerful for finding these groups of patients.

7.9.10 Text Understanding

What does this text mean?
Example: Is this a properly documented diagnosis of diabetes with peripheral neuropathy?

- **Natural Language Processing (NLP).** Natural language processing includes an extensive toolkit of different text processing tools and steps, combined with the goal of understanding the meaning or practical implications of a piece of text. In clinical text analysis, text understanding depends on being able to recognize distinctions among diagnoses attributed to a patient, those mentioned in a differential diagnosis, family history, and negations ("patient does not have diabetes mellitus"). There are a number of open-source tools for general NLP and for clinical NLP that can be incorporated into application development. Full NLP analysis of text can be very computationally expensive, both in terms of CPU cycles and memory required.

- **Text mining.** Text mining is the application of extensive dictionaries of terms to identify occurrences of key terms in text such as clinical notes, consult letters, and discharge summaries. Text mining has the advantage of being able to recognize vast variations in terminology, including abbreviations, misspellings, regional variations in usage, and transcription errors from scanned documents (often using optical character recognition, or OCR). Text-mining methods are often augmented with specific NLP tools to help understand the context of the terms that are identified in the text. For example, negation detection can be combined with search for diagnoses to help understand the difference between a positive statement of a diagnosis and a negative statement that a diagnosis does not apply.

- **Deep learning.** As described above, deep learning has the ability to learn key features of data without explicit programming. In the case of text understanding, deep learning has begun to show value for identifying complex ideas in text and interpreting the implications of their context.

Common uses in healthcare: Studies show that structured data in healthcare can be deeply flawed. For example, structured problem lists consistently suffer from extensive false negatives and false positives, even for impactful conditions such as heart failure. As a result, clinical text is one of the most reliable sources of usable information in healthcare, and the number of healthcare systems using text analytics as part of their reporting, decision support, and care optimization efforts is growing rapidly. Examples of applications include:

- Identify conditions that have been addressed in face-to-face encounters but not submitted to Medicare Advantage for capitated payment.
- Automated coding of typed or dictated encounter notes.
- Extraction of key findings in radiology reports to correlate with information in the EHR.
- Identification of medications and other key findings for inclusion in risk-prediction models.
- Automated chart review to identify care, such as annual diabetic foot exam, which is routinely performed without being separately coded. These reviews can directly impact reported performance measures.
- Mapping of patient care history, across multiple provider organizations, without requiring access to data sets from all providers.

Figure 7.4 shows how machine can be combined with other types of analytics to solve a large swath of business problems.

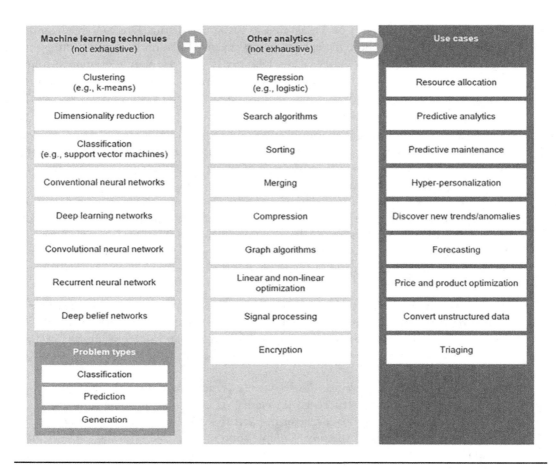

Machine learning techniques (not exhaustive)	Other analytics (not exhaustive)	Use cases
Clustering (e.g., k-means)	Regression (e.g., logistic)	Resource allocation
Dimensionality reduction	Search algorithms	Predictive analytics
Classification (e.g., support vector machines)	Sorting	Predictive maintenance
Conventional neural networks	Merging	Hyper-personalization
Deep learning networks	Compression	Discover new trends/anomalies
Convolutional neural network	Graph algorithms	Forecasting
Recurrent neural network	Linear and non-linear optimization	Price and product optimization
Deep belief networks	Signal processing	Convert unstructured data
Problem types	Encryption	Triaging
Classification		
Prediction		
Generation		

Figure 7.4 Machine learning can be combined with other types of analytics to solve a large swath of business problems. (*Source:* Exhibit from "The Age of Analytics: Competing in a Data-Driven World," December 2016, McKinsey Global Institute, www.mckinsey.com. Copyright © 2016 McKinsey&Company. All rights reserved. Reprinted by permission.)

7.10 Machine Learning and the Contextually Intelligent Agent

Machine learning will begin to realize its full potential in healthcare when contextually intelligent agents (CIAs) are put into widespread use. A CIA is a system that can interact directly with a human, via spoken or written communication, and that can understand context to identify what's important in a given situation. CIAs are a first, and crucial, stop on the journey to artificial intelligence. (See Figure 7.5).

Why is context so important? As we just described, most machine-learning algorithms have been created to answer a specific question. How can I compare two patients? Is this a heart failure patient? When will this patient convert from pre-diabetes to full-blown diabetes? But for any given situation, there are many, many such questions that could be reasonably asked, and then answered with a machine-learning algorithm. Intelligence depends, in part, on the ability to know which question to ask at any given time, based on the context of the situation.

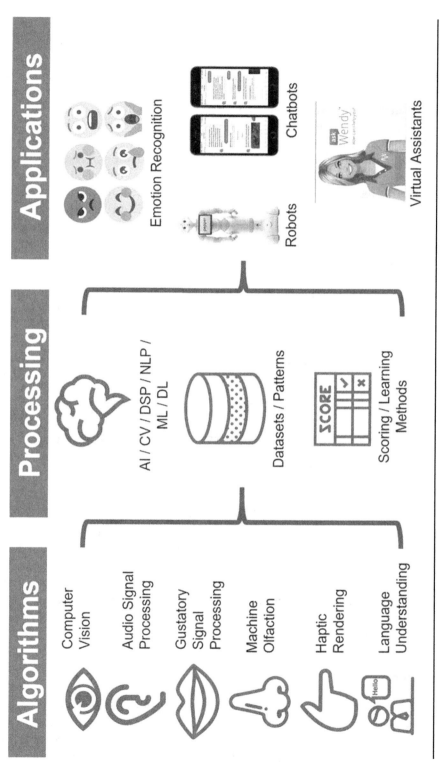

Figure 7.5 Learning algorithms, processing, and CIAs in healthcare. (Used with permission of Catalaize, Nardo Manaloto, and Wen Dombrowski MD.)

Who is asking the question? What has recently changed? Where is the question being asked? We refer to systems that are sufficiently contextually aware to be able to ask (and then answer) the right questions as CIAs.

CIAs are beginning to have an impact in healthcare. Chatbots are effectively communicating with patients to help them find an effective disease management intervention or to coach them through physical therapy following a surgical procedure. Or consider the portable ultrasound, a revolutionary technology that is being actively developed right now. To have non-invasive, highly actionable ultrasound information available in the field, where it can be most valuable, is a huge advance, but the challenge is that it has traditionally required an enormous amount of training for an ultrasound technician to be able to collect clinically meaningful images. How can a relatively untrained user in the field collect clinically useful ultrasound images? The answer is that the portable ultrasound comes with a CIA that can guide the user to collect good data given the circumstances that are driving the need for the imaging. Such contextually aware applications will become increasingly important in healthcare and will drive the value of machine-learning applications.

We would argue that, just as machine learning was a necessary technology to extract value from big data, the widespread availability of CIAs will be required for machine learning to realize its full value in healthcare. Not only do algorithms need to give the right answers, but they need to ask the right questions: questions that are sensitive to the current clinical situation, and which fit neatly into a clinical workflow rather than disrupting it. CIAs, which are appearing in many areas of healthcare, from payor disease management programs to patient wellness and diagnostic imaging in the field, are the key enabling technology to allow this transformation to happen.

7.11 Some Best Practices for Successful Machine Learning

7.11.1 Ask a Specific Question

Your machine-learning algorithm should answer a very specific question that tells you something you need to know and that can be answered appropriately by the data you have access to. The best first question is something you already know the answer to, so that you have a reference and some intuition to compare your results with. Remember: you are solving a business problem, not a math problem. Ask yourself, "What valuable action will be taken as the result of my analytics?"

Analytics and artificial intelligence systems come in two flavors: (1) knowledge management systems that interpret questions and provide information to answer these questions, and (2) very targeted quantitative systems designed to provide information for a specific use case. Don't try to build both types of system in a single effort.

7.11.2 Start Simple

This is true for model selection and the data you consider using for your analysis. You want your results to be robust, so less model complexity and fewer parameters are always beneficial. Regarding data, don't start by building a huge data lake with every kind of data you could possibly get your hands on. Instead, start with the minimal set of data that could get you to a good result.

7.11.3 Try Many Algorithms

Most machine-learning toolkits support multiple algorithms. Try a few to see how they work. This allows you to find the best tool for the job. Also, if one classifier works incredibly well and another doesn't seem to work well at all, be cautious. You may have an overfitting situation, which means you won't really have much predictive power. You may also want to combine methods: use deep learning to extract features from unstructured data and then use these features, along with others, in a classical machine-learning algorithm to get interesting results.

Remember that data is more important than the exact algorithm you use. More training data is always desirable. In addition, for classical machine-learning applications, the better your features, the better your performance will be.

7.11.4 Treat Your Data with Suspicion

Look at your data, dig into its details, look for correlations, suspicious gaps, systematic biases, errors, and flaws. Use statistics and visualizations here. Text has transcription errors, misspellings, and abbreviations. These challenges often exist for structured data as well: you will find that data is recorded inconsistently both across your data set and even within a single field.

7.11.5 Normalize Your Inputs

Machine-learning algorithms can perform poorly if there are large differences in scale between different features.

7.11.6 Validate Your Model

Separate your data into training, test, and validation sets, or if you are using K-fold cross validation, at least hold out a validation set. You need to keep some powder dry for most applications. Also, be aware of biases in your split. Remember: there is no such thing as a random set of data, only a random process to generate data. If you randomly flip six coins and they all come up heads, that's not going to be a very good validation set.

7.11.7 Focus on Data Fidelity But Ensure Quality of Training Data

Data fidelity is more appropriate for machine-learning systems than data quality for the reasons discussed in Section 2.4.2. For supervised learning algorithms, you will want to look closely at your training data. Does it cover all the use cases? Is it biased in some way? For example, did multiple humans create it? Can you see biases or differences among different folks?

This is particularly challenging in healthcare, where unstructured data is critical and source data comes from multiple silos. Extra effort in developing a high-quality training set will pay major dividends and will improve fidelity. Because of the variation in how information is represented in different healthcare settings, the more diverse the sources of data you use in your training set, the more transferable your results will be.

7.11.8 Set Up a Feedback Loop

Think through how you will use the output errors of your machine-learning system to improve it. Downstream users can provide feedback on when your algorithm got it wrong. How are you capturing this feedback so you can bring it back into training?

Note: This is great for false positives, but can miss false negatives, so you will want to pay special attention to false negatives as you train and use this experience to help you find missed results in production data review so you can include them in your next round of training.

7.11.9 Healthcare Doesn't Trust Black Boxes

Some machine-learning methods are more transparent than others. Clustering, topic modeling, and recommender systems tend to be easy for humans to interpret, because they create groupings of concepts that humans can associate with known influences. Linear regression can tell you how important each feature is to the final output. This is true to a lesser extent with linear classifiers. Random forests are difficult to interpret. Deep learning is truly a black box, with very little transparency to what is important in the decision-making process.

Note that there is a lot of research in this area of machine learning, so better tools for helping us understand the decision process are coming. In fact, some third-party healthcare analytics providers have instrumented interesting explanatory tools for their machine-learning algorithms.

7.11.10 Correlation Is Not Causation

It's easy convince yourself that two factors that move together imply that one causes the other. Just remember that in many cases there is a hidden factor that could be causing both factors to move together.

7.11.11 Monitor Ongoing Performance

How will you monitor the performance of your algorithm on an ongoing basis? Data drifts and systems evolve. You can do this manually by spot checking your results against the incoming data, and you can monitor data and algorithm statistics with a dashboard. Simple moving averages can tell you a lot.

7.11.12 Keep Track Of Your Model Changes

Always track the revision of your model and report it with your results. As you improve different parts of your data analytics pipeline, you will want to go back and re-analyze data. Recording which model was used at which time helps you understand what to recalculate.

7.11.13 Don't be Fooled by "Accuracy"

If you're looking for a rare event that only happens 1% of the time, and you never actually find it, you can report your accuracy as 99%. Obviously, that's meaningless. Instead, figure out before you start your project what precision and recall your application requires to be useful. Build your application to these metrics.

7.12 Conclusion

In conclusion, let us look at some next steps for machine learning and AI in healthcare—and what it means to professional practice, personal skill sets/knowledge, and jobs.

1. The current state of the industry, as evidenced by rapid recent progress and increasing investments, is promising. However, we haven't reached the Promised Land yet. We will get closer to it when the predictions and data-driven insights from machine learning are connected to contextually intelligent agents (CIAs), as described in the preceding section. CIAs and applications (see Figure 7.5) are necessary to complete the "data to action" or "data to behavior modification" workflow loops. They will be critical to the "mainstreaming" of machine learning within each HC organization and by individuals—patients, providers, and consumers included.

2. As you can expect, machine learning and AI in healthcare must deal with or account for the foundational five V's of big data in healthcare, as described in Chapter 2. Successful advanced analytics (predictive or prescriptive analytics) and CIAs will "need to be able to easily integrate more data sources, harness machine learning and advanced technology for faster, more sophisticated analyses, and extract insights that will improve business performance."[49]

3. Labeled data in healthcare remains a challenge and a time-consuming effort. While making more data available to machine-learning systems is always helpful, in healthcare setting that data must be prepared and labeled in the context of the source and intended use. Context-based labeling is essential to ensure the relevance and validity of learning, prediction, and action.

4. Feedback loops are essential to any healthcare machine-learning system. Period. Feedback loops can be of two types:
    *   Explicit annotation by human experts
    *   Implicit inferencing from downstream use of the data as evidenced by the behavior of both
        o   contextually intelligent agents, and
        o   individuals who are the recipients of the recommendations/actions suggested by the agent/application

---

[49] "How Analytics and Machine Learning Help Organizations Reap Competitive Advantage." (2016, December.) *MIT Technology Review*. Available at https://s3.amazonaws.com/files.technologyreview. com/whitepapers/Google-Analytics-Machine-Learning.pdf. p. 3.

5. The topic of data fidelity (as opposed to just data quality, as discussed in Sections 2.2.2 and 2.4.2 in Chapter 2) remains an important one in deep learning today. Some practitioners believe that deep-learning systems require the highest data quality as inputs for the predictions/results to be relevant and useful in healthcare. Other practitioners believe that imposing more stringent data quality requires more up-front investments and longer time to market. According to this school of thought, the advantages of deep-learning black boxes are proportionately reduced with increased attempts at enforcing transparency and management of uncertainty in hidden layers of a deep-learning system.

The reason for this debate is that current deep-learning experiences don't provide needed transparency and do a sub-optimal job of determining and managing uncertainty in hidden layers or can't always identify blind spots between input and output layers. We agree that more transparent management of uncertainty and weights will allow us to do more deep learning on healthcare data of lower-data quality than is currently required.

Given the current state of deep-learning architectures, we also think this debate is yet to be fully settled in healthcare. As a result, we don't yet have validated and settled best practices for this topic. However, given the coming importance of contextual usage-driven intelligent/applications for deep learning, we strongly recommend you use data fidelity (as defined in Section 2.2.2 of Chapter 2) instead of data quality in the design and deployment of deep-learning systems, both in the interim and for the future.

6. Questions for readers:
   - How are you approaching data fidelity in deep learning?
   - Do you think we're close to settling this debate or will that happen only when layers are "unhidden"?
   - What are the estimated added costs (or conversely, savings) of going from black-box to white-box deep learning or improving data fidelity?

7. In an Analytics 3.0 environment, the roles of data integration and MDM remain as critical as they do in the Analytics 1.0 and 2.0 environments. Analytics and workflows based on machine learning and CIAs must be integrated with all relevant data—both little and big—across silos in order to benefit the healthcare enterprise and users. Your EDW will continue to play a key role in supporting newer processes and technologies in an Analytics 3.0 world.

8. Questions on ethics and privacy as they relate to machine learning (and AI) are as relevant today (if not more so) as in the past. Current AI systems are not designed to account for the morality of learning algorithms and machine learning. It is useful to point out an important distinction between human and machine morality: "The moral constraints to which we are subject in our dealings with contemporary AI systems are all grounded in our responsibilities to other beings, such as our fellow humans, not in any duties to the systems themselves."[50]

---

[50] Bostrom, N. and Yudkowsky, E. "The Ethics of Artificial Intelligence." (n.d.). Machine Intelligence Research Institute. Available at https://intelligence.org/files/EthicsofAI.pdf. p. 7.

While it's beyond the scope of this chapter to provide answers to the various questions already being raised, we would like to suggest the following topics for more discussion and research.

a. How do we forward the knowledge coming out of machine learning and AI to the patient in a transparent and ethical way? How do we establish provenannce of insights being shared with the patient and provider?

b. Ethics of the human participant as related to providing inputs or acting on outputs.

c. Robo-ethics: ethics built into the machine-learning system by design or during learning.

d. Transparency around access to and inspection of the machine-learning system.

e. Reliability of predictions and validated performance.

f. Clear demarcation or sharing of human and machine-learning/CIA responsibilities when failure happens.

g. Legal, privacy, and innovation (patents, copyrights, etc.) considerations.

h. As you can guess, points a–g above will also create new discussions on the ethics of AI as related to public policy, reimbursements, population health management, SDoH, and access/cyber security at the global and individual levels.

9. Jobs: While applied machine learning and AI are here to stay/thrive, the impact on health-care jobs will mostly be positive (helping humans do their tasks or creating more jobs) in the immediate- to mid-term. As a result, we will see increased augmentation of human tasks in healthcare—and not the overblown wholescale replacement of physicians, sur-geons, radiologists, nurses, CXOs, or IT geeks as often portrayed in the popular press.

However, we do not recommend complacency. In the mid- to long-term, we fully expect to see more administrative roles and even some specialties to be eclipsed or replaced by machine learning and AI (and in certain geographies and organizations at an accelerated pace). So, how do readers prepare for coming changes in healthcare jobs?

a. Understand what's available and coming; we hope this book has helped you get started.

b. Do projects to investigate and be prepared for emerging technologies in this space.

c. Leverage your existing skills to drive question determination, feature definition, labeling, data integration, feedback loops, and promotion of data exchange and use.

d. Leverage intelligent bots, agents, etc. and try things out via smartphones, personal wellness applications, CIAs.

Case Studies

Prashant Natarajan

1. Introduction

The following case studies provide useful perspectives on the current state of big data, machine learning, and AI—and what the near future holds for healthcare professionals and policy makers. In addition to providing real-life examples of bedrock principles and best practices (as described in Chapters 5 and 7), these case studies also showcase the exciting developments and the rapid value currently being obtained by leveraging and integrating all healthcare data. As you will read, these case studies are not all alike; their primary focus is varied befitting the specific organizational/business needs they address. As a result, you will see that the big-data characteristics that make up the primary focus of these case studies can vary significantly, even as they achieve value: Velocity (streaming data from devices and monitors and just-in-time analytics), Variety (diverse analytics applications and heterogeneous data sources), Volume (large volume structured and semi-structured data), and Analytics 3.0 (machine learning and AI).

Put together, these eight case studies represent not only what's realistic today but also what's coming. They also provide excellent examples of how to go from Analytics 1.0 to 2.0 and 3.0. In the spirit of collaboration and peer-to-peer sharing, case study authors write about what worked, what did not work, and lessons learned in their journeys.

2. How Did We Get Started?

After our proposal for this book was accepted, I put out a call to healthcare organizations (providers, payers, and government/public-private collaboratives) on LinkedIn and Twitter. Separately, I reached out to individuals and organizations who were collaborators in the recent past and who had practical experience with topics covered in this book.

While the focus of case study recruitment was healthcare providers, we were also keen from the outset to include success stories from government and payers to provide ideas for collaboration and promote learning from allied healthcare domains.

3. Methodology

While we were thrilled by the tremendous enthusiasm and responses to our call for case studies, we also saw that some proposals lacked the qualities we required in order to include them in this book. We accepted only proposals in which the submitter could provide evidence of "production" experience and were able to demonstrate value and ROI or discuss integration or next steps beyond narrow use cases or silos. We were stringent about disclosing and applying the same evaluation criteria to each case study. These criteria were

1. The big data or machine learning case study has to be real and either in production or in the final stages of validated deployment at a provider or other healthcare organization (for example, governments or health insurers).
2. Each case study had to include sufficient background on business, clinical, or financial drivers and clearly document opportunities.
3. Contributors were requested to provide application demos and/or access to other business or clinical users, as needed.
4. Each case study was expected to review progress in going from Analytics 1.0 to 2.0 and 3.0, sharing lessons learned, and reviewing challenges faced.

4. Making the Final Cut

The case studies that made the cut in this book have been validated and are among the most real examples in healthcare today. They leverage data as an asset by incorporating analytics into daily decision making, business operations, and integrating with workflows.

The case studies are as follows:

1. Penn Medicine: Precision Medicine and Big Data, by Brian Wells
2. Ascension: Our Advanced Analytics Journey, by Tony Byram
3. University of Texas MD Anderson: Streaming Analytics, by John Frenzel
4. US Health Insurance Organization: Financial Reporting with Big Data, by Marc Perlman, Larry Manno, and Shalin Saini
5. CIAPM: California Initiative to Advance Precision Medicine, by Elizabeth Baca
6. University of California San Francisco: AI for Imaging of Neurological Emergencies, by Pratik Mukherjee
7. BayCare Health System: Actionable, Agile Analytics Using Data Variety, by Apparsamy (Balaji) Balaji
8. Arterys: Deep Learning for Medical Imaging, by Carla Leibowitz

5. Conclusion

Our case study contributors are world-class leaders with demonstrable and extensive track records of vision and success. The experiences and expertise they share here, in support of this book, will drive current and future conversations on

- Leveraging data as an asset that makes precision medicine and population health two sides of the same coin
- Going beyond reports and dashboards using analytics-driven workflows and advanced analytics
- Data fidelity, information governance, and stewardship
- Building learning systems, leveraging contextually intelligent agents, and symbiosis between humans and machines
- Evolution of healthcare informatics and jobs

Case Study

Penn Medicine: Precision Medicine and Big Data

Brian Wells
Associate Vice President of Health Technology and Academic Computing
Penn Medicine

1. Introduction

Penn Medicine is one of the world's leading academic medical centers, dedicated to the related missions of medical education, biomedical research, and excellence in patient care. The Perelman School of Medicine has been ranked among the top five medical schools in the United States for the past 18 years, according to *U.S. News & World Report*'s survey of research-oriented medical schools. Penn Medicine is committed to improving lives and health through a variety of community-based programs and activities.

The University of Pennsylvania Health System's patient care facilities include: The Hospital of the University of Pennsylvania and Penn Presbyterian Medical Center; Chester County Hospital; Lancaster General Health; Penn Wissahickon Hospice; and Pennsylvania Hospital, the nation's first hospital, founded in 1751. Additional affiliated inpatient care facilities and services throughout the Philadelphia region include Chestnut Hill Hospital and Good Shepherd Penn Partners, a partnership between Good Shepherd Rehabilitation Network and Penn Medicine.

2. Toward Precision Medicine

The following case study describes a big-data journey underway by Penn Medicine to pursue and enable precision medicine. In 2013, our organization made a strategic decision to invest in developing a program to support precision medicine. At this time, the scientific community was making significant strides in achieving a rapidly falling price of genetic sequencing and analysis, as well as discovering actionable genetic variants that were driving targeted prevention, targeted treatment therapies, and genetic counseling.

Penn was uniquely positioned in our region, given the depth and breadth of the underlying areas of expertise which support this evolving paradigm. Our experience ranges across many years of researching genetics and developing molecular-based clinical diagnostics and early treatments in targeted areas, the award-winning Abramson Cancer Center; our rich discrete clinical data warehouse (known as Penn Data Store); our success in implementing a common electronic medical record (EMR) across our enterprise, which provided a steady stream of discrete and unstructured clinical phenotype data; and the MyPennMedicine patient portal with over 300,000 active patient users who will be able to indicate interest in participating in clinical trials and submit data they generate into our EMR.

From an information technology perspective, setting the goals to align with our strategic initiative required making investments to enable the storage, management, and mining of "big data," which included unstructured textual documents and detailed genetic sequencing results, eventually leading to providing patient-supplied outcomes and ICU monitor data. Our first task was to address creating a holistic picture out of all the available data in our organization so that we could begin to architect an infrastructure to support precision medicine. Historically, our research data from sample inventories, clinical trials, registries, and genetic sequencing was not well organized and not linked to the research subject's clinical data, preventing the easy identification of patient cohorts suitable for recruiting into clinical trials based on this integrated data.

Genetic sequencing activity was rapidly growing among our research labs as well as within our new CLIA-certified Center for Personalized Diagnostics (CPD). The CPD was performing a growing amount of clinically focused somatic tumor sequencing and needed a place to store and analyze these targeted genetic test results. Much of our unstructured (free text) data was stranded in departmental systems supporting specific clinical service lines such as radiology, cardiology, and pathology. Our EMR visit notes and patient-to-provider emails exchanged through our patient portal became a rich and growing collection of untapped information. There was a strong consensus that the combining, linking, and liberation of this data would have a dramatic effect on research, education, and clinical care.

One organizational approach taken toward our technology strategy was to reorganize the information systems support for the Perelman School of Medicine by aligning our organization through joining the health system and academic information systems teams under a single CIO. Taking this approach enabled the AVP of Health Technology and Academic Computing (HTAC), reporting to the CIO, to bridge all three missions of Penn Medicine and position our focus on analytics, big data, data warehousing, and research computing. Unifying the team provided for a single point of accountability for the information technology required to achieve the vast majority of the goals of precision medicine.

The AVP of HTAC identified the need for an enterprise technology solution to holistically manage the large and growing collection of clinical and research data. An initiative was kicked off, dubbed PennOmics, to buy or build the necessary components. Executive sponsors from the cancer center, the CTSA institute, and pathology/precision medicine were identified to guide the overall initiative and provide institutional support. A broad governance committee was formed, representing health system and research members, to identify data and technology requirements while overseeing the implementation of new solutions to address. The highest priority was assigned to securing a research data warehouse that could house research data linked to de-identified clinical data. By developing this warehouse, it would be the first step in leading us to be able to simplify the task of answering complex questions about our patient and research subject populations. We wanted to enable research teams to quickly answer questions without having to contact the owners of six disparate databases and then synthesize the results on their own.

During our assessment in 2012, it was quickly determined that building a solution would not be a viable option, given the lack of available bioinformatics and biomedical informatics experts. At that point a market survey was completed in late 2012. Only one vendor existed that could provide a discrete data model for both clinical and genetic data in conjunction with a self-service web user interface enabling authorized users to easily query the data and identify research or clinical patient cohorts of interest.

The product and associated infrastructure was purchased in March of 2013. Data mapping from Penn Data Store's data model to the PennOmics data model was the focus for the spring and summer, while the hardware and software were being installed and configured. The years of investment in populating Penn Data Store from twelve separate source systems of clinical data stretching back to 2005, along with the mapping of that data to a common semantically interoperable data model, vastly simplified the development and validation of the data-mapping effort. In the fall, the loading of hundreds of millions of rows of clinical data began. Tuning the infrastructure to handle these massive loads was a big feat because of the need to cycle through multiple data loads to resolve data-mapping issues. By January of 2014, all clinical data was loaded and available for end users to be able to complete clinical queries with no assistance from the information systems team. In subsequent months, available genetic and research data was added. In subsequent years, the software and data models were upgraded, ultimately improving the end-user query tool and system performance, and leveraging the years of work mapping Penn Data Store content to national standards, such as LOINC, RxNorm, and others. The above work was completed by one dedicated end-user support resource and portions of time from an ETL developer, a DBA, and a manager.

As of June, 2016, the data in Table 1 was included in PennOmics and available for access by authorized users.

At the time of writing, the research data warehouse has 221 authorized users with 20–30 regular monthly users. The solution has received national recognition from numerous information technology publications and has been involved in the submission of multiple grants and journal articles. Using this self-service tool, users are empowered as never before. They are now able to ask and answer questions that can lead to a grant or clinical trial, such as:

- How many patients have had any diagnosis of a cardiovascular condition or experienced a concussion that has been shown to increase the risk for Alzheimer's or Dementia, have a recorded genetic variant on CR1, CLU, PICALM, SORL1, or TREM2 but not on APOE? What is the role of Apolipoprotein L1 in Atherosclerotic cardiovascular disease? This question took advantage of the combined clinical and genomic data within PennOmics to evaluate the connection between polymorphisms in ApoL1 in African Americans and their associated cardiac events.

- Can we identify patients that may benefit from Pharmacogenetic testing to prevent adverse drug reactions? This preliminary study found the patients who received medications

Table 1. PennOmics Data Content

Data	Start Date	Objects
Patients	2005	3,129,826
Encounters	2008	97,288,545
Diagnosis	2008	52,112,416
Procedures	2008	15,570,845
Labs	2008	348,479,369
Microbiology	2008	11,332,456
Administered Medications	2008	61,884,739
Vital Signs	2011	83,840,084
Tumor Registry	2010	85,308—Patients 375,032—Stage/Grade
Studies	2001	1,003
CPD Tests	2013	4,578
Research Genomic Sequences	Varies	6,770
Variants	Varies	1,700,000,000,000
Bio-Bank Samples	Varies	11,000 and growing

known to induce hypersensitivity reactions with corresponding diagnosis codes that indicated an adverse reaction.

The next priority in the PennOmics initiative was to make use of unstructured, free-text data. For this effort, we took a two-step approach. Our first step involved implementing a natural language search tool that we named PennSeek. We searched the market for a tool that could easily ingest and index hundreds of millions of clinical documents and then provide a powerful user interface that could combine unstructured search with key clinical discrete data items. We found a tool that had been popular in the online shopping marketplace and configured it to suit the unique aspects of healthcare data. Table 2 outlines the 31 million unstructured documents indexed from six separate source systems and available for search as of June of 2016.

As of June of 2016, there were 87 regular users, and PennSeek has supported 30 IRB-approved studies. In 2015, the tool placed ninth in the *Information Week* Elite 100 Innovation competition.

Step 2 of the unstructured data liberation efforts will be spent targeting the implementation of a natural language processing (NLP) tool and pipeline. By using PennSeek to identify rich sources of data that can be derived from natural language, we will configure the NLP tool to automate the nightly extraction of reliable facts and store them as derived discrete data in PennOmics for query by end users, scheduled for completion in early 2017.

Table 2. PennSeek Data Content

Data Source	Documents in PennSeek
Epic Visit Notes	18,003,801
Radiology Accession Reports	11,364,298
Pathology Reports	816,681
Echocardiogram Reports	193,955
Cardiac Cath Reports	24,613
MyPennMedicine Messages	367,117
Total	30,770,465

3. Conclusion

Throughout this journey, we have learned some valuable lessons:

- Adoption of the tool and realization on the part of the users of a return on the investment may be the most challenging aspect of our efforts. Communication with end users about the benefits associated with the tools often must be accomplished one department, division, and team at a time. As in most large companies, important messages do not always trickle down. We learned that teaching students was generally the best way to spread the word.

- Tool performance is paramount to success. In spite of the fact that the tools provide unparalleled access to information using intuitive interfaces, the response time must be under five seconds regardless of the complexity of the data request. Anything longer leads to end-user dissatisfaction.

- Self-service is not for everyone. In spite of attending training, many researchers do not have the patience or the understanding of the data complexities and nuances to successfully use the tool. In addition, the typically infrequent use of these tools reduces retention of the training material.

- Penn Medicine's investment from 2007 to 2013 (and beyond) in a centralized clinical data warehouse provided tremendous value to the team loading data into the research data warehouse. The backbreaking work of mapping 12 source systems to common standards had already been completed.

- Product customization is to be avoided at all costs. Customizing vendor product software and data models leads to long-term dissatisfaction and frustration tied to difficulty in future product upgrades, which inhibits the adoption of valuable enhancements or fixes.

- Small project teams are more productive and effective than large teams.

While we are pleased with our progress to date on the PennOmics initiative, we know that there are still unmet needs. Some examples of these are streaming data emanating at high volumes from our ICUs, Flow Cytometry data, and imaging data. We continue to investigate technologies and approaches to the leveraging of less structured data in areas such as cancer immunotherapy, predictive analytics, and gene therapy. While big-data technologies such as Hadoop appear promising and make it easy to quickly store unstructured data, they do not make it easy to retrieve and analyze the data in structured ways.

Case Study

Ascension: Our Advanced Analytics Journey

Tony Byram
Vice President, Business Intelligence
Ascension

1. Introduction

Ascension is a faith-based healthcare organization dedicated to transformation through innovation across the continuum of care. As the largest non-profit health system in the US and the world's largest Catholic health system, Ascension is committed to delivering compassionate, personalized care to all, with special attention to persons living in poverty and those most vulnerable. Ascension has approximately 160,000 associates and 36,000 aligned providers who serve in 2,500 sites of care—including 141 hospitals and more than 30 senior living facilities—in 24 states and the District of Columbia.

Growing organically and through acquisition, this national health ministry has been supported by a wide variety of healthcare applications. In 2000, an inventory found that Ascension had over 6,000 applications implemented across the system. Since that time, with the addition of new sites of care and health systems, the organization has undertaken several rationalization projects to standardize applications. In 2016, the number of applications in use at Ascension was closer to 4,000. While rationalization efforts continue, Ascension has embarked on an effort to pull together our data and build supporting analytics to support the organization's strategic direction promise to provide "Healthcare That Works, Healthcare That Is Safe, and Healthcare That Leaves No One Behind, for Life," in the communities it serves.

In 2009, an enterprise-level program began to consolidate and rationalize many of the diverse systems used for Finance, Human Resources, and Supply Chain to a single enterprise resource planning (ERP) solution. This project, Symphony, would also consolidate to a single budget and time and attendance system. As part of this large-scale business and IT change initiative, the organization had a vision to build an enterprise-wide data and analytics solution to help Ascension better serve our patients, support our mission, and adapt more quickly to the rapid changes in the healthcare industry. Before this time, most analytics and data initiatives were built and maintained at the local hospital or system level. The new solution, called the Ministry Intelligence Center (MIC), would be funded and managed under the larger system change initiative, Symphony. The MIC would begin to implement Ascension's advanced analytics strategy.

The organization was growing rapidly, the healthcare industry was changing rapidly, and the data was not consolidated in a manner that allowed for quick strategic decisions. When the Ascension system office wanted to analyze key complex components of the operation, data requests would have to be sent to the local hospitals and health systems to pull the data from their various IT systems. Problems arose if there were issues with data quality or misinterpretation of the data request, and it took a great deal of time to gather all of the needed data. The goal for MIC was to help solve these types of problems. It was determined that the work would begin with the operational side of the organization.

Ascension's advanced analytics strategy began the journey from an Analytics 1.0 capability to 2.0 and is proceeding to 3.0. This analytics strategy contains several aspects, but primarily data management capabilities, data governance, and analytical capabilities. I extend the definitions in Chapter 1 for the Ascension environment as:

- **Analytics 1.0**
  - o Data is managed in silos or in specific applications. The data may be available in a specific facility but not be easily available across the whole organization. Data quality is questionable or unknown.
  - o Data governance is virtually non-existent or minimal and in silos. Comparability across facilities are difficult due to few standard definitions.
  - o Analytics is made up of basic reporting and the occasional dashboard. Many leaders use Excel spreadsheets and/or make decisions by instinct, as getting the data and analytics together is difficult.

- **Analytics 2.0**
  - o Data is being managed centrally and being integrated into an Enterprise Data Warehouse (EDW), with data fidelity in addition to data quality. *Note:* Data fidelity is a an important undertaking and is a journey unto itself. The NRF Framework provides principles and guidelines on managing data fidelity in 2.0 and 3.0 environments (see Section 2.4.2 for further discussion on data fidelity and page 26 for a description of the NRF Framework).
  - o Data governance is being developed and enforced across the enterprise. Data elements are defined, metrics are consistent, and governance with representation across the various functions work together.
  - o Analytics is created with consistent, actionable dashboards and reports for the leaders of the organization. Dashboards are created that combine data across multiple domains to examine complex operational or clinical questions. Predictive models are being developed to help leaders move from instinct decision making to data-driven estimates about the future.

- **Analytics 3.0**
  - Data management is more automated. Machine learning is assisting with data mapping/normalization. Data is moving from normal structured data to tackling the unstructured or large external datasets such as social media.
  - Data governance is now part of the fabric of the organization and not considered a separate department or afterthought. All associates think about how their data fits into the broad data strategy of the organization and the impact of their data captures into the various systems.
  - Analytics capabilities mature to include more complicated dashboards, self-service Business Intelligence (BI), and predictive and prescriptive models. In addition, leaders do not have to monitor the vast sea of metrics and Key Performance Indicators (KPIs) or look for patterns, as machine learning will help point out patterns, help show the best visualizations of the data, and send alerts when attention is needed.

With any journey or model, as described above, there are exceptions and blurred lines between one version and another. For example, while in level 1.0, Ascension had a robust capability to look at financials, since this is fairly standard; while generally in level 2.0, predictive models were developed and more advanced analytics were available in key strategic or advanced departments. This is a roadmap for the journey and where we want to go. The development of the MIC would help Ascension transition from 1.0 to 2.0.

2. Advanced Analytics Journey

The architecture of the MIC was developed based on the traditional Enterprise Data Warehouse approach, as shown in Figure 1.

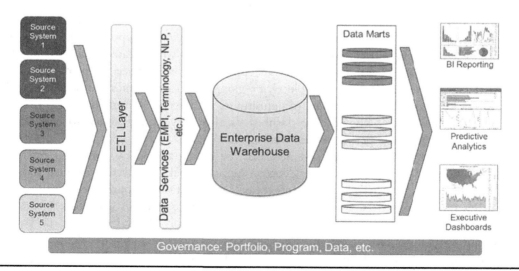

Figure 1   Typical data warehouse approach.

The initial build efforts included the creation of an infrastructure containing an EDW, Extract Transform & Load (ETL) toolsets, and a robust analytics presentation tool. The work began with purchasing an industry leading healthcare data model, adapting as needed, and integrating key systems from the operations side of the organization. The initial datasets loaded to the EDW were finance, human resources, supply chain, patient demographics, revenue cycle/patient billing, time and attendance, budget, and quality/safety. Later data sources from patient satisfaction, associate satisfaction, and more were added to the warehouse. Since we were replacing the disparate ERP-type systems with a single instance, this greatly simplified the integration effort, including the challenges of master data and data normalization.

This was not the case, however, with our Revenue Cycle/Patient Accounting systems. As mentioned previously, Ascension has many parts, and currently each facility or local health system has a separate system for patient billing. Therefore, the integration effort included interfaces from over 44 different systems, with more to be integrated. The data from these systems would supply information on each patient, including their payers, demographics, physician teams, coded diagnosis, coded procedures, payments, charges, and more. Pulling together data from different applications built by different vendors, implemented at different times, and containing different master data was a big challenge. One solution for minor data normalization was to build a tool that allows the various systems to crosswalk their data into a defined enterprise set of master values. This internally developed tool was called the Master Data Management Hub (MDM Hub). The MDM Hub would be used to translate items such as patient types, payer codes, earning codes, patient genders, etc. Since there were so many different patient accounting systems, each with their own disparate Charge Description Masters (CDMs), a more robust solution would be required. We chose to partner with a leading organization that has tools to support patient revenue cycle departments and leverage their toolset and best practice CDM to map all local charge values to a common CDM. This now allows us to look at all patient charges in a consistent manner.

At this point, Ascension had much of the operational-type data integrated into a single traditionally designed third normal form data warehouse. Analytics dashboards were built for key areas across the enterprise in human resources (e.g., Workforce Turnover and Diversity), finance (i.e., Profit and Loss Statements and Daily Volume Metrics), supply chain (i.e., Supply Expense and Inventory Turns), and more. These dashboards were created to allow leaders at various levels of the organization to see the data appropriate for their needs. The data could be viewed at a local hospital or department level, a region/market level, and the system/enterprise level. The KPIs and metrics had standard definitions, the data was normalized, and the data fidelity was managed and known. The dashboards also allowed drill down to help leaders determine the cause of the problems they were examining.

With all the key data integrated, we now had the building blocks to create an enterprise costing solution. The cost accounting or decision support capabilities were previously handled locally in different systems. To build the Integrated Cost Solution, we purchased a leading cost accounting application. These toolsets allow us to calculate cost factors (e.g., Direct-Variable-Labor-Patient Care, Direct-Fixed-Equipment) and then apply those factors to the patient encounter information. Our design was to use the cost accounting system to calculate only the cost factors and then apply them to the patient information stored in the EDW. This approach would prevent us from duplicating all the data in another system, allow us to scale to the level needed to support Ascension, and leverage the common CDM to enhance the comparability of the costs. This new solution gave us the ability to see our costs by charge code and by patient, and then roll up into Diagnosis Related Groups (DRGs) and service lines. Using a common cost accounting methodology and a common (albeit mapped) CDM, we can easily compare different hospitals, doctors, service lines, regions, and more.

Our EDW was growing and scaling as needed to support Ascension's growing appetite for analytics. By the end of 2015, the data in the EDW contained information for 75% of Ascension acute facilities. The production database held approximately 12 million patient records, 41 million patient encounters, 500 million patient charges, and well over 11 billion rows. Note that historical data was not back-loaded into the EDW as part of the implementation, and the rollout was over a four-year period. As new data is loaded and new facilities are integrated to the EDW, the growth is averaging approximately 400,000 patients, 1 million encounters, 20 million charges, and 1.3 billion rows per month.

Since the robust infrastructure and EDW became available, there have been several enterprise-wide implementations that could take advantage of the data. Ascension began work on implementing an enterprise-wide daily labor productivity tool. The core units of measure for productivity calculations would take advantage of the integration of the many revenue cycle systems into the EDW. A single feed from the EDW to the new system was built, which saved many months of effort duplicating the interfaces from the individual CDMs. Another win for this implementation was that we could use the common CDM codes as units of measures for productivity, which allowed us to map to external benchmarks more easily and bring comparability among facilities. In addition, an application was implemented at an enterprise level for safety event monitoring to replace the existing one, which was home grown. Using the EDW, we were able to build a single feed of patient admission demographic information to the new solution, which helped the nurses and other staff quickly enter events without entering all the basic patient information. This helped compliance and tracking, and the safety events were also fed back into the EDW to link with other analytics.

Another key to the success of all the work thus far was basic data governance. While at that time Ascension did not have a formal data governance office, the EDW implementation brought to light the need to help data become comparable and normalized. Some basic data governance was implemented as part of the EDW. Today, Ascension has created a Data Governance Office (DGO) and has set up a network of data governance committees, from operational to clinical. The office is maturing and beginning to establish key procedures and policies to help strengthen the validity and usefulness of the data. This work includes setting standards that will be pushed "upstream" to the source systems for use by front-line data entry associates into the core systems (i.e., Race, Ethnicity, Language, etc.) and those that would be used "downstream" in the warehouse for normalization (i.e., patient types, CDM, department codes, etc.). Having a data governance organization is key to ensuring that the data used for analysis is fit for purpose and that definitions are consistent before being used for comparability. Ascension's diverse systems, varied implementations, and different operations in multiple states with diverse regulations and payers require data governance to be successful into the future.

The Ascension journey to advanced Analytics 2.0 was primarily centered on operational data. However, clinical data must also be integrated into the solution. Key information challenges were coming, including population health management, Accountable Care Organizations

(ACOs), migration from fee for service to fee for value, and more. In addition, the healthcare field needed to view data and analytics across the continuum of care, not just acute care. Integration from the various acute and ambulatory electronic health records (EHRs), physician practice management systems, home health, senior care, etc. is a very daunting effort. In order to be successful, Ascension would need to look at newer technologies to assist.

In 2015, the Ascension Enterprise Solution Architecture (AESA) team was formed to look into these new technologies and architectures. The group would work on the data integration problem with key use cases surrounding population health and others from the clinical viewpoint. With the complexity of clinical data, the number of systems Ascension has, and the speed at which the industry is moving, the traditional ETL approach would not work. The goal was to utilize large-scale data dumps from these systems into a Hadoop cluster to speed ingestion in an Extract Load (EL) approach. We take data as raw as possible from various sources into the Enterprise Data Lake (EDL) and store it in the RAW area. Once there, we can easily profile the data, determine the needs for normalization, evaluate the fidelity and quality of the data, and make decisions on what needs to be transformed when loading into the second area of the big data cluster, known as the NORMALIZED area. Additional architecture technologies were evaluated, such as Enterprise Master Person Index (EMPI), data governance and data profiling toolset, and predictive model/pattern recognition tools. Having a separate team set aside to evaluate and pilot these new technologies and vendors allowed the MIC team to continue to complete its work on the operational side of the analytics.

The AESA team worked on a number of analytics initiatives to test the new infrastructure and determine if this new technology would assist with speed to value. Datasets were fed to the big data cluster via text file dumps and capturing Health Level Seven International (HL7) messages from our enterprise interface engine. One example of the rapid implementation and success was a predictive model created for readmissions. This model would use information from patients currently in our facility, calculate the chance for a readmission, and then feed a report back to the EHR system for use by the care coordinators. This would allow intervention to occur to decrease the probability of the readmission before the patient was even discharged.

Finally, in the spring of 2016, the time was right to bring these two teams back together. Ascension created a new organization structure called the Ascension Clinical Research Institute (ACRI) under the direction of our Chief Medical Informatics Officer (CMIO). The goals of this new organization are to commoditize the data across our various applications, create analytics, and support research. The newly merged groups are now working to determine how to combine the different technologies and approaches into a hybrid architecture to take Ascension advanced analytics to 3.0.

Efforts are underway to merge architectures, the traditional Enterprise Data Warehouse, and the newer Enterprise Data Lake. During the transition, there are many analytical needs that require data to be sent from the EDW to the EDL and vice versa. The ultimate design will be to feed raw data into the EDL into a raw/staging area. We will profile and determine what data to transform and normalize based on the current analytical needs of the organization. This data can then be fed to the EDW as needed to further integrate with the operational data and then ultimately into reporting data marts. As the technology matures, the opportunity may arise to forgo the traditional data warehouse approach by using solutions such as Spark. Ascension will continue to be cautious but will pursue newer technologies to speed our delivery and assist us to better serve our patients. Until then, a hybrid approach will be most prudent.

In addition to the technology journey, Ascension is on a path to build a more robust data governance organization. The goal is to have data governance be embedded into the fabric of the organization. We should always ask what data is needed, what is the definition, what is its intended purpose, and how does it integrate with other data to support our analytics. We will educate the front lines of data collection, set up procedures to ensure that we are using the information appropriately, and always keep the needs of the patient at the center. We will continue to pursue opportunities for machine learning to assist in this journey as well. Our mission is to serve the patient, and we have access to a lot of data that needs to be transformed into information and then knowledge.

3. Conclusion

1. **Create a vision.** Ascension had known for many years that it needed a more robust data and analytics approach. The leadership took advantage of a large-scale change initiative to start this work and begin to integrate it into the fabric of the organization. Having sponsorship at the top levels of the organization is extremely important, but we also needed to ensure that the vision and importance of this work could be understood and embraced at the lowest levels of the organization. Remember that the basic data entry is done by local associates, and they need to know how the data they input into these many systems comes together and impacts the larger analytics solution. Ascension's goal is to provide compassionate, personalized care, and the associates embrace that. Now we must show them how the small tasks they do affect that care, from registration, to billing, to patient care data entry. All our work serves one purpose: the patient!

2. **Build integrations and analytics in bite-sized chunks to create momentum.** We all know you shouldn't set up a project to "boil the ocean," but if you are not careful, that is exactly what you begin attempting. Come up with specific use cases that give you a reason to begin the data integration journey. Although you may have a few use cases initially, you will quickly find many more as you make the data available. The organization is starved for information and will continue to push you. Be sure that the amount of work you bite off is small enough to complete in a reasonable timeframe and that the fidelity of the data can be managed, or the organization will look for the information elsewhere. As we saw earlier, data fidelity is more appropriate in Analytics 2.0 and 3.0 environments.

3. **Test the hype.** Technology enhancements occur faster and faster with each passing year. However, you cannot always believe what the vendor sells you or what the magazines hype. Always test these newer technologies in a controlled environment. Be sure to have a specific set of test cases with specific success criteria for a pilot. Many organizations have believed they could move everything from traditional database technology to technologies like Hadoop, and many have failed. This isn't because the technology isn't good, but more because the technology wasn't fit for purpose for that use case, or that the technology hadn't had time to mature yet. Never stop innovating, but don't risk everything without testing the hype.

4. **Data governance is of critical importance.** Data governance is critical to ensuring that the data being used is of sufficient fidelity. Data governance is also hard! Most leaders in the organization will support data governance concepts, but it is difficult to get true action. Many times, one must put analytics into use to really get the attention needed to change the processes, procedures, or cultures of an organization. Be sure to keep pressing toward better data governance, and don't let perfect be the enemy of the good.

5. **Culture and politics can be a challenge.** As an organization works to centralize data and analytics, there will be challenges. Some departments may be afraid of losing control of their data and worry about the transparency of view or misinterpretation of their area. Others may be very comfortable with the local solutions that have been in place for years and are just nervous about change. These types of concerns can lead to political battles in an organization, and this is where sponsorship at the top levels must be strong. The purpose of the effort is to help the organization advance its mission. For Ascension, this is serving all with special attention to people living in poverty and those who are most vulnerable. We made sure that leaders, department heads, and associates understand how this initiative supports that mission and will help them better execute on that mission.

6. **Carve out time and resources for innovation.** As mentioned previously, technology is always changing. If an organization wishes to continue to innovate, it must set aside resources to test new technologies. No organization can test or try every vendor's product or new technology, but when one comes along that would appear to solve a business challenge, pull a special project team aside to test it. Ascension did this with the AESA group, and once there was a maturity of the technology and understanding, it was integrated with the existing technologies and teams. This innovation can be done by carving out a separate team or just by setting aside a small group to continue the research.

Ascension remains on the advanced analytics journey to bring better-quality, safer, more cost-effective, person-centered care. As we move toward an Analytics 3.0 level, we will be working with technologies such as machine learning. The thought of machine learning tools is exciting in that it may one day allow us to auto-create KPIs, automatically alert leaders for patterns in the data, automate mapping of the high-volume and diverse data we create and integrate, and, in the end, allow Ascension to continue to be a high-touch care organization.

Case Study

University of Texas MD Anderson: Streaming Analytics

John Frenzel
Chief Medical Informatics Officer; Professor, Department of Anesthesiology and
Perioperative Medicine, Division of Anesthesiology and Critical Care
University of Texas MD Anderson Cancer Center

1. Introduction

Personalized healthcare continues to be a rallying point that promises lower cost of care and improved outcomes for the patient. The idea of tailoring care and therapy driven by the patient state is appealing. While many of these efforts focus on big data use cases driven by genomics, personalized medicine has been practiced for years in the ICU. These environments receive critically ill patients suffering from disease processes of diverse etiology. Understanding the multifactorial nature of their acute compromise and rapidly reversing it, if possible, is the goal for these teams. Within these complex environments, large quantities of data are generated. Due to the limitation of human cognition, much of this data is unseen. While the physiologic state of a patient tends to be slow changing, trends and thresholds have been identified that can serve as predictors of patient deterioration. The following describes an ongoing effort to use real-time vital-sign data in the prediction of ICU admission for hospitalized patients.

Over the past decade, clinicians have realized the value of rapidly identifying and intervening in the care of patients with acutely deteriorating physiological status. An organized approach to care for these individuals saves lives and reduces the cost of care.[1] Hospitals have invested in the creation of specialized groups that can rapidly bring resources, skills, and training to the ICU for patients who show signs of rapid medical deterioration. Called *Medical Emergency Response Intervention Teams* (MERIT) or *Rapid Response Teams* (RRT), these groups are staffed with ICU-trained nurses, advanced practice providers, and a physician—often an

---

1   Beitler, J.R., Link, N., Bails, D.B., Hurdle, K., and Chong, D.H. (2011). "Reduction in Hospital-Wide Mortality after Implementation of a Rapid Response Team: A Long-Term Cohort Study." *Critical Care,* Vol. 15, No. 6, R269. Available at http://doi.org/10.1186/cc10547

intensivist—as medical director. When they are called, they evaluate the patient, and if necessary, take responsibility for the patient's care. If it is indicated, they will rapidly move them to a higher level of care in the ICU, enabling the staff to bring the full resources of advanced life support to bear earlier in the patient's course of illness, potentially averting a catastrophic outcome. Triggering the MERIT or RRT is usually the responsibility of the floor nurse. Currently, this is a more reactive process, with the burden of identifying deterioration using subjective assessment. To help structure this task, algorithms and flowsheets have been developed that include specific screening criteria and a scoring system. A well-validated, widely used scoring system, called MEWS[2] (*Modified Early Warning System*), is based on four physiologic parameters—systolic blood pressure, pulse rate, respiratory rate, temperature—plus the AVPU (Alert, reacts only to Voice, reacts only to Pain, Unresponsive) score. Of the five measurements, four are gathered by machine, and one, the AVPU score, is dependent on nurse evaluation.

MD Anderson recently installed the Epic EHR. Epic is an enterprise application that brings together patient data into a single comprehensive record. Using a third-party vendor, Capsule, the Epic EHR is able to collect and integrate data from bedside noninvasive monitors, ventilators, anesthesia machines, and infusion pumps. Data from these devices is extremely granular, usually sending updates continuously as new information is generated. Infusion pumps, for example, communicate data on alerts, errors, and alarms in real time. Ventilators send data with each breath administered regarding volume, peak pressure, FiO2, inspiratory time, and positive end expiratory pressure (PEEP) settings. At the time of any ventilator alarm or error condition, this data is relayed as well.

Across an enterprise environment, the volume of data is enormous. The Capsule infrastructure collects data from all connected and configured devices at a server, which then creates messages containing selected data elements at a reduced granularity for Epic to incorporate into the electronic record. The reduction in granularity makes sense from an end user's point of view, as physiologic data tends to be slow changing and must be validated prior to becoming part of the medical record.

The ability to store and analyze all data generated by these devices seemed compelling. The Capsule application had already created the framework and infrastructure to collect the raw information. We worked with the vendor to create a separate interface to open the entire, unfiltered, full-fidelity data stream for archiving and analysis. Predictably, this created a torrent of data that, while structured in nature, contained error, noise, and uncertainty.

Moving this information into an Analytics 1.0 structure was possible, but it would tax the performance of a relational database and require costly additional hardware. Considering this as an Analytics 2.0 use case, we harnessed our existing NoSQL environment based on Hadoop to manage the data. Hadoop is designed to use a distributed computing and storage model that lends itself to implementation on a commodity hardware platform. All data from Capsule was received as HL7 messages at the integration hub. Validated data from the Epic environment and raw data directly from Capsule moved into the Hadoop data lake, where it was post-processed and identified to the patient level using an ADT feed. This became the core data storage environment. Several development and exploration environments were built to support analysis by the data science team. Using the NoSQL environment forced the team to explore and embrace several different tool sets in the open-source ecosystem to help manipulate the data (see Figure 1).

---

2   Subbe, C.P., Kruger, M., Rutherford, P., and Gemmel, L. (2001). "Validation of a Modified Early Warning Score in Medical Admissions." *QJM: An International Journal of Medicine,* Vol. 94, No. 10, pp. 521–526. Available at http://dx.doi.org/10.1093/qjmed/94.10.521

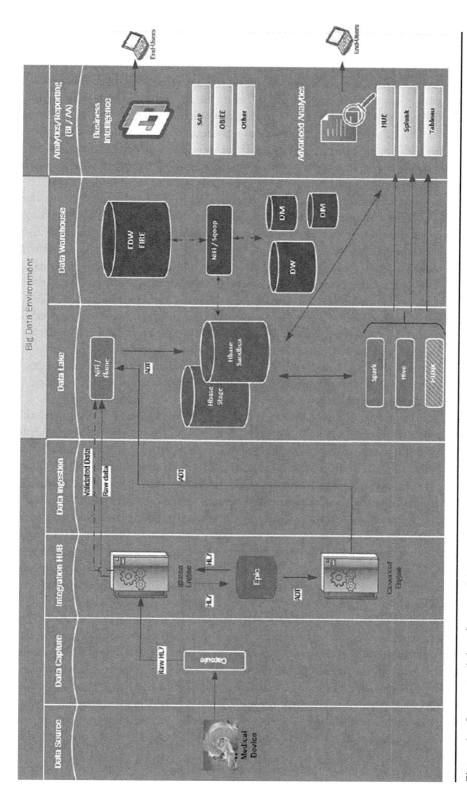

Figure 1 Conceptual data flow model.

2. The Analytics-Enabled EHR

There were several deliverables expected from this effort. The project plan was constructed in an agile manner. Environmental design with the configuration of the analysis toolchain and sandbox construction was undertaken first. The team used this time to dissect the problem space and validate that the sandbox environments would support the intended solution. They also used research, industry contacts, and local resources to create a short list of necessary software assets from the open-source ecosystem. These were configured and tested in the sandbox environment so that, as the project began to undertake modeling and analysis of the physiologic data, the capabilities and limitations of the tools at hand were understood.

As the sandbox environment stabilized, the project team began to map out the discovery roadmap. The first major deliverable was to decrease the time lag from measurement to intervention. As mentioned previously, noninvasive monitors such as blood pressure cuffs and pulse oximeters gather many more data points than just those appearing in the lower granularity validated Epic record. By combining new data with older observations of mental status, could we trigger the cascade of intervention sooner? This required data from the Epic environment to be sourced and combined with streaming data from Capsule. We identified and moved this data into the sandbox environment. The data science team worked to understand underlying data quality issues in the physiologic data stream. They created windows of analysis in which previous measurements helped to validate current measurements. This helped to filter spurious vital-sign results based on the assumption that vital signs over the medium term tend to be slow changing data. All of this analysis was done retrospectively on patients with known outcomes.

The second, longer-term deliverable was a broader effort to better understand the signals within the environment of care. The original MEWS study was published in 2001. Over the intervening 15 years, enterprise-grade EHRs have been much more broadly deployed, and within their data structures resides an extremely comprehensive longitudinal record of the patient. While physiologic parameters clearly were correlated with ICU admission, were there other findings in the medical record—consults, orders, or other interventions—which could improve the predictive ability? We built the capacity to add into the analytics environment these other data points. We created the ability to select a cohort of patients who were ultimately admitted to the ICU versus similarly scored patients who did not need the ICU level of care. While not in real time, this enabled us to wind back the data to a point several hours prior to the transfer and begin to understand how correlated these events were to the population at risk.

Results from this work are still ongoing. We are working to create an analytics that is able to construct a MEWS score out of Epic and continually update it with the newest physiologic data available. Next steps will include validation of any analytics created using real-time streaming data. Additional directions of analysis include understanding whether the variability and velocity of change augmented MEWS scores is clinically predictive. Are MEWS scores that have not reached the threshold for action, yet show a distinct trend toward the threshold, actionable? Are scores that demonstrate greater than normal variability important? These are two views of the score that are currently not possible in the static EHR world.

3. Conclusion

The EHR is currently the focus of activity for clinical healthcare providers. While fundamentally electronic, it continues to be remarkably close in functionality to its paper-based ancestor. Advanced analytics coupled with digital electronic records hold the promise to identify and intervene in the clinical trajectory of the patient to potentially reduce suffering and cost of care and extend life. Advanced decision support through analytics is something that the paper artifacts could never do and that our current electronic records are just beginning to demonstrate. By leveraging analytics, the EHR is set to become a partner in care for both the provider and the patient, as the data for each patient can be evaluated within the context of a much larger population, augmented with the insights gained to benefit society.

Case Study

US Health Insurance Organization: Financial Reporting Analytics with Big Data

---

Marc Perlman
Managing Director and Global Business Development Leader
Global Healthcare and Life Sciences
Deloitte Consulting LLP

Larry Manno
Principal, Insurance Analytics & Information Management
Deloitte Consulting LLP

Shalin Saini
Manager, Life Sciences & Health Care
Deloitte Consulting LLP

[This case study is from Deloitte describing a big-data implementation at an unnamed health insurance organization.]

1. Introduction

The Affordable Care Act (ACA) significantly changed the US healthcare system, with new demands and capabilities driving the need for advanced analytics to better manage risk, quality measures, and Health Exchanges. To remain competitive and grow market share, a US health insurance organization teamed with Deloitte on a multi-year journey to modernize the business and technology capabilities of their finance and actuarial functions. The modernization initiative provides improved analytics and business insights to the health insurance organization and uses big-data technology to enhance existing financial reporting processes.

The Affordable Care Act (ACA) is designed to reform the US healthcare system by providing more Americans with expanded coverage options and rights, as well as incentives and penalties surrounding quality of care versus fee-for-service. The changes in the law include new rules for insurance companies, which are driving new opportunities for the use of analytics.

Many health insurance organizations believe that in order to be successful, they require advanced analytics solutions, including tools for comparative and predictive analysis to better understand and manage issues around risk modeling and product structures specific to Exchanges. Strong and complete analytics are critical to align payer and provider incentives in new reimbursement models.

The basis of this case study is a US health insurance organization seeking advanced analytics to comply with ACA legislation and as a way to "future-proof" their reporting capabilities as regulatory requirements and product definitions continue to evolve.

Table 1. Why Implement Big Data?

Factor	Rationale for Big Data Solution
Cost reduction	With growth comes an ever-increasing volume of data capture. Deploying big-data technology to augment an existing data infrastructure can significantly reduce the total cost of ownership of data capture and processing by moving high-volume data storage into low-cost Hadoop clusters. The Hadoop environment can also be used to quickly deploy targeted analytics specific to one functional domain or slice of enterprise data. The traditional data warehouse can be evolved as needed for enterprise analytics and storage of highly conformed, structured historical information.
Capture of new data types	While traditional database technologies have enabled storage of structured data for several years, the capture and processing of unstructured data (data captured at the point of care in free text, images, sounds, etc.) represents an opportunity for competitive advantage in the healthcare industry.
Access to powerful new analytics	The capture of any and every level (and type) of data will facilitate the organization's use of next-generation capabilities such as text analytics, natural language processing (NLP), and machine learning.
Improving the quality of decision making	Large volumes of data brought together via big-data technology can be used to analyze and discern patterns and make better data-driven decisions. For example, advanced data mining techniques can allow narrower segmentation of customers and more precise tailoring of health plan products to the consumer.
Improving planning and forecasting	Identifying specific trends in healthcare premium and claims data (as well as causes of variability) requires a reliance on statistical methods that are beyond simple averages. Use of big data will enable the organization to pinpoint specific behaviors for planning and forecasting. In addition, access to interact with real-time sources will allow users to test these statistical methods in near real time and to a higher precision level.

The US health insurance organization in this case study operates multiple transaction systems to manage their day-to-day operations. The organization's "Data Presentation Layer" includes data warehouses, data marts, reporting marts, and statistical applications, all of which source their data independently from multiple systems.

This siloed, scattered view of enterprise data:

- Limits the organization's ability to run advanced analytics
- Requires the organization to invest in significant point-to-point integration using ETL effort to create data stores to support internal decision making
- Lacks the ability to capture and process unstructured and real-time data feeds
- Increases overall cost of maintaining the disparate sources and making them available through the Presentation Layer

Factors highlighted in Table 1 drove the decision to establish a Hadoop big-data solution to supplement the organization's information delivery capabilities.

2. Big-Data Strategies

There are two common big-data implementation strategies that can be considered in this scenario. One is to implement the Hadoop file system as an Archive layer, and the other is to do so as a Staging layer.

In the Archive strategy, it is important for the organization to define criteria for hot data (immediate operations data) as well as cold data (non-essential and historical data) and use Hadoop to store all cold data. The primary use of the Hadoop solution in this scenario is to run deep-data analytics to gain new insights not easily available from operational reporting and traditional business intelligence.

In the Staging strategy, all existing systems will be required to use the Hadoop file system as both the source and target for data operations. This is commonly referred to as a *Data Lake* strategy, wherein transactional data on the common data platform feeds to other information delivery solutions while storing all transformed and summarized data drawn from other (i.e., legacy) data warehouses and data marts. The Staging strategy often involves the use of high-performance processing to handle complex data transformations, which are often costlier to process on traditional data warehouse platforms. A key thing to note here is that even though there are multiple approaches available in big-data implementations, it is essential that the business issue at hand be the primary driver to determine the choice and scale of the solution.

At this US health insurance organization, the Hadoop solution would serve as a source for all Presentation Layer components. Termed the *Enterprise Data Lake,* this big-data ecosystem serves as a unified solution to store all data, for as long as required, in its original conformity. Integrated with the existing enterprise architecture, the Data Lake offers a path to reduce data silos, reduce latency and time to value, improve analytics and discovery, and significantly reduce costs. The finance division of the health insurance organization aimed to establish a link and audit trail to millions of detail-level transactions that roll up to general ledger accounts on financial statements.

3. The Big-Data Analytics Solution for Financial Reporting

Deloitte assisted the US health insurance organization in capturing financial information in its raw conformity within the Enterprise Data Lake, then applied summarization and validation rules within the Data Lake to automate and improve end-user consumption across the finance and actuarial functions.

Employing an Agile methodology, Deloitte built a Hadoop repository to access any transaction record at the lowest level of granularity. For example, if one wanted to determine the underlying details of a general ledger account balance in a billed premium, the finance and actuarial team would be able to access subscriber- and member-level detail that composes that general ledger account balance at a point in time within a specific accounting period.

In addition to providing the organization with the ability to perform deep-dive discovery analytics, Deloitte successfully integrated existing information assets that served specific business purposes. For example, a daily feed from the ERP system would support successful validation of general ledger account values when preparing the lower-level transactional detail for journal entries.

Authorized users diving into the Data Lake would be able to access any granularity of information they needed, all the way from source to target systems that they serve.

In addition to building the foundation layer in Hadoop that would support analytics, there was an executive emphasis on enabling self-service analytics (discovery analysis, investigative analysis, etc.). These capabilities can be provided through a variety of tools. In this case, the business requirement was supported through the use of several tools, including:

- HUE, a web interface that supports the Hadoop ecosystem
- Datameer, a third-party tool that offers self-service and schema-free big-data analytics

HUE provides the end user with the ability not only to browse the Hadoop file system but also to query HIVE table structures and execute scripts for complex data transformations. Datameer is optimized for analysis of large volumes of data and enables business users to perform statistical analysis on these large data sets.

4. Impact

Before the big-data solution, the summarization and transformation rules that applied to the high volume of transactions were captured in different Presentation Layer components for each line of business. As a result, several manual reconciliation processes had to be followed to summarize the same financial data to a financial journal entry. Deloitte worked with the organization's finance division to establish a big-data capability to most effectively provide finance and actuarial teams, as well as future auditors, the ability to drill down to the lowest transactional level while automating manual reconciliations and reducing the overall number of reconciliations.

In addition, the implementation of this big-data solution has enabled the US Health Insurance organization to:

- Provide timely, accurate, and standardized data from a single enterprise data platform with traceability to the source

- Integrate and modernize data management systems while enabling robust future reporting and analytics of enterprise financial data
- Improve reliability and auditability of data across the organization and optimize data integration across departments
- Define targeted use cases that support critical business decision making and continued build-out of advanced analytics capabilities

5. Challenges Faced, Lessons Learned

As with any set of next-generation methods or technologies, there are always challenges to gaining real business benefits from implementation. Like many organizations, the organization found the key areas of challenge to be around the themes of *technology* and *talent*.

- **Technology.** Although Hadoop has been around for some time, it is relatively new as an enterprise-strength standard in many corporate IT settings. The ecosystem is broad and continuing to evolve. Some tools and features may not be as mature as in other enterprise tools and technologies. While the Hadoop file system was originally designed to solve problems encountered by web organizations by capturing snapshots of large data sets, traditional RDBMS functions such as updates and deletes require a different development and implementation paradigm. Both paradigms provide value; however, there is typically considerable investment required to work through the details of an enterprise data architecture that effectively integrates and balances Hadoop with existing RDBMS platforms.
- **Talent.** Successful implementation of the big-data solution required a sophisticated team of developers and analysts with sufficient finance and actuarial domain knowledge to design technical solutions that provide high-value business insights on an accelerated timeline. Aside from the significant architectural differences among big-data and legacy-data management platforms, other challenges typically include the need to re-orient data developers that have worked in relational database environments (e.g., SQL, stored procedures) to instead use object-oriented programming languages and scripting (e.g., Pig) to perform data transformations.

Similar to other reporting and analytics implementations, big-data projects require a strong alignment with an organization's business goals. Often, key highlighted features of the new platform may not be critical business needs of the organization. For example, the distributed node configuration options and fault tolerance feature of Hadoop systems are key highlights but may not be necessary for the needs of all businesses.

The key elements outlined in Table 2 contributed to the success of the financial reporting and big-data analytics solution in this case study.

- **Technology Stack Selection.** Selecting a big-data solution stack is often a hard decision to navigate, with its overwhelming list of options. Ideally, the process should be driven based on a robust solution architecture directly tied to validated business requirements.

Table 2. Technology Stack Selection Criteria and Advantages

Criteria	Technology	Advantages
Select a mature commercial distribution of HDFS	Hortonworks	Documentation and warranty support against software flaws
Only enable big-data libraries that will be used in the implementation cycle	Hive, Ranger, Ambari	Improved system performance and ease of knowledge transfer to maintenance/support teams
Select a GUI tool for data integration efforts	Talend	Ease of translation of relational ETL concepts to big-data structures
Enable a web interface to access the Hadoop repository	Hue	Provide non-technical users with the ability to navigate and query without extensive training on Hadoop technologies
Statistical analysis tool	Datameer	Provide business users and data scientists with the ability to run statistical algorithms on large data sets

When seeking to accelerate the process, there are a few key factors to consider during the selection process. Deloitte and the US health insurance organization were able to quickly narrow down the options to a manageable set of technology choices using the prioritized decision factors in Table 2. Several example technologies are also provided to illustrate potential outcomes of the decision process, although other options are available.

- **Well-Defined Data Architecture.** A consistent, reliable, scalable, and reusable data architecture in Hadoop is critical to support a growing enterprise. The fundamentals of semantic consistency as the basis for security, governance, and usability still apply in the big-data world. A robust data architecture providing this semantic consistency is the foundation for sharing data across the enterprise and retiring redundant legacy capabilities. While many of these practices are extensions from the traditional enterprise data warehousing world, Deloitte and the health insurance organization focused on applying features such as those provided in Table 3 for maximum effectiveness in the Hadoop ecosystem.

Table 3. Big-Data Architecture Features in Financial Reporting Solution

Organize data into logical groupings	By defining each logical grouping with a specific processing purpose within the data lifecycle, there was better control over different schemas, file formats, and compressions.
Categorize data storage by Hive and HBase	Hive and HBase differ in their storage mechanisms in Hadoop. For example, Hive does not provide interactive querying and only runs batch processes on Hadoop data. As a result, data sets supporting analytical querying and time series/trend analysis is stored in Hive structures, while data that requires frequent updates and is used for real-time querying uses HBase structures.
Augment natural keys with an independent surrogate key	Creating a surrogate key that belongs to the Data Lake and is not associated with any data source or target system guarantees uniqueness across the Hadoop system, avoiding data inconsistencies when integrating across multiple source systems.

- **Agile Approach to Big-Data Implementations.** As the health insurance organization evolved in its understanding of its data assets, a blueprint and guide for current and future data projects was developed using enterprise data standards. A switch from the traditional waterfall big-bang approach to an agile approach was key in delivering quick solutions based on current needs with a quicker path to value instead of a time-intensive, big-bang development effort.

6. Conclusion

The health insurance market in the US is undergoing tremendous change, with new regulatory requirements driving the need to modernize business and technology capabilities of finance and actuarial groups. The modernization efforts described in this case study aim to enhance business insights by improving data management and analytics capabilities. With better, faster data and analytics, health insurance organizations increase their ability to predictively manage new products and risk. As the industry pivots to address the increasing number of newly insured entrants and medical cost, combined with the drive toward paying for care that is outcomes focused, it will likely continue to challenge health insurers' predictive and current reporting capabilities. In this case study, the health insurance organization has focused on improving its analytics and information management capabilities and is now able to:

- Provide more accurate, timely, and standardized data from a single enterprise data platform, with source system traceability.
- Deploy business-driven capabilities with streamlined integration between operational subsystems and the centralized data repository. The next-generation data platform and enhanced data integration enable more accurate planning and reporting, greater compliance and flexibility, reduced time to provide reporting to business, and strengthened governance to improve the reliability of reporting.
- Enhance automated integration with their ERP financial system while improving capabilities to drill down into underlying financial transactions and insurance contract details.
- Streamline processes and systems around financial close and governance.

With an investment in a scalable, modern big-data solution, and a path to optimize legacy operations and systems, this health insurance organization is well positioned for its business today and the evolution of its marketplace in the future.

Case Study

CIAPM: California Initiative to Advance Precision Medicine

Initial Demonstration Projects and New Demonstration Projects

Elizabeth Baca
Senior Health Advisor
Governor's Office of Planning and Research, California

Contributors
Lark Park, Senior Advisor, Governor's Office, California
Terri O'Brien, Associate Chancellor, UCSF
Uta Grieshammer, Program Director, CIAPM
India Hook-Barnard, Director of Research Strategy, UCSF
All the CIAPM team and demonstration partners

[This case study describes how the state of California launched a precision medicine initiative to leverage the vast amounts of varied big data to demonstrate the application of precision medicine.]

1. Background

California is internationally recognized for innovation. As the birthplace of high technology and biotechnology, California supports a vast ecosystem with a wealth of talent, data, resources, private companies, entrepreneurs, health systems, academic institutions, and non-profit and patient groups. This ecosystem will shape and contribute to the emerging approach of precision medicine. Governor Jerry Brown, in his 2014 state of the state address, announced, "Just as California has led the way with stem cell research, so too can we pioneer the new field of precision medicine," signaling California's interest in this emerging approach.

The term *precision medicine* has been used in varying contexts with multiple meanings. At the heart of precision medicine, though, is a paradigm shift for medical research, prevention, diagnosis, and treatment of disease. And *at the center of this shift is how data is utilized.* In 2011, the National Academy of Sciences (NAS) released *Toward Precision Medicine: Building a Knowledge Network for Biomedical Research and a New Taxonomy of Disease.*[1] This national report informs California's understanding of precision medicine.

Precision Medicine is the use of advanced computing tools to aggregate, integrate, and analyze vast amounts of data from research, clinical, personal, environmental, and population health settings, to better understand diseases and develop and deliver more precise diagnostics, therapeutics, and prevention measures.

Over the last several decades, medical research has resulted not only in our current ability to describe in astonishing detail the biological mechanisms of disease and to sequence the genome, but also in the technologies that have transformed how we measure, analyze, and aggregate data. Medical information, previously stored in paper charts, has largely migrated into electronic health records. In addition, technology has resulted in an exponential growth in our capacity to capture new forms of data through wearable devices, sensors on environmental quality, and transit and physical activity behavior. Most of this information is at our fingertips with cellular phones and handheld devices. At the same time, our capacity to collect information has surpassed our ability to use that data to fully understand and improve the health of Californians. As discussed in the 2011 NAS report, precision medicine holds the promise to aggregate, integrate, and analyze data from research, clinical, personal, and population health settings—to create a knowledge network and to enable more precise diagnosis, treatment, and prevention if we can fully access that data.

Although much of the conversation around precision medicine has been focused on the integration of genomic data, it is important to recognize that genomic data is one of many types of data relevant to personal and population health. Much like geographic information system (GIS) layers as noted in the NAS report, the data "layers" of precision medicine are manifold. They include the exposome, signs and symptoms, the genome, the epigenome, the microbiome, other patient "omic" data, as well as other patient information, from symptoms to patient-generated data. Together, this data is a vast resource for analysis and generation of health-relevant knowledge. In addition, social, economic, and environmental factors (also referred to as the "zip code" rather than the "genetic code"), can provide additional layers. With precision medicine, we can utilize this type of data at the individual level for more targeted prevention, early diagnosis, and treatment.

Shortly after Governor Brown's state of the state address, California appropriated $3 million in the budget FY 2014–2015 to support efforts across California to advance precision medicine. Following months of conversations with precision medicine leaders across California, the Governor's office launched the California Initiative to Advance Precision Medicine (CIAPM), choosing the University of California, San Francisco, as the lead partner to manage the Initiative and represent the University of California system, working in collaboration with the Governor's Office of Planning and Research, the state entity with programmatic responsibility for overseeing CIAPM.

---

[1] "Toward Precision Medicine: Building a Knowledge Network for Biomedical Research and a New Taxonomy of Disease." National Research Council (US) Committee on a Framework for Developing a New Taxonomy of Disease (2011). National Academies Press. Available at https://www.nap.edu/catalog/13284/toward-precision-medicine-building-a-knowledge-network-for-biomedical-research

CIAPM's goal is to provide limited funding to high-value, shorter-term demonstration projects; analyze precision medicine assets (such as data, research initiatives, infrastructure, expertise, etc.) across California; foster collaboration and serve as a network across California's private, academic, and non-profit institutions; and examine relevant policy issues. The bulk of the initial funding was awarded to two demonstration projects designed to harness expansive patient data, leverage additional resources from private and public partners across California, and ideally have direct benefit to Californians within a two-year period. In FY 2016–2017, the legislature appropriated an additional $10 million to expand CIAPM's efforts and fund additional high-value projects.

2. Initial Demonstration Projects

A powerful theme emerged through the CIAPM outreach process: for precision medicine to succeed, it would require a high level of collaboration, beyond the normal scope of partnership typical of academic projects. The request for proposals (RFP) outlined the eligibility requirement to bring in additional partnerships, and the competitive RFP process was hosted through a series of convenings that brought together precision medicine stakeholders across all fields. Not only did the convenings allow for networking and discussion with leaders across the state, it also allowed the demonstration project applicants the opportunity to bring in additional partners. Among the six finalists chosen during the first stage of a two-stage competitive review process, 40 private, foundation, and non-profit partners were proposed as partners.

A nationally and internationally recognized group of precision medicine leaders with strong clinical expertise, diversity of professional background, and history of leadership and selection processes evaluated the applications based on predefined criteria deemed necessary to advance precision medicine, including:

- Potential for tangible benefit to patients within two years, including the likelihood that the study will have immediate impact on patients
- Depth and breadth of data available and potentially available in the disease focus area across the UCs and from partnering institutions/organizations
- Prospects for efficient, effective data integration and analysis
- Expertise of potential team members
- Resources available for the project outside of CIAPM funds, including the potential for leveraging dollars
- Clinical and commercial potential of the platforms as assessed by outside experts
- Strength of connections between proposal team collaborators
- Potential to scale and to leverage the 13.6 million EHR from across the UC Health Centers
- Attention to particular challenges of interoperability, health disparities, privacy, participant engagement, consent, security, and ethical concerns and establish appropriate standards
- Potential downstream use of tools, measurements, and data, including open public accessibility of generated data and publications

During the first competitive, peer-reviewed selection process, two demonstration projects were selected and funded at $1.2 million each.

2.1 California Kids Cancer Comparison (CKCC) Demonstration Project

Principal Investigator:
David Haussler
Director, UC Santa Cruz Genomics Institute
University of California, Santa Cruz

The CKCC project uses large-scale bioinformatics to find new potential treatment leads for children with cancer in California who fail to respond to standard therapies. The project leverages already funded clinical trials at UC Medical Centers and partner institutions to employ genomic analysis. In current clinical trials through genomic analysis, only about 10% of patients yield new leads, in part because the tumor is analyzed on its own. CKCC places the genetic analysis of the tumor cell in the context of thousands of pediatric and adult tumors that have undergone a similar analysis.

Currently, the reference compendium has over 10,000 comparative samples and is growing daily as the project team adds new cases and partners. The goal is to at least double the number of new leads for children who do not respond to initial treatment with the ultimate goal for more cures. To date, CKCC has obtained genomic data from 95 patients and has presented to tumor boards on approximately a third of these. the CKCC team has already been able to identify new treatment leads. It is still too early in the project to mention outcomes, but the early leads are promising. An additional component of the project is developing MedBook, a social network platform for clinicians and researchers to work as a team through tumor boards and other collaborators to integrate genomic data in a private and secure way for cancer patients.

Partners in CKCC include Stanford University, UC San Francisco, Pacific Pediatric Neuro-Oncology Consortium, the Children's Hospital of Orange County, and the British Columbia Cancer Agency. The CKCC team is currently expanding their group of partners to include the University of Michigan, Children's Hospital of Philadelphia, and Mercy Children's in Kansas City.

2.2 Precision Diagnosis of Acute Infectious Disease (PDAID) Demonstration Project

Principal Investigator:
Charles Chiu
Associate Professor of Laboratory Medicine and Medicine/Infectious Diseases
University of California, San Francisco

The PDAID project is using metagenomic next-generation sequencing for actionable diagnosis of life-threatening infections in a timely fashion. Compared to current standard-of-care approaches that require sending multiple tests to identify suspected infectious agents, PDAID has created and validated algorithms to rapidly analyze samples of genetic material from cerebrospinal fluid and blood specimens, extract human sequence signals, and identify the causative infectious agent. Validation of the accuracy of the test is done in a licensed clinical laboratory certified for patient diagnostic testing.

Patient data is securely stored on local computational servers and in the cloud and linked to the electronic medical record. To aid with interpretation, impact, and integration into clinical care, a multidisciplinary "clinical microbial sequencing board" of experts meets online in real time to discuss cases. Decision analytics modeling using publicly accessible databases will be leveraged to assess the clinical utility and cost-effectiveness of the metagenomic sequencing test. A study of hundreds of critically ill patients to compare this test to conventional approaches in terms of diagnostic efficacy and cost-effectiveness is now underway at University of California San Francisco, with clinical partners at UC Los Angeles, UC Davis, and Children's Hospital Los Angeles.

The demonstration projects have several private sector partners and patient advocate support, and they are looking to expand their academic partnerships. They also have established milestones and metrics that are being monitored for success.

Lessons Learned

CIAPM has seen interest across sectors to engage with each other. The initial $3 million investment sparked substantial interest, which has been reinforced the additional $10 million state funding in FY 2016–2017. The state's investment in precision medicine has created opportunities to engage with national leadership in policy conversations on the federal Precision Medicine Initiative, to present at national conferences, and to discuss opportunities and lessons learned with similar efforts. Lessons learned of particular importance are:

Share a Common Definition

As a new paradigm, the term *precision medicine* has been defined several ways. Before the NAS report, a good deal of work focused on what could be termed *personalized medicine,* which is often confused with precision medicine. The terminology can be confusing and includes *precision medicine, precision health, precision public health, personalized medicine,* and *personalized population health.* The CIAPM definition of precision medicine attempts to incorporate the spectrum of precision medicine, from the very targeted and individual application to the population level. Creating a clear definition and reiterating the message through different forums has been key.

Leverage Other Assets

The initial cohort of demonstration projects was able to leverage the state funding and bring in additional investment. Also important was the ability to leverage institutional relationships, other research funding, publically available data, and knowledge from other fields. The initial $2.4 million investment leveraged over $15 million dollars in other investment, allowing the funds to have a much larger impact.

Partnership Is Vital

Although CIAPM is officially administered through the UC system, all partners acknowledged from the formation that it would require collaboration across multiple sectors and expertise within and beyond UC. Collaboration is central, but equally important is recognition that collaboration can be hard. Working across sectors, often with very different cultures, time lines, and processes, can be a limiting factor. CIAPM has created opportunities to collaborate, facilitated connections, and incentivized working together through the demonstration projects.

3. Next Steps

CIAPM recently completed a competitive, peer-reviewed round to select six new demonstration projects with funding up to $7.2 million. These new projects include application for both pediatrics and adults, and integrate and analyze data from sensors, digital health applications, radiologic images, the genome, the blood, and the electronic health record all with the aim to turn big data into knowledge and improve health. Over the next two years, CIAPM will continue to analyze and compile precision medicine assets across the state and host policy conversations on issues such as the cost and benefit of precision medicine, how to integrate health disparity improvement goals, regulatory challenges, and a host of other policy considerations.

4. New Demonstration Projects

4.1 Early Prediction of Major Adverse Cardiovascular Event Surrogates Using Remote Monitoring with Biosensors, Biomarkers, and Patient-Reported Outcomes

Brennan Spiegel
Director of Health Services Research
Cedars-Sinai Medical Center

Cardiovascular disease is the leading cause of death for both men and women in California. Tragically, many people develop a heart attack, stroke, or other complication of cardiovascular disease because they were under-treated, not taking their medicines, or not receiving the care they needed in the first place; this is especially common among younger women and racial/ethnic minorities. One reason for this is that early signs of disease can be easily missed, and also because people spend most of their lives far away from a doctor or hospital, making it challenging to monitor disease progression.

In this study, researchers will look for the earliest signs of impending disease by monitoring patients remotely, outside the four walls of the hospital or doctor's office. Patients will wear a specialized watch that measures activity, sleep, heart rate, and stress levels. They will also report their levels of anxiety, depression, and quality of life using a smartphone or computer. Finally, they will periodically send a small finger-prick blood sample by mail, allowing doctors to measure over 500 different blood chemicals.

By combining these different types of data, the researchers will seek a "signal in the noise" that predicts who may be about to have a heart attack or stroke. If successful, patients could greatly benefit from more effective prevention and treatment as a result of earlier disease detection, but in order to broadly implement innovative new technologies, it is also important to understand their potential cost impact on the medical system. The team will therefore perform an economic analysis to estimate the cost effectiveness of this remote monitoring approach.

4.2 Full Genome Analysis of Children to Guide Precision Medicine

David Martin
Senior Scientist
Children's Hospital Oakland Research Institute

Most inherited diseases become apparent in childhood, and many result in symptoms without a specific diagnosis. This is a difficult situation for parents and clinicians, often subjecting the child to a diagnostic odyssey. The project will advance precision medicine by developing methods that improve our ability to identify mutations that cause inherited diseases and to find the cause of previously difficult-to-diagnose genetic conditions. This will be accomplished by a full genome analysis that provides a more complete picture of abnormalities in an individual's DNA than is currently achieved. Interpretation of whole genome data remains a challenge, though, and the team plans to leverage the findings from this project for an even greater understanding of these often devastating childhood conditions by partnering with other international teams with the long-term goal of creating a catalogue of all DNA variants that can cause human disease. This project will also actively seek to include racially and ethnically diverse patient groups, which have traditionally been under-recruited for genetic analysis, thus adding novel and important information to improve diagnosis and care for the population at large.

4.3 Personal Mobile and Contextual Precision Health

Nicholas Anderson
Director of Informatics Research
University of California, Davis

Patients are increasingly gathering diverse and ubiquitous personal data through the mobile phones and devices they use in their daily lives. This data is potentially of unique importance to help both patients and their doctors improve the management of chronic diseases, but engaging patients to provide secure and personalized data, and integrating and interpreting this data in the context of their clinical health, remains a major challenge. In this project, the team will develop and provide easy-to-use tools and processes to track and contribute activity, blood pressure, and behavioral health data from mobile phones, and will engage patients to help design and evaluate a patient-centered mobile health system that will allow patients and their doctors to use this data for new approaches to managing chronic conditions such as hypertension and depression.

4.4 Artificial Intelligence for Imaging of Neurologic Emergencies: From Images to Precision Medicine

Pratik Mukherjee
Professor of Radiology and Biomedical Imaging, Bioengineering
University of California, San Francisco

Every 28 seconds, an American suffers a catastrophic neurologic emergency, most commonly stroke or traumatic brain injury (TBI). Neurologic emergencies affect 15 million US adults and children annually, at a cost of $115 billion, which is 7% of total US healthcare spending per year. Since the brain is susceptible to irreversible injury within minutes, immediate diagnosis and treatment are essential. Computed tomography (CT) scanning is currently the only type of imaging used worldwide to diagnose neurologic emergencies. Immediate diagnosis aided by rapid automated evaluation of head CT could greatly improve care in situations where minutes count.

This project will apply state-of-the-art artificial intelligence (AI) technology to automatically recognize life-threatening findings on emergency head CT scans in patients suspected of having TBI, stroke, or bleeding due to ruptured brain aneurysms, with the aim of assisting physicians to make a quicker diagnosis. Another important advance enabled by this technology is the ability to catalogue clinically significant "digital markers" that are recognizable across scans, which will facilitate future precision medicine research by combining data from quantitative image analyses with other types of data. The team will implement this AI system in the "cloud" so that its use does not remain limited to advanced hospital settings, and CT scans can be uploaded for analysis from anywhere in the world.

4.5 Precision Medicine for Early Prostate Cancer: Integrating Biological and Patient Complexity Variables to Predict Treatment Response

Sheldon Greenfield
Executive Co-Director, Health Policy Research Institute, School of Medicine
University of California, Irvine

Prostate cancer is the most common cancer in men, with over 200,000 new cases diagnosed each year in the US It is the second leading cause of cancer death in men, affecting roughly one in seven men over their lifetime. An important goal toward achieving better outcomes is to be able to predict, prior to treatment, which therapy will work best for each patient.

This proposal focuses on improving these predictions for patients with early-stage prostate cancer, based on diverse information, including (1) detailed patient characteristics and patient-reported outcomes such as socio-demographic information, health status, and disease management burden; (2) traditional prostate cancer severity indicators; and (3) an already established genomic test that measures the probability of cancer spread after surgery.

Another important objective of this project is to understand the validity of these predictive measures in an ethnically diverse patient population. The final combined prediction model will aid doctors and patients in personalizing prostate cancer treatment decisions to maximize effectiveness, and in choosing the treatment optimal for individual patients.

4.6 Precision Medicine for MS: Making It Work

Walter Stewart
Vice President and Chief Research & Development Officer
Sutter Health

Multiple sclerosis (MS) is a nervous system disease that affects the brain and spinal cord when the body's immune system mistakenly attacks healthy cells. MS usually starts between 20 and

40 years of age. Patients may face decades of physical disability and uncertainty around how the disease will progress. While precision medicine holds the promise of being able to predict and slow the course of MS, these advances in MS care have not yet made it to every doctor's office.

Sutter Health and UCSF are partnering with patients and the National Multiple Sclerosis Society to develop an interactive app that builds on technology created and tested at UCSF and shown to improve outcomes. For example, patients were significantly less likely to need a cane (10% versus 50%) when treated by neurologists using this technology.

In this project, Sutter Health's Research & Development team will develop the interactive app, called MS-SHARE, which will instantly combine the latest precision medicine data with real-time data from the patient's electronic health record, and with information that patients report about their symptoms between medical appointments. Doctors and patients will be able to view the app together during appointments to see how the patient's unique characteristics compare to other patients like them. Knowing how MS may develop over time for a patient can help the doctor and patient select the treatments most likely to slow disease progression and meet patient needs. The team will implement MS-SHARE in multiple Sutter general neurology practices and measure use and patient experience as first steps toward getting precision medicine into everyday care. This partnership holds the promise of bringing precision medicine—precise treatment decisions to address needs of individual patients—directly to the diverse populations living with MS in Northern California.

Further information for these projects can be found at www.ciapm.org.

Case Study

University of California San Francisco: AI for Imaging of Neurological Emergencies

Pratik Mukherjee
Professor of Radiology and Biomedical Imaging, Bioengineering
University of California, San Francisco

1. Introduction

Every 28 seconds, an American suffers a catastrophic neurologic emergency, most commonly stroke or traumatic brain injury (TBI). Neurologic emergencies affect 15 million US adults and children annually, at a cost of $115 billion, which is 7% of total US healthcare spending per year. Because the brain is susceptible to irreversible injury within minutes, immediate diagnosis and treatment are essential. Computed tomography (CT) scanning is currently the only type of imaging used worldwide to diagnose neurologic emergencies. Immediate diagnosis aided by rapid automated evaluation of head CT could greatly improve care in the emergency department (ED); and even ambulances, intensive care units, and operating rooms are increasingly equipped with portable CT scanners. Treatments begun early in the ambulance or ED hold tremendous promise for better outcomes in neurologic emergencies, including fewer deaths and less long-term disability. Reducing disability and shortening hospital stays also produces economic benefits.

New advances in machine learning and artificial intelligence (AI), including state-of-the-art computer vision techniques such as deep learning using convolutional neural networks (CNNs), have tremendous potential for extracting clinically important information from medical images. The design of CNNs has been inspired by the architecture of the early human visual system, with layers of computing units—sometimes called *neurons*—that communicate with each other to perform the necessary image recognition task. The neural networks are referred to as "deep" because they have many more layers than their 20th century predecessors, which enable them to perform much more sophisticated data processing. This dramatic increase in the power of neural networks during the past few decades has been enabled by cheap, high-performance, massively parallel processing in the form of graphics processing units (GPUs) as well as the aggregation of much larger datasets via the internet with which to train the CNNs. There have also been key recent advances in neural network design that allow deeper neural networks to function effectively. CNNs are now bieng used by technology companies to recognize objects in images, such as human faces or animals such as cats and dogs. The key advantage of CNNs is that they are general purpose and could potentially be used to recognize virtually any type of pattern in any type of image, unlike older computer-aided detection technology that required hand-crafted algorithms for particular specialized types of image-processing tasks.

Together with my neuroradiology colleague Esther Yuh and neurosurgical colleague Geoffrey T. Manley we have applied this state-of-the-art AI technology to automatically recognize life-threatening findings on emergency head CT scans in patients suspected of having TBI, stroke, or bleeding due to ruptured brain aneurysms. This image-recognition technology can be revolutionary for the rapid detection of emergencies, such as brain hemorrhage and swelling, so that physicians can be alerted for immediate action, thereby preventing medical errors from missed or delayed diagnosis in these life-or-death situations, in which every minute counts. We have already achieved high accuracy in detecting even small and subtle acute hemorrhages on head CT scans. We have also implemented a cloud-based version of this AI running on a website that can accept CT scan images from anywhere in the world and display in color overlaid on the images the areas of suspected hemorrhage, which can be viewed on any device running a web browser. Dr. Yuh and I are continuing to incorporate the latest innovations in CNN design, which are currently reported on an almost monthly basis, to improve the performance of our deep-learning system.

2. Project Goals

The aims of our project, which recently has been funded by the California Initiative to Advance Precision Medicine (CIAPM), are to: (1) further develop and validate this AI technology, including convolutional neural networks for deep learning, to extract quantitative biomarkers from head CT scans in neurologic emergencies; (2) scale up our cloud-based AI for detection of emergency features on head CT, which is robust to differences in scanner hardware and protocols; and (3) demonstrate that quantitative imaging biomarkers derived from the AI software are superior to current subjective head CT grading schemes for patient outcome prediction in TBI, hemorrhagic stroke, and aneurysmal subarachnoid hemorrhage (SAH).

Since "time is brain," increased speed and reduced error in this clinical setting would be a life-saving innovation, accelerating point-of-care diagnosis and treatment. A cloud-based implementation of this technology that is available worldwide would help address disparities in access to care, since CT scanners are increasingly available even in developing countries, but neuroradiologists who are highly trained in emergency head CT interpretation are very scarce in underserved regions. In the US and globally, TBI and stroke disproportionately affect the underprivileged. Cloud-based AI could rapidly identify emergencies and triage those scans for immediate attention by radiologists wherever available via teleradiology, and also could be delivered at low cost due to vastly reduced local hardware needs and the remote updating of algorithms.

Moreover, AI holds explosive promise for revolutionizing patient care by transforming the analysis of medical images into an increasingly quantitative science. This aligns closely with precision medicine's goal of "transforming healthcare through use of *advanced computing tools to aggregate, integrate, and analyze vast amounts of data . . .* to better understand diseases and develop and deliver more precise diagnostics, therapeutics and prevention."[1] The ability to extract, classify, and quantify clinically relevant features from medical images using fast automated methods for use in research and patient care would have a far-reaching impact on public health. This capability would meet the FDA's definition of biomarkers as objective measurements of pathology and thereby accelerate the development of imaging biomarkers. No imaging biomarker has been formally qualified by the FDA for TBI. Indeed, the FDA recognizes only "abnormal" and "normal" head CT for patient stratification in TBI clinical trials, despite the fact that an "abnormal" head CT spans a wide spectrum of pathological lesions, anatomic locations, and numbers and sizes of lesions.[2] The FDA, in particular, will not consider the subjective assessment of images by experts as biomarkers because they are "influenced by human choices, judgment or motivation."[3]

We will use AI to derive quantitative metrics that satisfy the FDA's definition of biomarkers as "objectively measured indicators of normal or pathogenic biological processes."[4] Such imaging biomarkers could be highly beneficial for TBI clinical trials, whose 100% failure rate has been attributed to heterogeneous pathology not accounted for by grading CT scans as "positive" or "negative."[5] Imaging biomarkers would also not only streamline the painstaking and costly process of image interpretation by central expert readers but also provide more granular data for research into outcomes and therapies.

3. Conclusion

A cloud-based AI that is robust to differences in scanner hardware and protocols would enable aggregation of imaging biomarkers across centers for high-throughput analyses of large imaging databases that can be combined with clinical, genomic, and other patient data in a precision-medicine framework. For example, we are working to validate our cloud-based AI

---

[1] "Toward Precision Medicine: Building a Knowledge Network for Biomedical Research and a New Taxonomy of Disease." (2011). National Research Council (US) Committee on a Framework for Developing a New Taxonomy of Disease. National Academies Press.

[2] Saatman, K.E., et al. (2008). "Classification of Traumatic Brain Injury for Targeted Therapies." *J Neurotrauma,* Vol. 25, pp. 719–738.

[3] "Clinical Outcome Assessment (COA): Glossary of Terms." (2016). US Food and Drug Administration. Retrieved September 28, 2016, from http://www.fda.gov/Drugs/DevelopmentApprovalProcess/DrugDevelopmentToolsQualificationProgram/ucm370262.htm

[4] "Group BDW. Biomarkers and Surrogate Endpoints: Preferred Definitions and Conceptual Framework." (2001). *Clin Pharmacol Ther,* Vol. 69, pp. 89–95.

[5] Saatman, et al. *op. cit.*

for automated measurements of emergency features on head CT scans, including amount of blood, degree of midline shift, and brain herniation. Applied to the billions of images residing in research and clinical data repositories worldwide, which can be analyzed cheaply and rapidly using deep learning on large-scale GPU clusters, this can generate the massive amounts of quantitative data needed for precision medicine research. These could include large-scale studies addressing prognosis, risk stratification, and best treatment practices in neurologic emergencies, as well as studies of the cost effectiveness of imaging tests and services in neurologic emergencies.

Improved clinical trials for effective treatments for TBI, hemorrhagic stroke, and aneurysmal SAH are sorely needed, because almost all such trials have failed up to now, in large part due to the lack of useful biomarkers for patient selection and treatment monitoring. Although head CT of neurologic emergencies is the focus area for this CIAPM project, we expect the AI methods developed to be applicable to other imaging modalities such as MRI and other major public health problems, including heart disease and cancer. It is an exhilarating time to be doing this work in an era of continual, dizzying advances in neural network technology.

Case Study

BayCare Health System: Actionable, Agile Analytics Using Data Variety

Apparsamy (Balaji) Balaji
Director, Enterprise Data Management & Web Applications
BayCare Health System

1. Strategic Plan

BayCare Health System (BCHS) has focused heavily on originating and servicing systems that streamline, support, and enhance processes needed to run a successful multi-million-dollar hospital system. This has resulted in a significant increase in organized data and a shift in focus toward analyzing information to improve performance. The healthcare industry is going through an unprecedented period of change and growth, which drives the need to use all the tools at our disposal to achieve excellence and gain a competitive advantage. The power of data is now viewed as an enterprise asset.

To maximize this asset to its full potential, stakeholders from different service lines were engaged to discuss the current state of BCHS's BI analytics and decision-making process, resulting in the identification of common themes and challenges to successful BI performance in this area (see Figure 1).

The primary focus for BCHS is to treat data as the new currency for innovation and promote data as a strategic asset in short- and long-term plans. Various firms from a variety of industries that are considered to be leaders in their use of analytics and have demonstrated their "world class" data competencies were studied to learn what works and what does not work. Processes that generate data have expanded rapidly in recent years, and the variety of data encompassed is across the spectrum. We focused on the various attributes that would stage future strategy and develop a roadmap for the data management program consistent with BayCare's goal of becoming a data-driven decision-making organization.

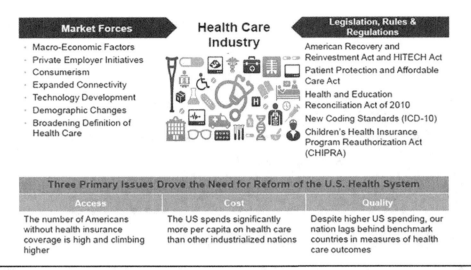

Figure 1   Drivers for changes and market forces in healthcare.

Cost reduction, faster delivery to consumers, greater agility, and improved communications are just a few of the immediate benefits realized by the business. These benefits are a direct result of our implementation of the self-service reporting model, with which individual business units can access and analyze their own data. This new self-service model was supported by our new data management and infrastructure changes. One of the principle positives is that the infrastructure leads to a streamlined environment by actively reducing the number of redundant and un-needed processes, resulting in reduced costs in key areas. The organization no longer needs to maintain the many legacy processes previously required to manipulate—often manually—raw data extracts from the various sources in order to create reports. This old approach is often time consuming and error prone. The new infrastructure is able to process data faster, more efficiently, and more safely. In the journey toward becoming a data-driven organization, our roadmap is to master the small data before we get into the big data.

An additional key benefit is the ability to take what was once not easily reconcilable data from various source systems and disseminate the information across a wide range of business units, resulting in faster and better decision making.

2. Building the Foundation

2.1 Data Governance

In the current healthcare delivery climate, there is an increasing need to ensure that information is trustworthy and actionable. Our data governance strategy seeks to provide a consistent methodology for the identification, standardization, and integration of trusted data into decision-making activities across the entire health-system landscape.

The first step in the roadmap is to build a strong data-governance structure, consisting of multiple tiers with good representation from across the organization to focus on implementing the data strategy. The primary objective of the data governance strategy is to help manage our data assets. It includes the rules, policies, procedures, roles, and responsibilities that guide overall management of both structured and unstructured data from the variety of sources that support BayCare operations. Governance provides the guidance to ensure that data is accurate, consistent, complete, available, and secure. (See Figure 2 on next page.)

In this initial planning phase, data governance must examine the current state of the quality and validity of data throughout the organization. As this examination progresses, it can be contrasted with strategic direction and, from this comparison, a prioritized agenda of governance effort can be developed. The priority of work can be driven by bottom-line impact or selected to address an extrinsic value driven by an external source; examples can be found in the regulatory landscape.

A key strategic initiative in meeting the organization's vision of "high-quality care and personalized, customer-centered health" is establishing *One Standard of Care,* which outlines a standard and best-practices way of operating. In order to support this far-reaching directive, the Governance encompasses a wide range of data to ensure the goals of the vision statement are met.

Information standardization is a key measurable objective for the Governance process. In order to standardize an individual unit of information, record providers must be identified, and the data elements they provide must be analyzed to ensure validity within each specific system. Given that several systems of record are producing the same data, a single system must be identified as the *primary provider* of the data element to the source of truth—the enterprise data warehouse. In the multi-year plan, the first stage is to apply the standardization and build analytics focused on the little data. As this goal is met, the plan is to evolve to handle the unstructured data and the variety of data coming from the slew of mobile devices, which must be processed to answer complex business questions and to provide greater insights for our business leaders.

While the ultimate responsibility for data governance resides at the executive level, the Governance strategy utilizes a multi-tiered structure to appropriately distribute governance decision making. A hybrid governance model is used to enable top-down strategic guidance while still providing opportunities for broad participation across the organization. A three-tiered governance structure consisting of Executive, Advisory, and Tactical levels is used to best address all the needs of the Governance stakeholders.

The Governance process focuses on any and all information associated with the patient or the provider giving care, such as a physician or a nurse. The sources of this information include clinical data as well as data from supporting disciplines. These supporting disciplines include such areas as finance, quality, administrative support, and operations, and include team-member as well patient information acquired through a variety of avenues. However, future unstructured data sources may include patient chart information, images, or even spoken language. The ability to gather and disseminate various data sources allows us to develop a more complete picture of patient and caregiver interactions throughout the system to better understand processes and work toward achieving the One Standard of Care objective.

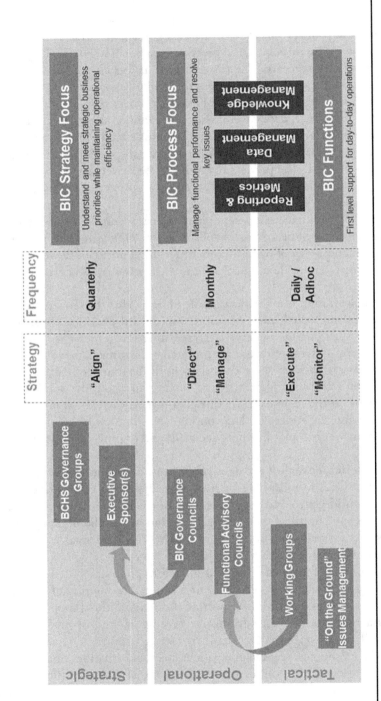

Figure 2 Data governance process, people, focus area.

Formalized data governance processes are in place to ensure data integrity and standardization from the highest to the lowest level of the organization. Executives rely heavily on data that is consistent, timely, and accurate and clearly understand the metrics for which they are accountable and work to proactively address performance issues. Analytics are used to drive accountability throughout the organization, which includes simple reporting and analytics to enable clear understanding and decision making allowing open access to data without management filtering. The implementation of formal data governance creates a clear vision for the future state of BI within the organization.

Established Governance Responsibilities

- **Program Oversight.** Oversees the administration, maintenance, and support of the BayCare analytics environment and major analytics initiatives.
- **Policies and Procedures.** Establishes policies and procedures that ensure that the analytics environment is free of duplicate, outdated, or inappropriate processes, tools, and data.
- **Decision-Making Process.** Introduces and maintains a prioritization mechanism by which major analytics initiatives can be approved, rejected, and sequenced based on specific criteria conforming to BayCare strategy.
- **Strategic Alignment.** Ensures alignment of BayCare strategic initiatives and processes with BI applications, investment, and usage.
- **Resource Allocation.** Takes an enterprise-wide view to ensure optimal utilization and distribution of technology and knowledge resources.
- **Communication.** Establishes BI communication plan across the organization.

The most visible business process in healthcare is delivering quality care to a patient. However, there are myriad, often hidden activities that support the care providers in this endeavor. Because the Governance process focuses on information generated through the interaction of patient and provider, any data that flows from these systems will be subject to governance. The business processes affected include admission/discharge/transfer, charge accumulation and billing, clinical documentation, and care delivery actions, as well as provider performance metrics derived from multiple activities. The desired outcome in this iteration of data governance is the achievement of One Standard of Care. Within BayCare, One Standard of Care may be defined as assuring that every patient receives the same standard of care with every BayCare service, every time.

2.2 Data Management and Enterprise Information Framework

A managed, centralized data environment will enable BayCare to meet its current data and analytics needs, as well as position it to meet challenges in the future with big data. Consumers of the data include the creators of data described above, as well as supporting disciplines consisting of business departments such as finance, quality, administrative support, and operation. The business process of data modernization must be in place at an organizational level to fully take advantage of these new capabilities. This is an area in which data governance will provide worth to the organization. The processes of monitoring data applications have historically been left to information departments in which the primary thing being monitored is system availability. In the new environment in which data is an asset, business teams must partner with technical teams and develop processes that will deliver Quick Response Information: the right information, delivered to the right person, in the right context, at the right time, for the right price.

2.3 Data Quality

Trust in the available data plays a critical role in healthcare delivery. Embedded in trust is the expectation of information integrity, which depends on the completeness and correctness of data. The breadth of the BayCare data governance process touches not only clinical information, but also nonclinical information, such as human resources and operational, financial, legal, and marketing information. By adherence to the data governance process, this information has passed numerous tests and can be spoken of as the source of truth for a particular subject. (See Figure 3.)

The governance process affirmatively answers the end users' questions about the integrity of the data used to deliver patient care. In the era of exponentially growing data mountains from a variety of data sources, by reducing data volatility, the Governance process eases the day-to-day information-driven activities of care providers and adds value to the organization.

Individual users can spend more time in data analysis and less time in gathering and validating the variety of data. This enables users to begin both asking questions that are increasingly more valuable for the business improvement and arriving at an answer in a shorter period of time. This adds incremental value to each work step they perform by removing hesitancy about the data they are using.

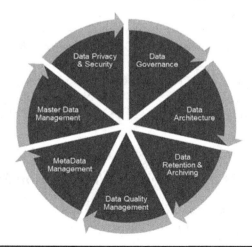

Figure 3   Various aspects of the data management.

2.4 Potential Challenges

- While the centralized self-service model has many empowering benefits for the organization, the process of gathering and transforming the data into a format that conforms to both the business needs and the data integrity rules can be difficult. Some of the bigger challenges presented by the data and infrastructure design involve data integrity, reconciliation, and downstream dependencies.

- Data in the healthcare ecosystem is multidimensional and represents a tremendous variety both in form and in source. The most straight-forward data classification to be governed is structured data. This data resides in a system and is defined in the context of an application. However, a large, unstructured component of healthcare data still resides in written notes and physical images, which must be visually interpreted.

- In other instances, data describing the same thing may appear or be entered in many different places within a given application (or possibly multiple applications). This adds to the complexity in that the source of the data, within an application, must be identified, validated, moved from the system of record to the data warehouse, and then recognized as a source of truth across the organization.

2.5 Analytics Foundation

The acquisition, enrichment, integration, and storage of data for use in analytics applications includes:

- Data acquisition
- Data quality
- Data integration/distribution
- Centralized storage of structured and unstructured data
- Corresponding master data, metadata, and unstructured data

Here are some of the established processes to support the Analytics Foundation:

1. Standardize the data acquisition and data integration/distribution-enabling technologies.
2. Publish **standards, processes, procedures, and best practices** for data acquisition and data integration/distribution (both batch and real-time, as well as structured and unstructured data).
3. Create a **logical data map** for all enterprise data, starting with little data and evolving into big data in the future.
4. Create a **centrally stored location** for enterprise master data, business metadata, and data lineage metadata.
5. Develop a **comprehensive strategy** for integrating and distributing data with external entities.

2.6 *Variety of Data Sources*

The multitude of data sources from which we are consuming data today and planning to ingest it in the near future to accommodate our long-term plans includes, but is not limited to:

- Clinical information from systems from different vendors and versions
- National benchmark data from regulatory boards
- Scheduling, registration, and billing information centralized and decentralized system
- Unstructured data, such as notes, from clinical and other related sources such as care-management solutions
- Claims data from commercial vendors and CMS
- Operational data from the family of mobile apps systems and app stores
- User behavior from various portals that we provided for our customers, physicians, and team members
- Internet-of-Things (IoT), mobile devices, wearables, and remote-monitoring devices from patient home
- Operational and financial data produced by internal and external operational systems

All these data sources produce data in a multitude of formats and layouts, at a tremendous pace. Our approach is to start little to cover the basic information from these data sources, and slowly and incrementally enrich the data inflow into our warehouse to support our data platform.

2.7 *Data Acquisition*

- Centrally managed batch data acquisition using consistent methodology
- Real-time/near real-time data acquisition approach that leverages HL-7 messaging for applications such as clinical alerting and real-time workflow management
- Capturing the operational data from mobile/smart devices from patients and customers to build on improving user behavior and creating better experience
- Expanded external data acquisition capabilities required for Clinically Integrated Networks (CIN), Accountable Care Organizations (ACO), and state and federal requirements

2.8 *Data Integration/Distribution*

- Centrally managed data integration/distribution hub for batch (structured and unstructured) data, real-time/near real-time data, and external data
- Enterprise tools and technologies for data integration and distribution
- Published and enforced standards, processes, and procedures for data integration and distribution
- Enterprise-level data integration utilities such as automated data integration/distribution job scheduling

- Secure data integration and distribution capabilities for external entities (CIN, ACO, patient portals, etc.)

2.9 Analytics Enablement

The consumption of data from the centralized data environment through analytics applications and business intelligence tools, including:

- Analytical applications
- Enrichment engines
- Establishment and promotion of self-service analytics
- Retrospective reporting and analytics
- Near real-time reporting
- Prospective (advanced) analytics

The initial analytics initiatives are focused on a unified analytics approach on small data, with full awareness the future will require us to evolve to start processing big data.

Establish these processes to promote analytics enablement:

1. Develop **standards, processes, procedures, and best practices** for analytical application development and for using retrospective, real-time, and prospective reporting and analytics capabilities.
2. Establish a formal **training program** for ensuring that data consumers are proficient in data and enabling technologies.
3. Develop **retrospective reporting capabilities** that are more interactive in nature.
4. Develop **real-time/near real-time capabilities** for operational and clinical use.
5. Develop **advanced analytical capabilities** to drive competitive differentiation.
6. Create **self-service capabilities** to meet long-term goals of the data consumers.
7. Employ a **role-based security and access approach** for access to the centralized data environment.

2.10 Infrastructure

BayCare identified the need to utilize the vast amount of data contained in various disparate ecosystems within the organization in a streamlined manner to allow timely use of the information, resulting in actionable items. The main forces driving this need were ever-changing market conditions, new regulatory obligations, and changes in the competitive landscape. The delivery method for the data had to be easy to use for the author and user community, readily accepted and trusted by the business stakeholder community, and adaptable to future changes.

The model required infrastructure change to accommodate the goal of a longitudinal data view, data integration from disparate systems resulting in a single standard source of truth, and ability to deliver information via a centralized publishing platform. The items the infrastructure and delivery method had to address were data acquisition, data transformation, and data presentation across the organization. The decision was made to implement an enterprise-wide data warehouse, leveraging Oracle Exadata as the database technology, Oracle OHF (Oracle HealthCare Foundation) as the foundational data model, and Tableau for self-service reporting and data visualization. The data from a variety of sources, both small and big data, could be used to monitor and address changes in market conditions, regulatory obligations, or competition (see Figure 4).

When we started this journey, we developed the plan in such a way as to ensure that the technology and toolset that we selected were scalable both vertically and horizontally. This means we can ensure that an increased volume of information can be persisted and processed to provide business insights. The topology also was established in such way as to accommodate and address new dimensions of data—structured and unstructured—to close the gap on the visibility of patient conditions to the care providers and care plans. In other words, we design the architecture and approach to handle the small data first, make an impact on the business process, and incrementally add value.

In the next phase of our evolution, we are well in position to start identifying the dark data to be acquired and processed to bring a completely new dimension to the analytics. This also helped to augment the analytics built from the structured data. Our plans in the next couple of years is to expand and build the profile around the patients, including their socio-economic data, as well as to tap into the Internet-of-Things to understand our patients and their behavior.

3. Collaboration and Partnership with Business Groups

The key takeaway learned by the organization is that executive support, data validation, and business collaboration are all needed to make a project of this magnitude a success. Executive support allows departments to work together and remove barriers that might have previously hindered the project. The validation of data builds trust within the various departments and continues the goodwill and collaboration needed for project success. Having the support of upper-level decision makers and stakeholders both builds a culture of result-driven focus and gives everyone involved the ability to overcome obstacles by allowing complete cooperation and sharing of data. Senior management is a key aspect in delivering policies and processes that further allow the team to focus on analysis and results.

A key benefit is the ability, discussed above, to take what was once not easily reconcilable data from various source systems and easily disseminate the information across a wide range of business units, resulting in faster and better decision making. Subject matter experts and department-level authors can now easily utilize data from a wide range of sources to better understand, monitor, and manage their business. Business and end users can now focus on their main tasks instead of spending time formatting and gathering data, and so further increase productivity. The organization overall is able to respond to changes in a very fast and agile manner because the streamlined, central, and consumer-centric delivery model is conducive to modification. Any modification to the business need driven by a change in the market or regulatory environment can easily be reflected in the self-service delivery model.

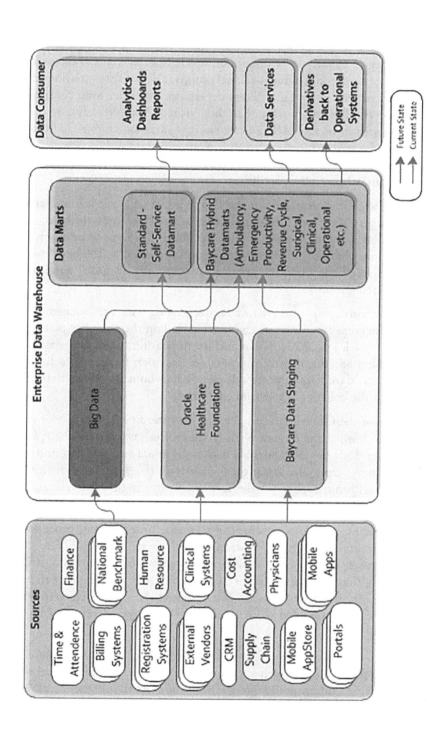

Figure 4 EDW data architecture.

3.1 Analytics to Influence and Benefit Business Process

1. Through the examination of physician order data, the Governance group members identified a high degree of variation throughout the facilities in terms of the orders generated for treatment of common diagnosis-related groups (DRG). This variation resulted in the potential for a patient to have a different experience in service for a common diagnosis, depending on the facility or time that they visited. These differences contributed to varying costs within the same DRG as well as cost variation among facilities, the patient experience, and overall patient satisfaction. Following established governance processes, the Governance committee members worked with clinical and business stakeholders to standardize clinical care across facilities.

2. One such standardization success is the development of a surgical analytics platform. Individual surgery directors from across the facilities worked within the Governance process to establish common metrics, which enabled the direct comparison of OR facilities that previously shared no common evaluation elements. The benefits of this standardization enabled the direct comparison of clinically identical surgical procedures across all operating rooms.

3. The same standardization approach was implemented with the emergency-room directors to establish common measures that are enabled on the analytics platform. By using the same "yardstick" decisions about facility utilization, plans to expand or contract services can be made on directly comparable, data-rich facts, not feelings or hearsay. Furthermore, standard data initiates a deeper dialog about true performance and how to maximize it to the benefit of the entire enterprise.

4. The influence of the Governance process involves the simple example of recording the weight of a newborn at the time of birth. Their concern was that without accurate birth weights, proper dosing was impossible without manual intervention and contact with the OB floor nurse. Upon investigation and analysis, the process was revised to enhance the workflows within the labor and delivery units, ensuring that all relevant information was getting to the appropriate care givers.

5. Answering specific questions concerning prescribed medication, procedures ordered, or readmission rates for each region, facility, and physician helps define the focus and pinpoint processes or services that need improvement or elimination. The main purpose is to bring that recommendation back to the EMR and flag it at the time of care to change the care provider behavior. We designed the same pattern for readmissions to promote the recommended clinician activity when we encounter a high-risk readmission patient.

6. We are currently working to release the spend analytics to improve efficiency and reduce cost for the supply chain management group. The plan is to get the derivatives out of the analytical platform and bring them to the ordering system, to present recommendations for the overall supply order to our vendors, and also to present standard preferred carts for the surgeons.

4. Implementation

Building discipline around data governance began by redefining information as a valuable asset—an asset that could be found across the entire enterprise and one that would require an enterprise-wide effort to protect. Achieving information standardization is a highly complex process, involving many variables, unknowns, and end-use idiosyncrasies. The process of information standardization begins by understanding the data that is available and being used in a given application or workflow. One way this is done is through the use of smaller focus groups.

4.1 Agile Methodology

Following an Agile methodology, the Governance process supports the formation of service-line–specific focus groups. These groups explore a specific information-driven initiative. Using the framework of the focus group, participants identify a desired outcome and begin an iterative process of identifying features necessary to a solution. Since this methodology is designed for speed, *Agile analytics* is the term we are phrasing around the process. It seeks to quickly understand the thrust of the issue and the impact an information-driven solution may provide. Detailed descriptions of how everything *is* and how everything *should be* are developed as the process moves forward—they are not a requirement to begin. The goal is to achieve quick resolution of a tactical issue.

A successful example of this process in action is the focus group addressing cardiovascular (CV) analytics. Through frequent phone and in-person meetings, the group identified necessary metrics to better manage detailed reporting of CV procedures within the larger context of general surgeries. By agreeing on these measures, the CV group has laid the groundwork for the exploration of CV clinical analytics, the next task in the iterative process of developing better, more actionable CV information.

The Governance model as implemented is really a model for change management. The pursuit of the One Standard of Care strategy provides insight into the change requirement at hand; its size, scope, and impact also become apparent when viewed through the lens of Governance. The operating nature of the model enables Governance requirements to scale the effort to align resource expenditure with the type and size of information change that is identified to support the strategy. Utilizing an Agile development philosophy, the quick delivery of business functionality was a key focal point of the project plan. Initial data components included elements from five dominant operational systems that supported the business processes of patient management, clinical documentation, and provider credentialing. Since that time, we have consistently delivered a major analytics solution every quarter.

4.2 Self-Service Analytics

It was at that point that the organization was able to verify that the self-service model of data delivery did indeed meet the goal of the business case. The various business communities were able to consume the information in a manner most familiar and efficient to their specific needs, resulting in the ability to make decisions and implement actions faster than previously possible. The centralized publishing platform allowed authors who were subject-matter experts to further glean knowledge from the data by combining the now-standardized data from various source systems.

The central self-service model has also led to improved communications across the business spectrum. By giving all the business units within the organization access to previously unobtainable data, it is now possible for various entities to communicate with each other to address issues or questions that were previously unknown due to data silos. This is greatly aided by the single source of truth/data integrity concept. By bringing many different source systems into one central repository, it is possible to transform data elements that were previously repeated across the different sources into one agreed-upon source-of-truth element. The result is reduced complexity, improved processing, greater trust by the business community, and the ability to utilize self-service data consumption faster and more easily.

4.3 Infrastructure Changes Based on Variety

The main areas of workload issues are a result of the amount of data being ingested and center around data-presentation performance. One of the primary drivers is the variety of data produced and analyzed for the needs of the business. In our road map, we started off with small data and reaped the benefits of that information through various analytical solutions. We are starting on the next wave to focus more on the big data, mainly driven both by the huge outpouring of information from the family of mobile apps and by exploration of the unstructured data from the various notes by the care providers. This data feeds at a rapid pace, and the variety of data coming into the centralized repository grows rapidly. In order to manage and process this data and to convert it into information, new architecture was required to manage this business need, using big data to handle the heterogeneous data in unstructured format. Also, the infrastructure needed to expand to handle the huge influx of data in the next couple of years to put us in a better position to answer the resulting business questions.

5. Conclusion

5.1 Mobile Devices and Healthcare-IoT

With the advent of smart phones and wearables, numerous healthcare-related apps and IoTs have come to market. The smartphone apps range from simple communication to telemedicine, generating lots of data about everything from user behaviors to actual patient care settings. On top of these, there are medical devices connected with patients both inside and outside the hospitals. These devices are producing very valuable data about the patient and for the healthcare vertical. As opposed to the manual readings, these vitals and readings are streaming in and accumulating quickly. In order to accommodate the increased processing needs, we are looking beyond the current architecture that supports our little data.

5.2 Diving into Physician/Nurse Notes

With over two decades of data captured in the EMR systems, there have been several waves of business analytics focused on the structured data in EMR. The natural progression of those analytics covered a lot of low-hanging fruit, which can be achieved with data in the EMR system. Also, our growth in the care-management area relies heavily on the data buried in the notes from physicians, nurses, laboratories, etc. We are working on some proof of concept to read these unstructured data in the EMR and help provide greater information to the care managers about the patients. In the near future, we expect to mature the analysis of this unstructured data and get those derivatives into part of the EMR to add value for our services at the point of care.

5.3 Information about Our Population

One of our major strategies is to know more about our patients/consumers. From a marketing and strategy perspective, this information is vital for the general market and individual segment analysis. In order to get the 360° view of customer behavior, we are capturing every bit of information about the process at the customer touch point. This includes our various portals, mobile apps, care managers, follow-up calls, and every other patient access point. The value of this information in understanding our patients' behavior and building our processes and systems accordingly is huge. In this effort, the variety of the data from those access points are across the spectrum, and we are well aligned in our progress with the data strategy to handle it. As the first step in this, we are building a data lake to capture all possible information from the mobile apps. We expect to use this to better design and build more engaging apps and improve user experience.

BayCare is committed to improving lives and health through a variety of community-based programs and activities. All the data we capture will be leveraged as assets for the initiatives that support our values.

Case Study

Arterys: Deep Learning for Medical Imaging

Carla Leibowitz
Head of Strategy and Marketing
Arterys

1. Early Development

In line with its vision to further develop medical imaging via cloud computation and advanced analytics, the company launched its effort to explore big data and machine learning to advance the state of the art of medical image processing and automation. At the time, most medical imaging processing happened on hospital premises with limited computing power. Measurements were performed manually, and automated tools were crude at best.

From a background in applying computational fluid dynamics to CT scans for sleep apnea, the team had built a cloud-based tool to perform advanced analyses of large image sets, but they realized over time that imaging alone was not sufficient to determine treatment for apnea patients. They believed that cloud computing and advanced analytics would transform medical imaging, so they set out to find an area in which real clinical value would result from the application of both technologies. They learned about clinical research on an advanced MRI technique called *4D Flow,* which resulted in a far more comprehensive cardiac study than was possible with existing methods using echocardiography or conventional MRI, but the exported files took days to process in the hospital's existing IT infrastructure.

The decision was made to combine the two technologies to process 4D Flow images in the cloud. Over the next three years, they developed a suite of software tools that could take these very large files to the cloud, process them quickly, and render them beautifully (see Figure 1). They also began working with GE Healthcare to make the 4D Flow sequence available to more locations on GE scanners. Academics and scientists around the world embraced the technology and started using it for research purposes. They now had a tool to scan the entire volume of the heart, compared to conventional cardiac MR studies that could scan just a few slices of

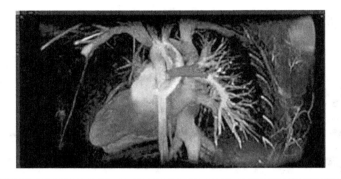

Figure 1   4D Flow visualization of the heart: gradient indicates blood flow velocity.

the anatomy and that had to be carefully planned and acquired. This enabled a faster scan and the ability to make measurements of both anatomy and flow anywhere in or around the heart after the scan was completed.

2. Roadblocks to Early Adoption

With the feedback of these early users, the team continued to refine the software, but they encountered two major roadblocks: First, hospital administrators and clinicians were not comfortable with sending patient data to the cloud. And second, measuring key physiological functions from cardiac MRI studies was a manual, tedious process and could take about an hour per scan—whether acquired via traditional methods or via 4D Flow. Combined, the two roadblocks pointed to very limited adoption of the 4D Flow technology.

The second half of 2014 was frustrating and difficult. Attempts to automate the time-consuming manual measurements were producing sub-optimal results. Models created with traditional machine learning and conventional techniques did not work well enough to be included in a clinical-grade product. They were also extremely labor intensive and were taking a toll on the developers.

The team had been hearing about deep learning, a nascent technology that was revolutionizing computer vision. While the technique had many skeptics, they nevertheless realized that there was a real limitation to creating models with hand-crafted features. It was clear that the same class of deep-learning–based tools, already in use for state-of-the-art facial recognition at Google and Facebook, could better perform the complex tasks of identifying anatomical structures in a moving, beating heart. This meant entering the uncharted territory of allowing machines to craft the features for their predictive models. This also meant that cloud infrastructure was as important as ever, as these advanced analytics tools required significant amounts of computation (specifically, using GPUs and not CPUs), especially if they were going to be used in real time.

That was when the team doubled down on their commitment to the cloud, proceeding both to build deep learning tools and to resolve the security issues around cloud processing of medical information.

3. Building a Clinical Product

A team of engineers began planning software that would manage security. Very quickly, the option of attempting to create a hyper-secure cloud was deemed unattractive. Not only was it an enormous technical challenge, but hosting identifying patient information (also known as *PHI,* for *protected health information*) would increase insurance bills tenfold. Thus, the team set out to create a sophisticated system called *PHI Service,* which strips identifying patient information from medical images before they are sent to the cloud, and then re-identifies them only when users with the right credentials log in.

Fortunately, because the existing infrastructure of deep learning tools was 100% cloud based, all of the scans and the measurements that had been performed with the software were already on the company's cloud, meaning that they could look at which measurements were most time consuming and could then go about automating them by building deep learning models for each task. Furthermore, the fact that the data came from 30+ research facilities meant that the model was being built from a representative sample of users. Still, creating these models was challenging for several reasons:

- First, all of the scans did not have all of the measurements that they set out to automate. Therefore, data processing and augmentation became critical steps for every model the team set out to create. In some cases, they acquired additional ground truth through collaborations with clinical partners.

- The team also found that following best practices for software development was critical to ensuring that multiple projects could be worked on simultaneously and that experimentation and iteration could proceed quickly with contributions from multiple team members. This practice led to significant economies of scale, where one project's software improvements immediately translated to other projects.

- Third, there was a real tradeoff between accuracy and time for inference: a deeper model (one with more layers) usually created a more accurate result, but it took longer to process an image. It was important to identify the point at which the model's accuracy was satisfactory without becoming excessively slow for inference.

- Because the models are complex and are applied to very large data sets (one study is 22K images), they needed to augment their cloud infrastructure. To ensure hundreds of users could simultaneously use the model with minimal onsite computation requirements, they created a distributed computational platform that parallelized the processing of multiple studies as well as the inference on different slices of the scan.

- Finally, delivering the model output in a clinically useful way was not simple. The team iterated this delivery with end users to make sure that the automated measurements were not interrupting their normal workflows and were also easy to adjust. They also added a closed feedback system that captured these user edits. When enough data was collected, the model could be re-trained with these edits for further improvements.

Once the first model met rigorous internal accuracy requirements, the next step was seeking regulatory approval for its use in clinics. The model automatically contours the insides and

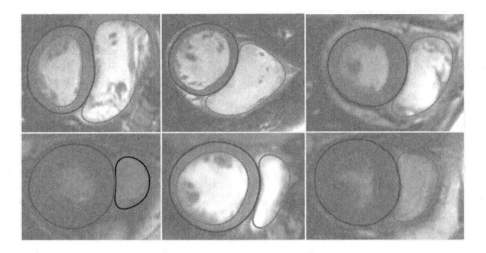

Figure 2   Deep learning model applied to one slice of a short axis stack. (Right: right ventricle endocardium. Left, outer: left ventricle endocardium. Left, inner: left ventricle epicardium.)

outsides of the ventricles of the heart in what is called a *short axis stack*. The model (Figure 2) proved to be as accurate as expert annotators performing the same task (with expected error similar to that of an expert reader), but much faster. One of the most experienced clinicians performing the validation claimed that each study currently took her ~1 hour to perform. In contrast, the newly developed model inference took 10 seconds total, required no user effort, and could be done automatically when a scan was uploaded.

As of this writing (late 2016), the PHI service has been thoroughly tested, and one of the first-ever 510K applications for deep learning on MRI images has been submitted to the FDA.

4. Key Learnings

Some key learnings on cloud and big data for clinical applications:

- Deep learning is the most powerful tool available today when it comes to pattern recognition in images, and it can work on low-definition, skewed images as well as on pristine scans.
- Models that are trained using data from multiple scanners, users, and facilities are more reliable, flexible, and applicable than those that have limited sources of ground truth. Models should also be validated on a variety of scans to ensure broad applicability.
- Securing PHI and adhering to local security, privacy, and regulatory rules is critical in building a big-data system that both serves patients and improves clinical practice. Data that is simply de-identified, while useful for big-data applications, cannot be used to treat the individual patient, especially when it comes to longitudinal monitoring. On the other hand, applying a model to patient data without a closed-system feedback hinders the improvement of the model and clinical practice.

5. Conclusion

The company is now furthering its cloud computing and deep learning capabilities in different spaces in several ways:

1. Aggregating data over time from a consortium of researchers to jointly create faster and more consistent tools for measuring and tracking tumor volumes.

2. Predicting outcomes based on imaging data from clinical trials. Predicted outcomes include response to treatment as well as risk of disease progression.

3. Adding other data, including genomics and other lab results, to create more comprehensive predictive models that will help individualize patient care.

Because of the way the cloud platform is built, the time to develop a new application is significantly shortened: infrastructure from the scanner to the cloud and into PACS enables fast aggregation of data for the creation of new applications and new deep learning models. The next goal is to enable the consistent quantification of medical images and the use of these standardized measurements in the advancement of individualized care.

Big Data Technical Glossary*

Shalin Saini
Manager, Life Sciences and Health Care
Deloitte Consulting LLP

Accumulo. A sorted, distributed key-value store that provides robust, scalable data storage and retrieval. (*Source:* https://accumulo.apache.org/)

Ambari. A web-based Hadoop management project that makes it simpler to provision, manage, and monitor Hadoop clusters. (*Source:* http://ambari.apache.org/)

Atlas. A metadata framework for Hadoop that helps enterprises meet their compliance requirements with Hadoop and facilitates integration with the whole enterprise data ecosystem. (*Source:* http://atlas.incubator.apache.org/)

Avro. A data serialization system that relies on JSON schemas to read, write, store, and integrate data. (*Source:* http://avro.apache.org/docs/current/)

Cassandra. An Apache database management system that is designed to manage large amounts of data across many servers and provide scalability and high availability without compromising performance. (*Source:* http://cassandra.apache.org/)

Chukwa. An open-source data collection and analysis framework that monitors large distributed systems. It is built on top of the Hadoop Distributed File System and MapReduce framework. (*Source:* http://chukwa.apache.org/)

Columnar. Stores data in columns rather than rows. Important in optimizing analytic query performance because it reduces the amount of data necessary to load from disk and the overall disk I/O requirements. (*Source:* http://docs.aws.amazon.com/redshift/latest/dg/c_columnar_storage_disk_mem_mgmnt.html)

---

*NB: All definitions and sources below are open source.

ELT (Extract Load Transform). A data integration process that involves moving data from source systems into a data warehouse. Similar to Extract Transform Load (ETL), however, instead of transforming data before it is written, ELT takes advantage of the target system to do the transformation. (*Sources:* https://docs.oracle.com/cd/B19306_01/server.102/b14223/ettover.htm, https://www.ironsidegroup.com/2015/03/01/etl-vs-elt-whats-the-big-difference/)

Falcon. An Apache feed management framework for governing the data life cycle in Hadoop clusters. It addresses enterprise challenges related to Hadoop data replication, business continuity, and lineage tracing. (*Source:* http://hortonworks.com/apache/falcon/)

Flume. A service for streaming logs into Hadoop, Apache Flume is a distributed, reliable, and available service for efficiently collecting, aggregating, and moving large amounts of streaming data into the Hadoop Distributed File System (HDFS). (*Source:* https://flume. apache.org/)

Hadoop. Open-source software library project administered by the Apache Software Foundation, which defines it as "a framework that allows for the distributed processing of large datasets across clusters of computers using simple programming models." Hadoop is unique because it detects and handles failures at the application layer, rather than relying on hardware to deliver high availability. (*Source:* http://hadoop.apache.org/)

Hadoop Common. A set of common libraries and utilities that support the other Hadoop modules. (*Source:* http://hadoop.apache.org/)

Hadoop Distributed File System (HDFS). A file system that is designed in Java to provide reliable and scalable data storage spanning large clusters. Typically, the file system software stores data in a temporary local file until there is enough to fill a complete HDFS block. These files are usually stored in blocks of 64MB and are sent across the network and written to multiple servers in the cluster. (*Sources:* http://hadoop.apache.org/, http://www.aosabook. org/en/hdfs.html)

Hadoop MapReduce. A software design framework that facilitates writing applications that process large amounts of data in parallel. It typically splits the input data set into independent chunks, which are parallel processed by the map tasks into a series of keys and values. The framework then sorts the outputs of the maps, which are input to the reduce tasks. MapReduce schedules and monitors tasks, and if they fail, re-executes them. (*Source:* https://hadoop.apache.org/docs/r2.7.2/hadoop-mapreduce-client/hadoop-mapreduce-client-core/MapReduceTutorial.html)

Hadoop YARN. A framework that divides and handles cluster resource management and job scheduling as separate functionalities: a global ResourceManager (RM) and per-application ApplicationMaster (AM). (*Source:* https://hadoop.apache.org/docs/r2.7.2/hadoop-yarn/hadoop-yarn-site/YARN.html)

HBase. A Hadoop database that allows storage and access to large quantities of sparse data. (*Source:* http://hbase.apache.org/)

Hive. An open-source data warehousing library that provides the ability to program Hadoop jobs using SQL. While it provides a convenient relational database view of underlying storage structures, because of Hadoop's focus on large-scale processing, the latency can cause even simple jobs to take minutes to complete. (*Source:* http://hive.apache.org/)

Hue. An open-source Web interface that supports Apache Hadoop and its ecosystem. The interface can be used not only to view files, hive table structures, etc., but also to code and monitor script runs. (*Source:* http://gethue.com/)

Impala. An open-source, analytic massively parallel processing (MPP) database for Apache Hadoop that is supported by Cloudera, MapReduce, Oracle, and Amazon. Impala allows for querying data, whether stored in HDFS or Apache HBase, in real time. (*Sources:* http://impala.apache.org/, https://www.cloudera.com/products/apache-hadoop/impala.html)

Key-Value Store. A simple database that uses an associative array, such as a map or dictionary, as "the fundamental data model where each key is associated with one and only one value in a collection." (*Source:* http://www.aerospike.com/what-is-a-key-value-store/)

Kite. A high-level data layer API for Hadoop that speeds up development. (*Source:* http://kitesdk.org/docs/current/)

Knox. Also known as the Apache Knox Gateway, it is a secure entry point for Hadoop clusters. It provides "perimeter security so that the enterprise can confidently extend Hadoop access to more of those new users while also maintaining compliance with enterprise security policies." (*Source:* http://hortonworks.com/apache/knox-gateway/)

Kudu. A part of the Apache Hadoop ecosystem that enables fast analytics on rapidly changing data. Kudu "provides a combination of fast inserts/updates and efficient columnar scans to enable multiple real-time analytic workloads across a single storage layer." (*Source:* https://kudu.apache.org/)

Mahout. A scalable machine learning and data mining library. (*Source:* http://mahout.apache.org/)

Metron. A scalable advance cyber security application framework that helps organizations detect cyber anomalies and rapidly respond to the identified anomalies. (*Source:* http://metron.incubator.apache.org/)

MongoDB. An open-source document-oriented NoSQL database program. MongoDB is different from traditional relational databases because it makes use of a unique document data model that stores data as documents in a binary representation called BSON (Binary JSON). (*Source:* https://docs.mongodb.com/)

NewSQL. A modern database technology designed to preserve SQL and the relational data model and also to provide the same scalable performance of NoSQL systems while still maintaining the guarantees of traditional database systems. (*Sources:* http://dataconomy.com/sql-vs-nosql-vs-newsql-finding-the-right-solution/, https://www.datavail.com/blog/what-is-newsql/, http://newsql.sourceforge.net/)

NoSQL Databases. In general, NoSQL databases provide a mechanism for storage and retrieval of data modeled in means other than the tabular relations used in relational databases. (*Source:* http://nosql-database.org/)

Pig. A high-level procedural language platform developed to simplify querying large datasets in Apache Hadoop and MapReduce. Apache Pig features a "Pig Latin" language layer that enables SQL-like queries to be performed on distributed datasets within Hadoop applications. (*Source:* http://pig.apache.org/)

Ranger. A framework that monitors and manages comprehensive data security across the Hadoop platform. (*Source:* http://ranger.apache.org/)

RecordService. A Cloudera high-performance security layer for Apache Hadoop that, when complemented with Apache Sentry, "delivers complete row- and column-based security, and dynamic data masking, for every Hadoop access engine." (*Sources:* http://recordservice.io/, http://www.cloudera.com/about-cloudera/press-center/press-releases/2015-09-28-cloudera-introduces-recordservice-for-the-apache-hadoop-ecosystem.html)

Sentry. An Apache real-time error tracking system that provides insight into production deployments and information to reproduce and fix crashes. (*Sources:* https://sentry.io/welcome/, https://sentry.apache.org/)

Solr. An open-source enterprise search platform powered by Apache Lucene. Solr provides distributed indexing, replication and load-balanced querying, centralized configuration, and many other features. (*Sources:* http://lucene.apache.org/solr/)

Sqoop. An open-source tool designed to facilitate the transfer of bulk data between Apache Hadoop and relational database management systems, such as SQL Server and MySQL. Sqoop stands for SQL to Hadoop. (*Source:* http://sqoop.apache.org/)

Spark. A fast and general engine for large-scale data processing. It provides a simple and expressive programming model that allows applications to be written quickly in Java, Scala, Python, and R. (*Source:* http://spark.apache.org/)

Storm. An open-source distributed computation system that helps process unbounded streams of data. It adds reliable real-time data processing capabilities to Enterprise Hadoop. (*Sources:* http://storm.apache.org/, http://hortonworks.com/apache/storm/)

Tez. An application framework that provides a "powerful and flexible engine to execute an arbitrary DAG of tasks to process data for both batch and interactive use cases." (*Source:* http://hadoop.apache.org/)

ZooKeeper. A centralized service that enables high-performance coordination for distributed applications. It maintains configuration information and provides distributed synchronization and group services. (*Source:* http://zookeeper.apache.org/)

Index

Printed in the United States
by Baker & Taylor Publisher Services